The CRANE DANCE

TAKING FLIGHT IN *Midlife*

BY WILLIAM R. FINGER

Printed in the United States of America
ISBN 978-0-9965875-0-1

Library of Congress Control Number: 2016909604

for Ellis and Mamie Finger

and

for Georgia

TABLE OF CONTENTS

PROLOGUE. Passage to India

THE TRAIN STATION IN DELHI IS TEEMING with people, suitcases stacked three and four tall on heads of coolies, huge bundles of goods waiting for loading, small fires smelling like burnt charcoal at the edge of the platform. The driver from the five-star Delhi hotel, where I had attended a meeting, is striding in front of me, determined to get me to my train. He guides me through throngs of people as thick as the afternoon dust. In his crisp beige suit and chauffeur's cap, he is as conspicuous as I am—a six-foot-tall white man a head taller than most of the Indians jostling on the steps of the bridge that leads to the second set of tracks.

Passengers hang on to luggage and to each other as they press along the steps, moving toward the exit or with us toward the departing trains. No one seems to notice the person sleeping with a thin, dirty wrap across him on a step. Perhaps he's a holy man, I think, or maybe he's dead. A scene from my visit to Calcutta more than 30 years earlier dashes through my brain, a dead body on the street not far from the railroad station. But there's no time for staying with the past, that year I spent in India as a Peace Corps volunteer. I need to concentrate on staying with the driver and finding the Gondwana Express, scheduled to depart at 14:30.

Walking across the bridge and onto the Gondwana track, I realize now that the driver is as lost as I am. His usual job is to take guests on tours of the city, to and from the airport, or sometimes on an all-day trip to and from Agra to see the Taj Mahal. The train station presents a challenge with its swarming chaos holding out the promise of order but only if you can decipher the code.

Dodging mounds of baggage, coolies, children, and animals, we see "Gondwana Express" on the lists posted on the cars to our right. I begin searching for my name next to a seat reservation but see only a long list of Indian names. The driver and I look on a few cars with no luck—all Indian names. The line of passenger cars stretches as far as I can see. The train is due to depart in less than 15 minutes now, and I can feel the adrenaline boiling up. I do not intend to miss my train to Jabalpur. I left there in 1970. Now, in 2003, I am on my first trip back. I have come too far not to make it back to see the family with whom I lived for nearly a year.

Holding out my ticket, the driver tries to ask a conductor for directions to my car. But too many are asking the beleaguered conductor questions at once, and he points vaguely down the track towards the second-class cars. We go back where we have just been and see another conductor. The driver repeats the process with the same result.

Adrenalin pumping now at full force, I grab the ticket from the driver and look more closely, seeing the "A1" under the column "Coach" in small print under the Hindi script. I run back to the first conductor again, lift my ticket over the shorter Indians surrounding him.

"A1, *kahan hai*?" I shout, pressing my ticket under his nose. He points two cars down in the direction opposite from where he had sent us before, his Hindi a blur of sounds but the meaning clear enough. At the entrance to the car, I scan down the list and see my name with the seat reservation number that matches my ticket, clear and organized. The famous efficiency in the train system, built in the English colonial era, appears as rock solid as ever in the midst of this chaos.

The driver and I confirm the pick-up time in two days on the return train and I watch him walk away. I am on my own, back to the resources that I relied upon in 1969, when I joined the Peace Corps organized through the vision of John Kennedy. Now, at age 56, on my occasional trips to a developing country for my job, I am accustomed to staying in well-heeled hotels in capital cities and having my company's local office available for backup needs. But now I am boarding an overnight train in India, a laptop computer hidden in my bag, no food, and basically no Hindi.

Moving down the aisle, I see mostly Indian men and a few families settling into the seats that will turn into beds before too many hours. No Americans. I find my seat, push my backpack under me on the floor, take a deep breath, and glance out the window at the harried conductor. The scene minutes before comes back to mind.

Kahan hai. Somehow, I remembered how to say "Where is it?" I had long forgotten the basic Hindi I had learned so long ago. If someone had asked me how to translate that phrase, I could never have conjured up the answer. Nevertheless, buried somewhere deep in my memory, the Hindi emerged. I smile, thinking that it came from a soul or spirit place, where important life messages and deeply rooted patterns of behavior lodge.

THE GONDWANA EXPRESS PICKS UP speed gradually as it moves through the miles of Delhi slums that border the tracks. Dirty children are playing on hard red clay. Cots are pushed to the edge of living areas, and old men squat nearby. Sheets of heavy plastic cover the houses. Two oxen lumber across an adjacent field, a rail-thin man guiding them with a stick. Three women move in another direction, carrying firewood on their heads. Through the window of our car, the waves of poverty and people merge together like a painting. Slowly, the rattle of the wheels over the tracks speeds up, and the fields begin to appear, first with zigzag trails of people and oxen, then gradually into open farmland. A field thick with corn and another filled with graceful white cranes. A single man squats watching four water buffalo.

The accumulation of images—accented by the clacking from the tracks below and the fast-paced Hindi in the car—activates the kind of memory that goes beyond the specific details of a past time and place. I am feeling the same kind of openness and vulnerability that I carried with me upon arrival at age 22, but now with the life skills accumulated through adulthood.

The feelings well up from a place deeper than thought or memory, as when a 56-year-old like me gets on a bicycle for the first time since youth. I would not think to lean this way or that but simply pedal. The memory of balancing on the bike lodges not in thought but in muscles and bone. The Gondwana Express is moving at breakneck speed now, and my body memories are alive—activated not by thought but by smell, sound, impulse, emotion, and some would even say through grace, whatever that word may mean in this melting pot of religions called India.

"Are you from America?" asks the small, quiet man sitting across from me on the long, padded seat. He was quiet before the train left. A friend sat next to him for awhile before de-boarding the train, but the two did not talk. He seemed deeply sad, too absorbed to speak.

I nod. "I'm going back to Jabalpur, where I lived many years ago. Are you going all the way to Jabalpur?"

"Yes, I live there." He introduces himself as Ashok and then is silent again.

"Were you visiting in Delhi?" I ask.

"I went to be with my daughter for awhile. My wife has just died. And my daughter thought it would be a good idea to go and stay with her. But now I am returning." His eyes grow even darker. Still, he manages a question for me. "Why are you going to Jabalpur?"

"I'm going to visit the family I lived with when I was a Peace Corps volunteer about 35 years ago. I was right out of college. It's a kind of reunion. I'm excited to see the change."

"Did you come all the way from America to see them?"

"I attended a meeting in Delhi, part of my work. When I realized I was coming, I got in touch with them. We made our plans by e-mail. The new technology has even gotten to Jabalpur." I smile, seeing his eyes coming to life just a little.

He smiles slightly. "I was a bank manager in Jabalpur until I retired a few years ago. We didn't have computers yet but they are putting them in now."

I think of my trips to the Jabalpur bank once a month so many years ago, when the manager insisted that I drink tea with him and visit before he would present my Peace Corps paycheck, as if part of a formal ceremony. The pace of business in these India offices was no more urgent than the conversation we are having on an overnight train ride.

"Amazing how many changes have come to India," I say. He nods. Several minutes of silence pass before I push the conversation forward. "How did your wife die?"

THE CRANE DANCE v

He picks up the question easily, apparently willing to tell his story. "She was downstairs watching TV when her heart gave out. I was upstairs. When she didn't come to bed, I went and found her. She was only 53." This quiet man begins to talk with more animation, telling me he is 59 years old, which is the same age as my own brother. He seems to appreciate the opportunity to share details of his life with a stranger. "When I saw she was dead, I called the doctor and he came right away. The next day, friends and relatives came. And, my daughter came, of course, from Delhi. We cremated my wife. It was so sad. She was so young."

In his simple white shirt and cotton pants, this small man looks more vulnerable than the Indian bank managers I remember. The national bank had moved him from Bengal, a state near Bangladesh, to Jabalpur in 1988, he tells me. That same year, I am thinking, losing my job prompted me to reflect on the patterns of depression in my life. Ashok had to start a new life, leaving his roots in Bengal, where he spoke Bengali and English. In Jabalpur in his mid-40s, he had to start over, including learning Hindi. I too started a new life in 1988. I began to learn a new kind of internal language, which I eventually learned to think of first as awareness, then acceptance, and finally action.

Ashok is returning home to an empty house. "Tomorrow, my new life begins," he says with eyes black as before, no sparkle.

A porter arrives asking if we want to order anything to eat. Ashok translates with his Hindi. I order chicken curry and chapatis. Then we fall into silence. I pick up *A Passage to India* by E.M. Forster, a last minute purchase at the Raleigh, N.C., airport. I pause on page 24, where a young English woman named Adela Quested, just arriving in the country, announces her desire to see the real India. I realize I'm thinking the same thing, now that I've left the protectiveness of my hotel in Delhi. Forster's images from the 1920s and Ashok's story of his wife's recent death spin together with my own memories of Jabalpur.

I know that televisions have reached cities throughout the world, but I have a hard time picturing the living room in Ashok's house in Jabalpur as his wife spent her last moments looking at television. His impending loneliness conjures up the slow rhythm of my days in Jabalpur so long ago, when I often succumbed to worrying about my future, my thoughts far from daily realities. No television offered temporary relief, only books and the teeming life outside my door.

Early in the Forster novel, an angst-ridden young Muslim, Dr. Aziz, pauses for a rest in his mosque. To his surprise, he comes upon an older British woman, who has traveled to India with the young Adela Quested. The older woman has slipped into the mosque out of curiosity, moving past the stage in life where she observes the strict conventions of the 1920s British. The meeting prompts Aziz to host the two women on a trip to the nearby caves, a bold step of showmanship, hospitality, and disdain for the British rulers. This impulsive decision to cross the lines of culture, class, and race almost costs Aziz his life.

As I read deeper into Forster's world, the train rattles on. I think about the Indian world I entered, including the Muslim family where I stayed. Now I am about to see the Razas again, for the first time in more than 30 years. The dusk through the portrait formed by our window is no longer enough to read by, and I flip on the tiny light above my bunk. Across from me, Ashok folds the back of his seat down to make his bed.

About three hours after leaving Delhi, the train stops at Agra, the home of the Taj Mahal. I want to stretch my legs and get a snack. Another 10 or so passengers are moving quickly to the same vendor I spot. I get no special treatment and wonder if I can come up with another Hindi phrase. I stand pondering how to proceed in this press of customers. I breathe the pungent smells from the tiny fires built on the platform by less prosperous vendors and waiting passengers.

People are moving back onto the train now, prompting me to lean in with rupees. I point to a baked vegetable pie and give him a bill, which is probably far too much. My only advantage is a long reach, and I take it and run, not pausing for change. I hear no "All Aboard," only the hiss of steam and flapping of flip-flops and sandals on children and adults alike. As I step back on the train, a man using a long stick hooks a woman's shoe that has fallen off the platform to the ground beside the rails. He gathers the sandal and follows his stout Indian wife, who fidgets nervously with her sari across the top of her head. The bouncing, coal-eyed children bound onto the car just as the train starts rolling south again, now into the vast state of Madhya Pradesh, one of the poorest states in India.

MY SECOND PASSAGE TO INDIA offers an opportunity to return to the place that launched me into adulthood without the anchors of home, family, school, and culture. My return to Jabalpur means revisiting that place and the Razas—and to some extent, the emotions of that time. This trip provides a chance to help me frame the central theme of my adult life.

The transitions in my life, both large and small, have triggered what I have learned are symptoms of depression—worry, lack of hope, workaholism, irritability, and sleeplessness. Ironically, in 1969, I was far more prepared for the challenges of going to India than I was for the transition back to the States. The trip to India proved difficult, but the return home triggered a depression that sent me spiraling down a tunnel.

Even so, in 1971, I regained firm ground. And when other major transitions arrived, I continued to sidestep recurring cycles of darkness, as if in a children's dodge-ball game. Not until I lost my job in 1988 at age 41, with two young children, did the direct hit occur. Only then did I address the patterns long ingrained in my brain and behavior. Only then did I realize the stakes in changing deep survival patterns and face the task of rediscovering the unique spark that arrived on earth in me.

BOOK 1. GOING IN
(1969–1971)

CHAPTER 1. No Fair Going to Sleep

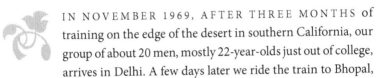 IN NOVEMBER 1969, AFTER THREE MONTHS of training on the edge of the desert in southern California, our group of about 20 men, mostly 22-year-olds just out of college, arrives in Delhi. A few days later we ride the train to Bhopal, the capital city of Madhya Pradesh, where the Peace Corps has an office. We spend a few days there, practicing our language on the street and attending final orientation sessions. The second day, they take away the toilet paper from the guest house, preparing us for a key cultural step. We know about washing with our left hand after squatting in often makeshift latrines, and eating with our right hand—not a fork. But taking this step hits many hard.

"I can't do it," yells the volunteer who has taken Sudhir as his Indian name. He is running down the little hallway in our lodge. "I'll go nuts! I can't deal with this." And, as we watch him, we can all tell he's not playing a game.

"Sudhir! Sudhir!" several of us yell. "Calm down. You can do this."

He runs back and forth in the hall before stopping and looking at us in the eye. "This is crazy. I can't make it."

Sudhir is being placed alone in a small town to the north, and we encourage him to be patient in the adjustment. I am going to Jabalpur, along with Rick, another liberal arts graduate with little college training for our agricultural outreach project.

On one of our last days in Bhopal, Rick and I are taking a walk. We stop to chat with a group of children maybe four or five years old. I'm staring blankly as one of the boys waits for me to answer his question.

"Listen to him," Rick says to me. "You know what he's asking."

"*Naam kya hai?*" the boy asks again. I smile now, picking up the abbreviated version of one of the first phrases we learned in our Hindi classes back in California.

"*Mera naam Vijay hai,*" I say, enjoying using Vijay, my Indian name, as we have been doing since training. Walking away, I feel my insecurity with the language, doubts from training drifting into my thoughts. In college and high school, I relied on memorization and long hours of study for French classes, but I never really heard the language easily. During training, Hindi was the same, even when we spoke no English in classes. I know I need to relax and just listen, not worry so much. But concentrating and relaxing at the same time is hard for me, a new way to try to trust myself.

The next day, Rick and I board the train for Jabalpur, saying goodbye to the others as they head to different parts of this large central state in North India. We have to find a place to live, set up a house, and figure out how we can contribute to the mission of the Peace Corps. We have enough money to buy bicycles, rent some type of lodging, and buy cots and other basic furnishings. We have a few contacts and addresses, including our supervisor at the local government poultry extension office and several Peace Corps volunteers who have been there from one to two years.

GREATER JABALPUR HOLDS SEVERAL hundred thousand people; no one really knows how many. The city boasts a medical school, a Christian seminary, a Sikh-dominated military post, a Chinese restaurant, and a major railway station on the main route between Calcutta and Bombay. The narrow streets teem with bicycles, rickshaws, and hand-pulled carts holding everything from coal to cauliflower. Sprawling slums surround the central areas, actually small villages tacked on to this source of survival. Many in Jabalpur speak English; a cinema offers diversions from the slow days with a taste of the growing Bombay film industry.

We have an address for a Peace Corps volunteer who lives in town and is scheduled to leave in a few weeks. We understand he has worked with the poultry office where we are assigned. Before we get to his house, though, a wiry old man hails us down as we walk along a busy street. We sense some purpose beyond a street beggar, and we stop to talk with him.

With a wispy voice, he says, "Namaste, Sahib. My name Motilal." Rick and I say hello, wondering what he wants. He races ahead, this gnarled, unshaven face indicating his preparation.

"Cooking *kay leeye* [for you]." In a rapid-fire presentation, he splices Hindi and English into a clear, compelling invitation. Alternating between a deferential Indian to the white man and an assertive, experienced household manager, he offers his services with an animated pitch that we mostly understand. "I cook for British Sahib," he says in his sing-song throaty voice, hoarse from decades of chewing beetle nut and smoking beedies, cheap Indian cigarettes.

"The British?" I ask, pulled by romantic notions of his working for the pre-independence sahibs and by skepticism that he is lying through the two long teeth he has left.

"Ah, Sahib. Cooking plum pudding for Christmas for British Sahib." He smiles impishly. His blend of deference and braggadocio is so transparent as to be endearing.

He certainly looks old and frail enough to date to pre-1947 British cooking, which leads Rick and me to consult on how long we thought he would last. But we barely have time to consider such issues before he insists on taking us to the place he has found for us to live. This is too good to be true—lodging and a cook. He somehow learned about our arrival and hatched his plan.

Rick and I nod at each other and decide to go with Motilal. We will check in with the other volunteer later. We follow the spindly man at a rapid pace down several turns and streets. Eventually, we come to a stately clock tower in the middle of a large British roundabout where three streets meet. After a short walk down one of them, we turn left into a gate and move into what appears to have once been a stately family compound. We follow him down a curving driveway around modest gardens and reach a rambling bungalow at the back of the lot. Wicker chairs are empty on the wide porch under a tiled roof. Rickshaw tracks are clear on the circle around the driveway, where they drop passengers under an extended roof.

Motilal introduces us to Mrs. Raza, a young schoolteacher raising her two pre-adolescent boys alone. She greets us with a brisk, efficient manner. "My husband died some years ago," she says matter-of-factly in perfect, staccato English. "I have far more space than I need. This half of the house would be fine for you, I think." She walks us through the left side of the house pointing quickly to the separate rooms. "Motilal can cook your meals here," she says, standing in the back room, a small door opening to the backyard. Our feet rub against large stones. I wonder if Motilal can work his magic on plum pudding with fires of dung or charcoal. I feel relieved and excited— a neat place to live, a nice family, and a quirky old cook. So far, so good.

RICK AND I SPEND A FEW DAYS WITH MOTILAL shopping for the basics—simple wood-frame beds with taut woven hemp for support. Heavy fabric stuffed tight with cotton lies directly on the hemp-mesh mattress. Our cook selects his pots and pans, haggling at every turn for the best price. Vendors put the items on one side of a set of scales balanced with weights on the other. I smile as we set up our household using an approach that resembles the symbol for American justice.

After settling into our home, we find the poultry office and meet the director, a handsome Indian man who is expecting us. With sparkling jet-black eyes and a razor thin mustache, he introduces us to his staff and invites us to ride with them in the jeep as they make the rounds to the area farmers. He and his staff are implementing in Jabalpur a national five-year agricultural and nutrition initiative from Prime Minister Indira Gandhi.

Over the next several weeks, we ride in the back of the jeep on rounds to families with mostly small flocks of chickens. We begin to understand the basic system and its challenges. The district office guarantees a minimum price for the eggs to those who receive 300 free chicks. In turn, they must sell the eggs to the government office rather than sell them on the open market. The office has to generate reliable markets for these eggs, such as the military base or booths in the market. Rick and I are supposed to help bring together the supply and demand sides for the eggs marketed through the government office.

Our three months of training in southern California alerted us to a basic cultural problem. Most Hindus are vegetarians, and many object to eating eggs because they think an egg potentially contains a new chick. We learned that chicks can be identified as male or female at a young age (called "sexed") and then separated, so that females will lay only unfertilized eggs. All large chicken farms in the United States use this sexing system, which we learned how to do during training. Now in Jabalpur, we can teach families taking in chicks the importance of sexing and separating the birds, and how to do it. If they don't use this approach, a hen can lay a fertilized egg. This can be a problem.

The refrigeration in the government office is not very reliable, nor is the sexing of the chicks among the small farmers. More than once, consumers in town have cracked an egg from the government office and found an embryo. This has led to a lack of confidence in the area in the government supply. In the few chilly winter months, when Indians are more likely to eat eggs, the price is higher on the open market, and fewer embryos are likely to develop, even in a fertilized egg. In the summer months, when eggs need to be refrigerated, prices fall because of a surplus of supply. Meanwhile, the government has to guarantee a steady price to the farmers for the eggs in all seasons.

After several weeks of riding in the jeep and getting to know a few farmers, Rick begins to sort out how he might help expand the distribution of the chicks into new households. My job is to work with marketing arrangements for the eggs, to help ensure a steady market, especially in the summer months when they are harder to sell. My business/economics degree from Duke University provides some theoretical background. But the cultural issues seem intimidating, to say the least. Our supervisor is happy for us to try out a few things on our own, reporting back to him as we go.

One day, I ride my bicycle to the edge of town and find the large Jabalpur military base. I see groups of tall Sikh soldiers marching briskly with their turbans and manicured beards. Another group is on the athletic field. I've learned that Sikhs eat eggs more regularly than Hindus and think the military base might be a good outlet in a marketing plan. I stop my bike near the gate of the base and consider going to the guard to ask about seeing an officer. But where do I start? What would I say? I don't know if I have the authority to represent the government poultry office in such a visit. Even if I do get in to see someone, I would first have to go through a long tea drinking ritual.

I decide to ride away instead of pursuing the visit, thinking about the protocol of sipping tea and the slow pace of life here. Having work be so nebulous, so unclear, is new territory for me. I don't know whether to feel discouraged or hopeful. For now, I just try to notice how things work in this country.

Soon after, Rick and I meet with the head of the district office to discuss our orientation to the project. "I went out to the military base and thought about talking with one of the guys in charge," I say. "Maybe they can buy eggs on a regular basis." The handsome Indian officer smiles but offers no comment. Rick tells a little of his early but unsuccessful efforts in marketing more chicks. Still, no response.

He finally leans towards us and says with a twinkling eye, "Read a lot of books while you're here." He stands up from the little table in the cramped office. We rise as well, realizing our little meeting is over. He reaches his full six feet and looks at me eye to eye. "This is a complicated business. Don't worry about the work."

Going home, Rick and I don't talk about the comment. But I can sense he is already feeling discouraged in his work. I feel a little numb. My Indian boss doesn't expect much from me. So how much do I expect from myself? I try not to get discouraged and manage to focus on the street, where everything is so interesting. A man in simple sandals is pushing a large cart down the middle of the street with vegetables piled in beautiful, artistic stacks.

RICK AND I ATTEMPT TO SETTLE INTO a productive work routine, but instead, our days unfold as our Indian supervisor foretold. Rick has trouble finding a niche with the outreach activities. I make no progress developing a marketing plan. I feel isolated, without a real team to work with. The guys at the poultry office are polite but seem pre-occupied with their own work. Gradually, Rick and I drift away from regular hours at the office.

A daily work routine has always been an anchor for me, as a student and during summers in college. Without such a structure, navigating the Jabalpur cultural landscape becomes the central task of the day. My senior year at Duke, I had an excellent interdisciplinary course on India, gaining a thorough intellectual grounding in the Hindu caste system and the country's social norms. But nothing could prepare me for the daily press of poverty, the loud film music broadcast night and day, and the squats at the latrine with water. My sensitivity hardens as I follow the guidepost one ex-volunteer suggested during training: give only to the beggars who are missing a limb.

Finding some solace in the privacy of our home, I try to tune out the ragged multitudes without losing the larger hope of trying to make things better. But even sitting on the verandah, I cannot escape the bombardment of stimuli that often immobilize my feelings, as well as my actions. I watch the women laborers just over the border of Mrs. Raza's compound as they balance bricks and other building supplies on their heads. They carry the loads from a pile at the road to the wobbly wooden scaffolding going up around the shell of a new building. The women throw faded saris across boney shoulders. Their eyes suggest they are about 30, maybe 35, but their bodies look like they could be 50, burdened by too many children, too much lifting, and too few rupees.

One day, not long after arriving, I walk back home from the Chinese restaurant beside the clock tower. Motilal has the day off, and I have just eaten lunch. Rick is off somewhere. The omnipresent blare of Indian film music competes with the ringing of bicycle bells as men, women, and children negotiate their cycles and rickshaws through the crowded street. The sounds are dreamlike, not distinct. Then I notice a voice calling my name, as if from a distance. I lift my head and realize I've been in a kind of trance.

The veteran Peace Corps volunteer who is returning home in a few days is standing before me holding his bike. "Are you okay?" he asks.

"Yeah, why do you ask?" I jerk back into the present.

"I called your name several times, and you didn't answer. You were kind of shuffling your feet." I remain silent, feeling his words sink into me like a drink of water. "Maybe you're a little depressed about being here?" He stands at his bike, stroking his full beard.

Looking at him closer now, I realize that I was in fact staring at the ground, not thinking and not seeing, but numb to my surroundings. The sharp ring of the rickshaw bells now penetrate this mental fog as well, men glaring as they pedal around me. The word ricochets through my brain—*depressed*. As I start to think about answering his question, he continues.

"Don't worry about the rickshaws," he says. "You'll get used to them."

I notice people getting water at the public spigots beside me. A filthy stream flows behind the Chinese restaurant. I dodge a rickshaw rolling my way, one more bell avoided. I realize that I don't remember walking down the hill from the little restaurant.

"I guess it's a little overwhelming," I say, alert now, attuned to the sights all around me. "Everything will be fine," I tell the veteran volunteer. "Don't worry." But I don't feel so confident.

LIVING WITH THE RAZAS PROVES TO be one of our finest contributions as Peace Corps volunteers and a comforting anchor to the day. We provide a contrast to the conspicuous American jeeps that nudge through Jabalpur's crowded streets from the fenced compound of the U.S. Agency for International Development (USAID) on the edge of town. Middle-aged Americans retreat in these jeeps from the dusty streets into a suburban-like life behind wire fences. They use finely granulated sugar and toilet paper shipped from the States. We speak Hindi with the rickshaw wallahs, and on Motilal's days off, negotiate with vendors in the market. I help with the boys' basketball team at the Catholic School where Mrs. Raza teaches. The boys call me "*lal admi*" for "red man," my freckled, fair complexion now a permanent reddened hue in the Indian sun. Meanwhile, Rick, shorter and with a dark complexion, cycles about the city in his new Nehru jacket, passing for a native.

While we do not share meals with the Razas and live in separate quarters, Rick and I are adopted as quasi-family. Taqi, a bright, intense 12-year-old, acts as the man of the house. He races from homework to chores and then to visits with us, enjoying our stories of the States. He also monitors his younger brother, Moin, who would prefer playing with us on the verandah to settling down to his homework. Often, we ask Mrs.

THE CRANE DANCE   9

Raza about routine matters of transportation and logistics when Motilal's judgment seems shaky or his Hindi is beyond us.

One night, Mrs. Raza invites us over for a visit after dinner, with her and her best friend, Ala. We settle into the living room at the front of her section of the house. A small platform with colorful fabric sits next to the wall that separates the Razas' space from ours. A stunning teak divider with carvings of animals and birds on several hinged panels functions as a living room wall, containing our conversation in the front part of the large room.

I have met Ala a few times in passing on the verandah. This is our first real conversation. The talk turns to religion. "Bill and Rick have been singing in the choir at the Anglican church," Mrs. Raza says, using our American names, which she prefers.

"Did you grow up in a Christian church?" Ala asks.

"Yes, we both grew up Christian," I say. "We're attending the church here to meet people. And, we both like to sing." Rick and I have become adept at answering for each other at times. Often I find myself jumping in first, probably out of nervousness. Rick is patient with me. Perhaps he's more secure.

"I'm a Parsi," she says. "Do you know that religion? It's from Persia."

"I know a little. Fire is important, right?"

She explains about the key deity and the relationship with fire.

The conversation continues on this religious turn. "I'm sure you know," Mrs. Raza says, looking at Rick and me, "that many Muslims stayed in Jabalpur when independence came in 1947. East and West Pakistan were too far for many to travel."

"Were there problems after that?" asks Rick.

"Many times over the years there were conflicts. But that has mostly calmed down. We all get along much better now. We have not had any recent problems in our compound."

We sip our tea and continue to chat about Jabalpur and religion. My mind wanders as I listen. The melting pot of religion here has been stimulating to me on many levels. I think about the contradictions of the Christian church where I was raised, about segregated congregations in my hometown in Mississippi. Christian messages seemed confusing to me as a child, because the church preached brotherhood but kept people apart. Now, I find the Christian concept of salvation equally limiting, as my Indian friends follow such diverse worship systems. Then I hear Mrs. Raza speaking and turn away from my daydream of the Methodist Church in Jackson, Mississippi.

"These boys have been taking music lessons."

"Really. What have you learned?" Ala asks, looking our way.

"I've been studying the tabla," says Rick. "And, I've started on the sitar as well. Vijay plays the bansuri."

With a little encouragement from Mrs. Raza, Rick goes next door and fetches our instruments, the two small drums that function together as the tabla and my small reed flute. We sit cross-legged on the platform near the teak divider, as if in formal concert, and warm up briefly. Then, we begin in unison, as we have been practicing. I play the raga melody that we have learned from our teacher, and Rick anchors the tune with his tabla. Our Indian friends applaud when we finish, amazed at our proficiency. And we are amazed too, after less than four months of lessons and practice.

WE HAVE LEARNED OUR INDIAN MUSIC from a master, both in his music and his ability to inspire us. A former backup sitar and tabla player for Ravi Shankar in Bombay, our teacher is happy to have eager pupils from the West. Returning to Jabalpur from his peak years as a world-class musician, he misses the more cosmopolitan city and friendships. He enjoys our lessons and organizes picnic outings with us and a young Brit working in another development project. We become friends.

We work with him one or two nights a week in a little hut not far from our house. He writes out simple ragas in small composition books, and we carry them to our lessons like schoolboys. We ride our bicycles in the dark, ringing our bells at the few carts on the road. He sits cross-legged on a mat on the floor, ample belly providing a table of sort for his sitar. His smile reflects years of chewing beetle nut.

We go through the ragas from our notebooks, and he adds nuances of rhythm and pace. "Listen to the end, how it picks up," he says, going through the final phrase of a raga. We go through it again, this time, speeding up for the ending.

I take a break as he works with Rick on some tabla techniques and walk outside. In just ten steps, I am standing in a small empty field looking up at a crystal clear and moonless night. The stars seem as close as gumdrops on a Christmas tree, as if I can pluck them out and eat them. With no pollution in Jabalpur in 1970, the lights from millions of miles away seem as near as the fireflies I caught as a kid. I lean back and stare, absorbed in the heavens. Such moments satisfy me in India, when I feel most alive and energetic.

I head back inside, and we settle into another round on the evening raga. Rick has become quite proficient on the tabla, the anchoring rhythm in Indian music, and I have an adequate skill on the bansuri. With our teacher at the sitar, we strike quite a pose, sitting here on the floor of this little hut. The starlight shines down on our cross-cultural concert, illuminating the dark corners through the door and the square gaps in the sides of the mud-baked walls.

Tonight, no worries of daily Jabalpur routines or future life back in America penetrate the protective bubble forged by our music and companionship. We are carried away into the rhythms of the raga. The high pitch of the bansuri marches across the sky. Anchoring us below are the rapid rhythms of the tabla, as Rick massages the drum-heads with fingers and the base of his palm. Our teacher leans his balding head back, eyes closed, as if chasing the gods of music across the long neck of the sitar. Then just as we hear him moving towards the final phrase that we have been practicing, he looks at us and smiles and we race to the finish, picking up the pace. We end in perfect unison.

MANY VIBRANT MOMENTS OCCUR—in the music hut, on the verandah, or riding my bicycle and soaking in such sights as the men navigating their vegetable carts in busy streets. I try to absorb and feel grateful for the mystery and humanity of this cultural experience. But the spiritual transformation of the ragas does not ring through the entire day. Without structure or a sense of my future in Jabalpur, I often slip into a routine of self-absorption, thinking especially about the future.

I sit at my small desk in our bedroom, trying to read or study Hindi, just as I have relied on discipline and routines all my life. But my mind wanders. What will I do when I return? How will I deal with the draft and Vietnam? Can I make it through two years here? As these thoughts return day after day, I sink downward. Many days move forward as slowly as the huge vegetable carts I watch men pull down the street. I work hard to keep my dark moods from preoccupying me, forcing myself to pay attention to the sights and sounds just outside the door.

I think Rick is also absorbed with such doubts, but we never talk much about these issues. One afternoon in the hot season, five months after arriving, we are trying to sleep under our mosquito nets in the afternoon heat, as does the rest of the city at that time of day. In this ritual of the hot seasons, everyone sleeps. No one worries. It is too hot to think. Sleep provides the only respite. I start to drift off but Rick wakes me up.

"No fair going to sleep. Wake up, Vijay." Vijay wakes up and worries more about Bill's future. I also worry about what Rick is thinking. He has been even quieter than usual in recent weeks. I have a hunch he may leave.

Lying under the mosquito net on my cot, I think about days I spent as a kid, often alone on the college campus where I grew up in Mississippi. I also felt alone during much of my college years. I am used to moving into an internal world and know I will survive. I flash back to the psychologist at Peace Corps training. His evaluations were rigorous, and he rejected several promising volunteers because he did not think they could handle the stress of India. The psychologist was right to let me come, I think. I can survive India. But at what cost?

Not long after that afternoon, in the middle of the night, I wake up on my own this time, to sounds like chalk against a blackboard. I roll over and see Rick across the room outside his net furiously scratching something on the wall. "What are you doing?" I say, half asleep.

"Go back to sleep, Vijay. Don't worry about it."

The next morning, I see an abstract drawing of some sort on the caked mud wall of our large bedroom. I start to ask about it but stop. Rick seems more restless than I am, even more detached from any semblance of structure by now. Not long after his mural night, Rick comes up one afternoon when we are sitting on the porch and says he has something to talk to me about.

"I've decided I need to go home, Vijay." He looks at me with his dark eyes. "I feel really bad about leaving you here alone but I just can't manage anymore." He does not say a lot more, only that the work doesn't make sense to him. "The music has kept me sane. It's time for me to go, Vijay. I've got to." We haven't been here a year.

The Peace Corps has recently changed its rules about early departure and will pay for a direct flight home. Previously, they would not pay for an early departure. Rumors abounded that volunteers were evacuated from India after mental breakdowns. True or not, Rick is sure that he needs to leave before things get worse.

After he leaves, I have an even harder time making it through the days. I feel more alone than ever now. Even though Rick and I rarely discussed how we felt about things, he was a good companion for meals and for music. Now, I am mostly alone. My work has dwindled to working with one young man who is only a little older than I am. He received a batch of 300 chicks from the government office, and I show him how to raise them. He invites me to eat at his house and wander the streets with him and his best friend, talking about our futures. "I wish I could be like that bird," he says one day, smiling. "And fly away from here." I wonder about where I will fly in my future. One night, I go with them to a night-long Muslim festival. We watch barefoot men dash across red-hot ashes and then join the crowd parading to a nearby lake, where they sink large flowered decorations, part of the symbolism of the holiday.

The cultural stimulation keeps me going, barely. Not long after Rick leaves, I get news that my only brother is getting married in the summer. Missing the wedding does not seem like an option to me. In 1970, the Peace Corps does not allow a temporary trip home. I decide to leave too.

"SLOW DOWN, YOU MOVE TOO FAST," I sing aloud as I pedal past the rickshaws on my right. "Got to make the morning last." I smile as the popular Simon and Garfunkel tune helps me to absorb the sights on Jabalpur's streets, just weeks before I head home for the wedding.

Today, Mrs. Raza and the boys are away at school. I have told Motilal I'm leaving, and he's now rarely around except to produce an evening meal. Rick's bed, thin mattress, and mosquito net are gone. I live as if in a vast, abandoned house. Back home by mid-day, I try to concentrate on packing some papers at the little desk in the corner before I try to sleep through the worst of the afternoon heat. Ruminations about my future, as well as my past, circle about... the military draft that surely awaits me ... my failure as a Peace Corps volunteer.

I re-read the letter from the Peace Corps office in Bhopal, which explains my travel arrangements. Not sure what else to do, I need something to engage my mind. I pick up the copy of the resignation letter that I sent to the Bhopal office and study the first line. "John Kennedy often paraphrased Aristotle by saying that happiness is the full use of one's faculties along lines of excellence." I look up. I still believe it—excellence is what I long for. But I have not achieved it here. I feel like I might cry, but the excitement of returning to my family feels stronger than the sense of failure. The range of emotions is too much to absorb. Instead of sorting through the feelings, I turn to thinking.

I review the debate about why I joined the Peace Corps in the first place. Should I apply for the domestic Vista program or the international Peace Corps? I pondered the question from the winter break of my senior year well into my final semester. I should stay and work at home, perhaps with the poor families I have seen for years when I traveled to Appalachia during the summers. But no, the pull of the overseas adventure proved to be stronger. As a kid, I loved getting postcards from my grandmother as she traveled around the world. She would bring little dolls in exotic dress home to us from her trips. I never saw such items in my friends' houses in Jackson, Mississippi.

My senior year in college, the government was drafting more and more young men for the Vietnam War. The draft was almost certainly going to reach me. I was convinced that Kennedy was right, that I needed to do something for my country, not ask what it could do for me. When I thought about the draft, the Peace Corps looked even better. When I decided to join, I understood I could not be drafted if I was a volunteer. Even so, in California during our Peace Corps training, a notice ordering me to take a physical arrived. I spent an afternoon at the massive Los Angeles recruitment facility and passed all the tests. My draft board sent out the notice, which reached me in Jabalpur.

Not long after the letter to report for duty found me in India, our supervisor from Bhopal came through on a planned visit. He said he would get it to the right people in Washington, where the national board did in fact overrule my local board. Now I'm giving up the protection from the draft afforded to Peace Corps volunteers.

The hot afternoon moves as slowly as my rudimentary Hindi. *Surely, I'll get another draft notice, as soon as the paperwork catches up with me.* But enough thinking. It's time to go to sleep, to toss worries to the heavens, slip under the mosquito net, and forget. Yet, I am drawn again to the letter, to review my thoughts, my words—how I articulated this decision to leave. I pick it up again before going to sleep.

"During the last several months, my inadequacy for my particular position has become increasingly evident." I resist the tears forming deep in my eyes. Admitting inadequacy is not familiar territory. In school, I worked hard, and grades mostly came easily. This measurement helped build my self-confidence, even if that barometer took no reading on my emotional health.

India has shaken that confidence, and I feel vulnerable. Still, I know leaving is the right choice. My job proved too elusive, and I need to be at my only brother's wedding. While I feel burdened by failure, I also feel a glimmer of hope as I again read the end of the letter. "I still feel the need for a life of active involvement in a field of usefulness and relevance to one's particular surroundings." I tuck it into a pouch for the journey home.

CHAPTER 2. A Cold Winter Flame

GEORGIA HAS A LATIN BOUNCE TO HER step as she heads down the cobblestone walkway from my family's log cabin in western North Carolina. After six months traveling to Peru, Brazil, and other Latin American countries, her long dark hair seems a sugary brown. A colorful purse dangles from her shoulder.

"We'll be awhile," I say to my parents and brother, who are on the large screened porch discussing final arrangements for his rehearsal dinner. Georgia accepted my invitation to the wedding, returning from Peru via North Carolina. Only a week back myself, I am quickly losing the fast-paced, sing-song English I acquired in Jabalpur.

As my language shifts back to the familiar, my thoughts continue to race across distant lands—real places in India and psychological locations that remain dark and unknown. I focus on the specifics of the day as best I can, delighted to see my family and Georgia. But mostly I feel disconnected, lacking the familiar backdrop of loud, ever-present Indian film music. The cars are so big. Television and telephones now jangle me instead of cows in the street and the familiar sounds like, "*Hey, kaila*" from the street vendor selling bananas.

Georgia and I walk up Littleton Road, the narrow lane in front of our cabin. Two cars can barely pass on the streets of this little community called Lake Junaluska. Having Georgia beside me after nearly a year feels surreal, like a mirage. "I hope you don't mind visiting with Mrs. Hawkins," I say. "Mother likes to put people together who have things in common."

"Oh no, this will be interesting. I love looking at fabric and weavings." Georgia is making her own adjustment, from her arrival yesterday straight from Peru. She'll stay for my brother's wedding and then head to her family in Washington, D.C. She smiles. "I'm just glad to be here."

I look at her sky-blue eyes and hold her hand as we walk up the hill. We met my last semester at Duke University and had a strong connection by the time I graduated. But our separate dreams, along with the specter of the draft, pulled us apart. Since I last saw her in August of 1969, on a break from Peace Corps training in California, we wrote occasional letters. We weren't sure if we would pick up our relationship. On a vacation in Nepal before leaving, I sent her a letter from the post office in Katmandu inviting her to the wedding. It somehow found her via the American Express office in Lima.

Mrs. Hawkins is delighted to have company, especially someone who can talk about South American weavings. We settle into the living room of the little summer cottage with exposed beams over four modest rooms. As she brings out woven rugs, hangings, and linens, I watch these two textile enthusiasts discussing color, fabric, stitching, and culture. Feigning interest, I find myself more engaged with a vigorous internal conversation than the bright-colored fabrics.

It's great seeing Georgia so happy, but I wonder how she does it. I wish I felt like that, one voice says, as if addressing a committee. *I mean, it's nice to see Georgia, but I feel like I'm in a dream. How is she happy?*

People aren't really happy like that, another voice says. *They just fake it. You're just not good at faking it.*

Then a third voice pops up. *Why should you be happy? Life is hard. But at least you're not fighting in the jungle right now. Dying for your country in Nam. Right? Count your blessings.* As I sort out these messages bouncing through my brain, I realize that a real voice is addressing me.

"Bill, I was asking if you wanted something to drink."

"Oh, sorry, Mrs. Hawkins. I was just thinking about India. I'm afraid you and Georgia have gone way beyond me on the textiles."

I look now at the curiosity in Georgia's eyes and remember how quickly I became absorbed with her when we started eating lunches together after the mid-day class my last college semester. When I described how Junaluska gave me a sense of freedom in the summers, away from the heat and pressures in Mississippi, she seemed to have a genuine understanding of what I meant. And she sparkled, talking about learning Spanish or volunteering at a nursing home.

Watching Georgia unfold another set of fabric with Mrs. Hawkins, I remember how we moved quickly from our common interest in the Religion and Contemporary Literature class to the common experiences of our families. Growing up I had never felt so at ease talking to a girl. Soon the after-class lunches expanded to dates. She came to my tennis matches, where the Duke team would struggle against higher caliber teams that offered scholarships. She was a regular fan by the end of the season, cheering me on.

I snap back to the present as I realize that Mrs. Hawkins and Georgia are winding down, the last piece of fabric now folded neatly and stacked with the others. "Thank you so much," Georgia says as we head to the door. I nod my thanks to my old friend as well.

The dream-like quality of my return from India blends into the following days. At the little chapel next to the lake, my brother walks in from the side door. I'm his best man and stand beside him, along with our father, who is performing the ceremony. I look handsome in my tux and am glad Georgia is there. It's a happy occasion, and I laugh with relatives and friends.

After the reception, Georgia is off to her own family. In a few weeks, she will start law school in Washington, part of the first great wave of women going to law school in the 1970s. Even though she majored in religion and loves so many sides of art, she is the last of the three girls and neither of the other two has followed in their father's tracks to become a lawyer. "We'll see how it works out," she says as I drive her to the airport. We promise to be in touch, to schedule a visit after we both get settled into the fall semester. I'm sad to see her go but know she and I have a lot to work out in our respective careers and in the relationship as we head to different cities.

In a few days, I'll be driving through New England for a last trip before entering the Boston University School of Theology. When I decided to leave India, I applied and got accepted to the alma mater of Martin

Luther King, Jr. Studying ethics and religion in a new city seemed like a good way to start life again in the States. I had lived only in the South. Maybe Boston would provide both a landing and a launching pad. The acceptance letter reached me in Jabalpur.

Religion has always interested me, growing up as a preacher's kid and going to the Southeastern Methodist Assembly grounds at Lake Junaluska every summer. I do not have a clear religious belief now, after drifting away from the church in college and embracing Muslim and Hindu friends in Jabalpur, but I welcome an opportunity to sort out some of my feelings about ethics and religion. I don't plan to apply for a IV-D draft deferment, the classification for divinity students and ministers, because I do not plan to be a minister.

I don't want to hide from the draft behind this deferment. Nor did I go into the Peace Corps primarily as a way to dodge the draft; the mission and the opportunity took me there. But avoiding being drafted was a relief. Now, I'm not sure what I will do. I have a low number in the new lottery, a draft system initiated by the government when I was in India. The lower the number, the higher the risk of being drafted.

THE DORMITORY ROOM ON COMMONWEALTH AVENUE has no phone. Neither I nor my roommate brought a television or stereo system. But we do have a picture-book view looking onto the Charles River from the seventh floor of the School of Theology Building. Bustling Kenmore Square lies on the other side of the building, but in this room, the energy of a captivating city seems far away.

Lying on my single bed against a bare pea-green wall, my energy is slowly moving through another day of withdrawal from the world, a kind of hibernation. I feel inside like a summer beach house being boarded up for the winter, one window at a time. Even so, I am managing to keep up with my courses in this first semester of graduate school, a testament to several excellent teachers and the discipline I learned from my father.

At dusk, the pale light off the Charles River is starting to shade the green plaster, as I drift into a restless nap. A knock on the door surprises me. My roommate, an eager student who will be an excellent parish minister one day, often has visitors, but he is out. Rarely does someone come to see me. The knock comes again. I open the door to two familiar but unexpected faces.

Rick, my Jabalpur roommate, stands before me, along with Dirk, my traveling side-kick to Katmandu. In Boston, I have seen Dirk a few times and he told me he was in touch with Rick.

We chat for a few minutes, not sure whether to begin reminiscing or jump right into our current lives. "Come with us to the movies," Rick says, Americanized fully again with long, flowing hair.

"No, I don't feel like it. I'm tired."

"Come on, Vijay. You can't lie there all night, like we did in Jabalpur." He pauses. "We can just go out and catch the MTA. We don't have to arrange for a rickshaw." His twinkling eyes reflect the energy he had when he played the ragas. "It looks like you could use some getting out. Plus we're going to see MASH—it's funny."

I let the invitation settle. "I don't think so. MASH sounds too military to me. I know it has funny parts but I'm worried about the draft. I don't want to think about it." They try to persuade me, but instincts draw me instead to hibernation.

The next day, after class, I pack my gym clothes in a bag and throw in some reading from school. My classes engage my intellectual curiosity, and the energy of other students rubs off enough to keep me going through the days. The lethargy from the night before seems at bay for now. I hustle to Kenmore Square, five minutes from the Theology Building, for the long commute to my work-study job.

I have gotten familiar with the logistics of my urban commute. First, I ride the old-style trolley car into the middle of Boston, about four or five stops. Then, reaching the center of this spoke-and-wheel subway system, I change lines and head back out of town to the last stop, going southwest towards a section called Roslindale. Finally, the last leg by bus takes me to the YMCA. Roslindale borders the conservative Irish section of South Boston on one side and the predominantly black, poor area of Roxbury on the other. Racial tensions over school desegregation are high in the city. The ride one way is at least an hour if I make smooth connections.

Today the bustling student energy at Kenmore Square and the rattling trolley into the city feel like an adventure. I arrive at the YMCA late in the afternoon, when the high school boys are about to start a basket-ball game. My supervisor has figured out that although I'm in divinity school, I have no real idea of how to work with these boys. The supervisors at the Y know far more about what kind of activities will work best.

My job has become mainly playing basketball and hanging around afterwards. My credibility comes not from any ministerial wisdom but from my prowess on the basketball court. After playing basketball for my high school team and serious intramural games at Duke, I can hold my own with these teenagers.

This is the first time that I have gotten to know a racially mixed group of kids, mostly black. I lose myself in the frenetic games, thoughts about dull green walls and ethics gone in the intensity of speeding down the court. Even racial memories from Mississippi fall away as I run down court for defense or go up for my own jump shot. As we wind down, panting for breath, I'm smiling and energized by the exercise. Many of my happiest times at Duke were after playing hard basketball games, soaked in sweat, with thoughts and emotions on hold.

After the game at the Y, I often go to Jimmy's apartment in a nearby housing project. A charismatic black man in his mid-twenties, he has found a niche in this mixed race neighborhood. His wife and toddler wander about the little living room, with maybe ten boys crowding in. "The Bruins are going to be great this year," says Vinnie, who is white, as he shoots a plastic puck towards one of his buddies by the door. These kids carry street hockey sticks and plastic pucks everywhere.

On the couch, playing with his own little one, Jimmy glances at the clock. "You guys can stay a little longer, but you've got to get home soon," he says. "Homework. Don't play hockey all night."

"Come on, Jimmy, just a little longer," says a strapping 15-year-old who has no father at his apartment down the street. Everyone laughs at the familiar routine of protests.

As the guys start to drift out, I say good-bye. "You were tough today. Took all I had to stay with you," I say. The young man smiles.

Jimmy and I talk about the afternoon a little. "A lot of these kids don't have steady males in their lives," he says. "Even though you're not here much, it's good for them. Just being here, playing ball with them."

On the long commute back, Jimmy's words and the lingering adrenaline from exercise carry me forward for maybe the first leg. But nightfall is mingling now with the darkness of the subway as it leaves the above-ground trolley tracks and shoots into the underground tunnels. As my energy fades, I remember the familiar Kingston Trio lines about the man whose "fate is still unknown," who may "ride forever 'neath the streets of Boston, he's the man who never returns."

As I head into the central station in the middle of the city, I try to read my assignment for my Old Testament class, taught by an energetic and engaging scholar. After concentrating on several paragraphs, I put the book down and stare out the window. The bright lights of the transfer station startle me into action, and I make my way over to the line that goes back out to Kenmore Square. Settling into my last leg, a now familiar numbness begins to spread through me. From my final stop I shuffle back to the seventh floor room and plop down on my bed.

The next day and the next, I keep going. Willpower has gotten me through much of my childhood in Mississippi and through Duke and India. I can do this too, I tell myself. I force myself to explore the city. One evening, I press into a standing room only crowd in the Student Union, just a few buildings down from the School of Theology. A middle-aged black journalist named Alex Haley is speaking. He describes the research project that took him to ship logs, wind patterns, and slave lists from West Africa to the Eastern seaboard. He takes us through a breath-taking mystery of how he pieced together evidence that eventually led him to the actual African village that brought him to his roots. That night, I think about my own history in Mississippi and the riddles that are yet to be solved.

Several weeks later, anthropologist Margaret Mead, who is barely tall enough for me to see from the back of the packed auditorium at Northeastern University, speaks with the vigor of a graduate student. Now nearing the end of her notable career, she describes the excitement and wonder she experienced in other cultures. I nod, recognizing these same feelings—still fresh and vivid with the Razas, my flute teacher, and Muslim poultry farmer friends.

These many opportunities and inspirations in Boston do not give me what I need, however. I find that willpower alone no longer sees me through. More than once, I call in sick to my work-study job, something I would never have done growing up. Each time, Jimmy's reminder that these boys need steady male figures in their lives burns in my heart. I am letting them down, even by missing the basketball games—another male figure who doesn't show up for those boys. But I just can't summon the energy for the long commute. I manage to complete the minimum number of hours to keep my work-study funding for the semester but plan to drop out of the program at Christmas, despite the nagging guilt.

MY WILLPOWER WANES FURTHER as the semester drags into the edge of my first winter in the northeast. To save money, I often walk across broad Commonwealth Avenue to a low-priced grocery store. It lies beyond the Massachusetts Turnpike, the multi-lane freeway that slices through the city into downtown. The walkway over the turnpike has a high fence, maybe eight or nine feet, curved inward at the top so that a pedestrian could not possibly fall over.

One evening, bundled against the December wind, I pause as I walk over the turnpike and take a closer look. "I wonder how hard it would be to *climb* over it," I think, looking at the construction more carefully. I realize there is no way to fall or even toss myself over that fence. I would have to climb over it, deliberately and with effort. The details bounce around in my brain through the walk over the bridge to the grocery.

As the trips across the bridge get colder in December, the question keeps jumping into my mind, trip after trip. I begin to see an image—the physical task of climbing over and then having the nerve to jump. But other details are also pressing into my time and thoughts, so I usually put it out of my mind by the time I get back to my dorm room on the seventh floor.

I turn to my assignments. One course taught by the dean of the school, a well-respected veteran teacher, emphasizes the development of a life plan. The process requires us to determine what parts of life are important to us, how decisions need to be part of long-term goals. But I can barely get through the night. Another day seems so hard, so pointless. Where is this studying taking me? The self-absorption turns negative and dark. A few tasks keep me going. Travel plans for Christmas need my attention, to get to my parents' house in Nashville, Tennessee, and perhaps see Georgia along the way in Washington. Dealing with logistics for the upcoming holidays keeps me focused enough to get through my courses.

Georgia and I have not actively pursued our relationship during the fall, nor have we let it totally die. She is busy with her first semester of law school, while I am sorting out Boston. I manage to share a little of my feelings with her but am guarded. I don't want her to drift out of my life. Who would want to believe in someone with no sense of direction?

I confide a bit in a friend at school as well. "I don't know if I can make it through another semester," I tell John, another first year student who lacks direction. We talk more about school and why we each long for something more. But I stop short of discussing with him the thoughts I have walking over the turnpike. These are too scary and private to share with anyone.

Christmas provides a needed break. Pickup basketball games in Nashville with my high school buddy Jim Tramel help. And I connect briefly with Georgia. I tell her some of my ambivalence about school but do not go to any personal level, afraid that I will blurt out the truth of how depressed I am. I'm too embarrassed and scared to even talk about these dark thoughts. With relatives, I deflect questions about my future. I worry about the draft but don't tell anyone. Mostly, people leave me alone.

The time away races by, and I return north to another semester in my first really cold winter. The walks across the Turnpike get harder—braced against the chilling wind, hunkered down in my thoughts. Darkness descends earlier, outside and within. I start to lose interest in my courses. The complex theology of Rudolf Bultmann requires an intellectual curiosity that I cannot muster. No longer does discipline work. My father would rise early in the morning for study and working on a weekly sermon, before the family breakfast ritual and his short walk on the campus to his job as the president of Millsaps College. Dad's spiritual center anchored his discipline. Lacking such grounding, I rely on willpower, which is not enough.

One night in a bleak January weekend, I have a stomach bug. Focusing on the bare, pea-green plaster in the wide corridor, I hear snatches of words as I shuffle towards the bathroom—a few older students in animated voices on ideas about their future. No sign of John, my only real buddy on the seventh floor. Bent nearly double at the waist, I make it to the first stall and lift the commode seat before I vomit. Breathing heavily, sweat covering my fevered body, I lie down on the cold, tile floor. The retching continues long after my stomach is empty. I hang my head over the toilet bowl. Then I crumple back down on the floor and cry. I can't think of anyone who would care that I am sick or even if I died.

While the fever passes from my body that night in the bathroom, it is growing deeper at the psychological and spiritual levels. Walking across the turnpike, I start obsessing about the tall fence, a kind of thin veil between two lives. I study the patterns of the crossed wire. I stop and watch the pace of the cars—how close they are together, how fast they go. *Would I jump over the wire like I might a fence in the woods, just happy to cross over to the other side?* Questions ebb and flow as I walk through the winter, across that roadway, from practical to philosophical. *What if I didn't die? What if I ended up like a vegetable in a hospital?*

I pad through the winter cold, clutching sliced bread and cheese and milk against my chest on the return trip back to the dorm.

Mostly, I think of jumping only when I walk high above those lanes of speeding cars and trucks. One day, the questions get more personal. *What would my parents do if I died? How would they feel? How would it affect them?* Looking down at the speeding traffic, bundled against the cold, I think about Georgia. *If I stay on this walkway and don't jump, will we get married someday?* My mind moves forward. *Will we have children? Have a home of our own? Will I have a career? A life that interests me?*

Back at the dorm, these accumulating questions overwhelm me. The future is so hard to imagine, and I spiral deeper into a dark void. I stop going to most of my classes.

Even so, some faint flame is still burning. Some deep pulse of life finds its way into the darkness, pulling me toward specific images and people—toward life. And so, slowly, some answers begin to form in my thinking as well as more questions. In the stillness of the dorm room, my desk is a familiar anchor.

My mother and father... they would care. The thought that comes is soft but distinct, as if from a distant mountaintop. *It would hurt them. They would manage and move on. But it would make their lives harder.* I try to imagine my parents living with my death.

My brother and sister would care too. And, Georgia. What difference would it have on her life? It would make things harder. Jim would care too. And, my friend John here at school.

As January lumbers along, this debate consumes me. I lie in my bed. No more trips to Roslindale and the basketball games. I manage to get up and continue my Sunday morning routine at the Boston Commons, where I read *The New York Times* cover to cover. That keeps my mind going. But I still have to cope with the rest of the week, including the cold walks across the Massachusetts Turnpike.

ONE DAY IN FEBRUARY, I OPEN my little mailbox in the basement of the Theology School and see a return address that's vaguely familiar. I open the letter and realize the day has finally come. Initially, I feel panic reading the letter from the draft board ordering me to report. But I walk outside beside the Charles and the sensation washes away, as if carried away by the river. I head back to my desk with a burst of energy and pull out a notebook. I start making a list of the options that have been going through my head for months. Now, I have to make a decision.

"Go to Canada," I write. "Be a medic." Then, "go to jail." I study them a long time, the first time I've written them out and looked at the black and white of my choices. "I can't kill people," I write. More of what's in my head falls onto the page; my beliefs are getting on the paper. "Didn't even like hearing about deer hunting." I smile a little, remembering my uncles in Mississippi describing their trips into the woods and the time my cousin killed his first buck.

The next day, with energy as well as a little panic, I find a booth set up by the American Friends Service Committee, mostly Quakers, at the Student Union. I start chatting with an earnest young man who is handing out materials. "Here's a pamphlet about Conscientious Objectors or COs for short," he says. "You can start with that. It lays out the history, from Thoreau on civil disobedience through A.J. Muste, who was a pacifist."

I thank him and take away a pile of literature. I have heard of conscientious objectors but don't really know what that means. I've never read *Civil Disobedience*. Never heard of Muste. At the dorm room I feel a surge of urgency. A sense of purpose. A veil begins to lift.

The next day, I go back to talk more at the Service Committee booth about peace options and the CO status. I feel a bounce in my step as I walk along the Charles. Over the next several weeks, the details begin to fall into place. I decide I am in fact a CO. I do object to war, and my beliefs are consistent with the history of those who have come before me. I will have to make this argument to the Nashville draft board.

The Quakers coach me on my presentation, strategy, and content. I read Thoreau and others on standing for conscience, against war. I write drafts of answers to expected questions and compose an opening statement for the board.

In late February I fly to Nashville for the hearing. My father drives me downtown to the office building where the draft board meets. My wingtips grind against the snow as I step out of the car. He waits in the car, allowing me to go through this rite of passage alone, as a 24-year-old should. He supports me in following my conscience, but he doesn't tell me his personal position about my seeking the CO status.

I take charge of the meeting as I walk into the room, just as I have been coached. Bare and simple, the room has several official-looking flags that I don't pause to sort out. I introduce myself, handing out a packet to each of the seven board members. I am already beginning with my opening statement as I move to the front now, facing the men around the U-shaped tables. I explain what I am giving them and why I am happy to talk with them today. The chairman never has a chance to set the tone. Seven men in suits are listening to me. I have control of the conversation and keep going. I address the high points of my thick file, starting with my Peace Corps deferment from the National Board, which had overruled this local draft board when I was in India. "I want you to note that I chose to come home from the Peace Corps early. I could have stayed in India and kept my deferment. But I did not want to stay just to hide from the draft." I look around and they seem to be listening.

"Then I went to divinity school but please note that I did not choose to seek the IV-D deferment, which I could have done legally." I move quickly to the major issues for a Conscientious Objector, addressing them one by one, including the key question that they could raise: What would you have done against Hitler.

"I am not living then. I am living now," I say. "I know that I am against war. It is something that I cannot support."

When I finish, I ask if they have any questions. They have no ammunition for an attack. A few ask about information I've already covered, and I patiently go over the material again. An hour after I first stamped the snow off my shoes, I slide back into the Pontiac next to Dad as I loosen my tie.

"I thought it went well."

He shakes my hand. "I'm proud of you for standing up for what you believe." Then, with no particular celebration, we drive home that February afternoon past Vanderbilt University where Jim Tramel and I played basketball at Christmas. We pass the large Methodist Church I attended my senior year in high school, after we moved to Nashville. Finally, we reach my parents' house. I feel relieved and alive, ready for the next step in life. My winter hibernation seems to be coming to an end.

BOOK 2. AWARENESS
(1988–1989)

CHAPTER 3. The Journey is at Hand

"THIS COMMISSION MEETING is now open to general business," says Representative Richardson, a burly African American legislator, who co-chairs the N.C. Study Commission on Aging. "We have completed our personnel session and have an announcement." He glances at me, sitting across from him in the small audience of lobbyists and advocates for senior citizens.

It is August 1988. Since the beginning of the year, I have been the staff consultant for the Commission, sitting beside the legislators and working together. Just weeks before, our efforts led to the passage of a $1.9 million package through the legislature. But now I'm sitting on the outside.

Hold your head up high, I think, as Rep. Richardson continues. I have had only a day's notice of what he is about to make public, not enough time to sort through my emotions or the ramifications for my work or family. I remember the pressure situations my dad faced. *This is nothing compared to the stuff he went through in the civil rights movement*, I think.

"The Study Commission has voted in personnel session to end the contract for staff services with Mr. William Finger," says Rep. Richardson. He explains that legislation passed in August limited the use of outside consultants for study commissions and that the action in no way reflects on me personally. He then reads a resolution that expresses appreciation for my hard work. Little other business takes place, and it becomes clear to the group monitoring the Commission activities that this meeting was called for the sole purpose of ending my contract. Rep. Richardson gavels the meeting to a close. I knew this action might come but was warned about the secret agenda only just before the legislators walked into the session.

As the small group leaves the committee room, I feel emotions percolating up, from embarrassment to anger to fear to panic. I feel people's eyes on me as I head out into the hall. The few who stop to speak did not expect this, since they knew that I was scheduled to work for the Study Commission at least through the end of the year and possibly for a second year.

"Anything I can do, let me know," says an ex-state employee, now lobbying for several advocacy groups for the aging.

I manage a strained grin. "Thanks. I'll be in touch." I take a deep breath, steadying myself from the varying emotions darting about inside, calling for attention. After the few well-wishers leave, a reporter from the Raleigh paper comes up.

"Did you get a chance to read the memo?" I ask. When I learned the Commission might end my contract, I wrote a memo to the Commission members making a case for why I should continue my work through the fall. I knew the reporter had seen it. "You know, they didn't really *have* to let me go. The legislation did not require them to let go of current consultants. It was about future contracts."

"Yeah, I understood that. But looks like the deed is done," he says.

"But look at this," I protest slightly, pointing to a spot on the first page of my memo that explains a few of the technicalities about the earlier commitment of funds, how my contract was made before the new legislation. But he's right: it didn't matter.

As a news item, it is minor. Commission consultant's contract ends. Study Commission on Aging will turn to legislative staff members to help oversee how the $1.9 million funding is administered. End of story. But funding for aging issues is an issue in the governor's race, and it is a slow news day at the legislature. Few commissions meet so soon after the full legislature adjourns. I realize that the Associated Press will pick up this story. At Lake Junaluska for the summer, my parents will see it in the paper and worry about me losing my job.

I return to my tiny office in the large square legislative building, with its multiple courtyards, angled skylights, and confusing halls and stairways. I have some tasks to complete before leaving. Notes about the new projects for the legislative staff. Time sheets to fill out, receipts for travel. I try to stay focused, keep functioning. But I feel the emotions stirring about, not sure what they are. As long as I stay in the office, I feel like I can manage. I try to do a little more. Finally, I tear up, feeling overwhelmed by it all—the public way that I was laid off and the looming specter of needing money. Plus I think, *I've been good at this job and enjoyed having an impact, helping shape a major funding bill.* Now I'm starting to get angry as well.

Less than a year ago I got the consulting job at the legislature so that I could quit my longtime editor's job at a public policy research group. I wanted to write on topics other than state government—about fathers and family life and cultural issues. I need the Commission job for a base salary.

Driving home, a 15 minute trip down Wade Avenue, I'm calculating expenses and income. *Now I have more time to write but no money.* Small paychecks might come in from freelance articles for small weeklies and another smaller consultant job. But the figures don't come close to adding up without my half-time legislative gig. *What am I going to do?*

I turn in the driveway to our home, a modest Cape Cod two-story house built in the early 1950s on a one-acre lot just inside the beltline. I slump over the steering wheel for a second. Then, the large bamboo patch and stream beckon me. I take some deep breaths as I walk along the mostly stagnant water next to a swampy area. Dodging the briars, I hop over the stream into the thicket of four-inch-thick bamboo towering overhead and engulfing me. These wild parts of the yard always help me get out of my head, to notice something besides my worries. I squat next to the stream and watch the wispy tadpoles dart through the murky water. Dusk is approaching now; I hear the crickets chirping. "Burrumph," a frog bellows. I breathe in the cooling air that burns off the steamy August heat. My head clears. I feel relaxed hearing the sounds of the woods around me.

Heading toward the house, I pick a few tomatoes from our garden before I go inside. Rosebud barks from her pen. Everything seems more manageable as I clip on the leash and run up the sidewalk at a sprint, trying to keep up with the little mixed terrier. Back in the house, I feel calmer, but looming financial problems quickly jump back into my mind.

Georgia is in Illinois with the children, visiting her parents. Now married for 12 years, we have children ages four and seven. I told her things were a little rocky at the legislature, but I hadn't expected my contract to end so suddenly. "Why worry her tonight," I say out loud to myself. "She's having fun. This news can wait." I call my parents to let them know what they will read in the paper tomorrow, but they aren't home. I think again about calling Georgia but can't face it. I need to get clearer about the money so she won't be so worried.

I need to talk to someone, but calling people to talk about a problem is not my style. I have a lot of acquaintances, mostly through work or church, but not people I would call close friends. I can't ever remember calling a friend and asking for support. I've always dealt with stress by jogging, playing basketball, or hiking in the woods. Still dazed but feeling restless in the house alone, I go to a nearby deli to get a takeout order. An acquaintance from church is there with his wife. I order and then sit down with them to wait.

"How was your day?" asks Karmen, offering a goofy grin, his wavy gray hair disheveled. He and Edna are well into retirement, always friendly at church, but I know little about them.

"Well actually, I just lost my job."

A silence settles in. I'm surprised that I reveal such a vulnerable detail, and then I share some details about the legislative hearing. "And Georgia's out of town. So I'm feeling pretty bad right now, actually."

"I lost my job several times," Karmen says, smiling.

Why is he smiling about such news?

"It all turned out better in the long run," he continues and begins describing how one job led to another. "And the last job was in Raleigh, where I met Edna. We've been happy ever since." Edna is nodding as she listens intently. "Try not to worry about it. Use the time you have and see what happens."

My order is ready and I get up. "Thanks, Karmen. I'll think about that."

TWO WEEKS LATER, WITHOUT THE legislative job, I'm spending more time with the children. I take them to the swimming pool a week before school starts. I swim some laps but feel like I'm swimming crooked, like the water is about to knock me over. It's an odd sensation. I can't tell if I'm sick or dizzy or just so slow as to be pushed around by the water. My body seems to be telling me something, but I don't know what.

I cut my laps short and wait for the kids as they splash about. But I'm restless from the odd feeling I had swimming. Finally we are ready to leave. Walking out into the parking lot, thoughts race through my mind about work, the start of school for the kids, and money. I barely notice my children running along toward the car.

As we get into the Blue Goose, as we fondly call the old Dodge station wagon, the kids start jumping between the middle and back seats. Now behind the wheel with key in the ignition, I'm still preoccupied. *Why was I so dizzy swimming? Is something wrong with me?* I think.

I'm ready to go but realize the kids are still bouncing between the seats. I don't see this as a game. "Put your seat belts on NOW!" I snap, loud and without warning. In their playful summer mood, they look startled but settle down. I turn around and start driving to the end of the parking lot.

Dana, age four, chimes in. "Daddy, you need to go upstairs to time-out when we get home."

Her words penetrate deeper, and I take a deep breath, thinking about her pre-school teacher's time-out system. "You're right." I finally say. "That would be a good idea." Like a spear cracking my grown-up shield, her simple logic breaks down my anger. Calm now, I drive along and the kids settle down, cooperative and quiet.

When we get home, I turn toward the stairs. "I'm going to have a time-out now," I say. They nod, understanding.

That night I write in my journal. "When I stopped swimming I felt like I was rocking with the tiny wake of the lapping waters of the pool. Is there a chemical imbalance or am I depressed—or both?"

WHILE I AM BEGINNING TO HAVE some awareness that I am depressed, I try to focus on my responsibilities. Two small consulting jobs have deadlines, and I need to find better paying jobs—quick. Georgia has enrolled in a graduate program in art, her true love. She won't be increasing her portion of the family finances. So I have to keep up my monthly earnings, which depended on my legislative job. My money ruminations are hard to shake. At the same time, the kids are starting back to school, which means new schedules and transitions.

Focusing on being available to the children comes a lot easier than finding work. Several days before school starts, Lee is writing a thank you note to his grandparents for the summer trip but gets stuck on some of the letters. "I can't do a big 'G'. I've forgotten how!" Suddenly, he tears up and puts down the pencil.

I look up from my notebook and think about what to say. "Are you worried about forgetting how to write?" I ask.

"Uh-uh."

"Are you worried about second grade?"

"Yeah." He pauses. "Miss McDaniel will think I don't know how to write." The fear begins to find its voice. I offer some reassuring words that others will be rusty from the summer too. Then the spigot opens and he starts to sob.

"Robert has a different teacher and won't ask me over anymore. I won't have any new friends." Of course, little Robert will continue to play with Lee. But logic is not the issue now. Just as suddenly as the tears came, he calms down, breathing at a normal pace again. He picks up the pencil and copies over the sentence, capital G looking fine. Crisis over.

I am learning a lot from my children, especially when I take the time to really notice their ways of solving problems. As I listen to Lee and give him support, his worries about a transition to the second grade are manageable today. Solutions do not seem as easy for me, moving into middle age.

I struggle through the fall, worrying about money and work and parenting schedules. I like being around the kids and don't really want to work more. But I need money for the family. One night I scrawl on a yellow legal pad: "I've got to make new friends, contact with people. O.K. to feel down but don't feel down about feeling down. It's natural and will pass."

More and more, I'm beginning to acknowledge, at least to myself, that maybe I'm depressed. On October 17 on another yellow page, I reflect on meeting Georgia my senior year in college. "She helped me begin to feel and see the world around me and not be depressed."

I start to wake up in the middle of the night. I get up, fix warm milk, and write things down. On November 20 at 2 a.m., I write: "I feel at such a loss. I don't see how to make money. Have to find a job and give up what I want. No money. What am I going to do?" And my tears start flowing.

One of the factors that keeps me from getting more depressed is focusing on my children. On a beautiful Monday morning late in the fall, Lee rides his bike the half block to the neighbor's driveway where the elementary school bus picks him up. Dana rides her tricycle. When the bus comes, I push Lee's bike home behind Dana. At the house, Dana gathers up the spider she has to take to pre-school.

We drive to the old elementary school that now has a pre-school. I park and am about to get out when Dana asks. "Where does it pee?" She is watching the spider inch up the side of the glass.

"That's a good question. I bet Mrs. Thompson will know." We get out of the car and start walking in, holding hands. She carefully cradles the spider against her with her other hand. *Life is good*, I'm thinking.

Then she stops and puts the jar down on the concrete ledge to the sidewalk. She sits down on the sidewalk herself. I watch, wondering what she is doing, then notice she is looking at her feet. "Do you want to change your shoes?" I ask, noticing for the first time she has her little tennis shoes on the wrong feet. She starts taking them off. "Do you want me to help?" She nods.

For most of my adult years, my sense of self-worth revolved around work, but through the fall I feel that anchor slipping away. Some days I try to replace that identity with being a parent. But I come back to worries of work, money, my marriage, and my future. This transition feels different from other times when I have gotten depressed. I need to be a good father. That feels so primary that figuring out the depression seems more important than just finding a way to move on.

I AM BEGINNING TO SHARE MY DILEMMA with a group of men once a week. About the time I started working at the legislature in early 1988, I learned about support groups sponsored by the Men's Center of Raleigh. Seven of us meet, usually at one of our homes; all of us are fathers. One of the few rules for these groups is that you speak from your heart, trying to address feelings, not talk about politics or sports or opinions about issues.

Late in the fall we decide to have our first outing, a day-long canoe trip down the Neuse River. On a clear December day six of us drive east from downtown Raleigh in several cars. We take one car to the take-out spot, planned for about eight hours later. We carry our three canoes about a quarter mile to the river, which trickles down from the N.C. Peidmont and meanders to the Atlantic.

Burned out campfires, scraps of candy wrappers, and a rusty beer can signal previous visitors. The tall winter grasses obscure other signs of civilization. As we prepare for the departure, I look more closely at the grasses and began to pick a few tall cattails and long weeds with thistles. I usually take for granted the tall grasses in a roadside field, but today, viewing them separately and with slow attention, each stem and dried bloom seems as spectacular as a perfect rose petal in May. Without planning it, I form a bouquet in my hands. A spectrum of color blossoms in shades of brown and mustard and earth tones, muted in color but as bright as a rainbow in spirit.

As we wait for Frank, David checks on the food he has packed for our midday cookout. The occasion is feeling like a ceremony for me. The woods feel like a cathedral, the space sacred and calm. I feel safe, unworried about daily affairs. I jot down a poem, pulling in themes that echoed through our conversations over the weeks as we planned the trip. This first group outing beyond the predictable structure of our Monday night meetings needs to be recognized. Plus, it is David's birthday. That deserves some mention! Poem finished, preparations complete, and Frank now with us, we are ready to depart.

"I think we should have a blessing for this trip," I say. "Some simple kind of ceremony." A few look puzzled, restless to climb in the canoe. Maybe it's the word *blessing*. All of us are familiar with ceremony, mostly through churches. One of us is an ex-preacher, another a minister to be. One hates church. Sensing reluctance, I add quickly, "It won't take long. I just have a poem I want to read and this bouquet of flowers to offer to the river."

"Sure, read us a poem," Hugh says as we move down to the canoes.

I wait until all are quiet. Even the birds seem still. In the silence, the current sounds like a steady drumbeat. "This is our first outing," I say. "I hope we have many more. I offer these dried flowers from the shore to the river, to give us a safe journey." I toss the grasses into the pool near the shore. We watch them catch the twist of water and head eastward. Then I read "The Journey":

On the occasion of this outing of ours... and
On this solemn day one of David's 43rd year... and
On this day of joyous, boyish pleasure
We give thanks indeed
For a sparkling day of December sunshine
For a glistening water surface for us to glide upon
For each other—each of us alone... and
For all of us together.

On those days of sorrow, of hopelessness and helplessness
In our nights of sleeplessness and worries and
weights of the world and private burdens and demons
We can remember this day of ours... spent together.

And it will be ours—it is ours
To enjoy and to relish
Now... for the journey is at hand.

CHAPTER 4. A Man and His House

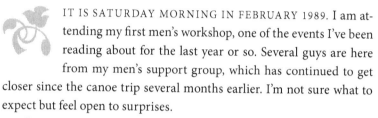 IT IS SATURDAY MORNING IN FEBRUARY 1989. I am attending my first men's workshop, one of the events I've been reading about for the last year or so. Several guys are here from my men's support group, which has continued to get closer since the canoe trip several months earlier. I'm not sure what to expect but feel open to surprises.

"When you listen to a story, listen for the part that pulls you in, the entry point for you," says Michael Meade, who is cradling a West African conga drum between his knees. "This is where you are in the story, the place you are in your life." A short man from New York with dark, close-cut hair, Meade gazes out at us, more like a street fighter than a storyteller. The urgency in his voice sounds like a cross between a teacher and an evangelist.

In the fairy tale Meade is telling, a young man sets off on a long journey. One of the first obstacles he faces is a three-headed monster that shoots fire out of all three mouths. "To get by, the prince has to find some meat to feed each of the heads of the monster," Meade says. "After the prince occupies the monster with the meat, he is able to pass."

The monster immediately pulls me into the tale. I feel it like a magnet. I see myself as the dragon, stuck in the ditch needing to be fed and feeling like everyone else in the family needs to be fed too. And I'm letting everybody down by not feeding them or me enough. In the ditch, I feel hungry all the time for something to help me climb out.

Meade drums as he tells the story, his words speeding up as he finds a faster cadence on the goatskin. Listening, totally absorbed as I sit among 70 other men, I move into a separate time and space, like one of my intense basketball games in high school. Everything else falls away except the immediacy of the action. I feel as if I'm in the story, going with the young man as Meade takes him past monsters, across plains and rivers, through adversity, and finally into a final phase where he begins his new life as a man.

Meade is quiet as the story ends, and then says we'll take a break. "During the day, when you hit the bathroom, notice the difference in the men's and women's. We have both of them today, so take a look." The event has the entire Raleigh clubhouse rented; no women are around.

Men start to stretch and mill about the large semicircle of chairs three-deep. I take a look at both bathrooms and notice a remarkable difference. The men's is stark, no decorations or character, just the plumbing and fixtures. A painting of flowers and other art greets me in the women's restroom. Even though the framed prints remind me of cheap yard sales, they do add a softness, even beauty.

When we return, Meade leads a short discussion on the significance of flowers for women and nothing for men, which keeps bubbling the emotional pot that he stirred with his story. Then he asks us to move to a place in the room that corresponds to the segment of the story that grabbed us. He motions to the right edge of the space as the beginning of the story.

I sit down on the floor near the front on the right-hand side, where the story begins. Others drag their chairs to various parts of the large room in the clubhouse. Then he takes us through the tale again, this time with our own stories as the plot.

"This dragon feels like home," I say when he calls on me. "I need to be fed, along with my wife and two young children. I guess we're all the heads of the dragon."

"Tell me more," Meade says, standing on the side of the room where several of us are situated in the dragon segment.

"Well, it's everything I guess. Work, getting the kids to school, earning money, breakfast routine, bedtime. Everything."

"That sounds like regular daily life. What about it is hard?"

"I'm not sure. I just seem stuck. It often seems like I need to be fed but ought to be feeding them."

When I get home that night, Georgia and the kids are asleep. I sit in the living room, staring at the large wall filled with art that Georgia has made—modern abstract quilts and paintings—and carefully hung in a well-designed arrangement. I feel invigorated by the day, not sleepy. Mouths of dragons. Princes and obstacles. Flowers on the wall. Women and beauty. Men and empty walls.

I don't know where I really belong in this house. I have a desk where I work, in a small room. But I need a wall—a place to see myself, to put drawings, photographs. Suddenly, I get up from the chair and take down the art on the wall. My breathing is fast, like I'm working hard at some physical task. I sit down. The empty wall looms like a blank movie screen and the home movies start rolling.

I SMILE NOW, LOOKING AT THE EMPTY WALL. I am picturing Georgia and me walking into our house in 1981 with our first child. I was 33, Georgia 32. A sharp January wind blew through the cracks in our old rambling house near downtown Raleigh. Months earlier, the agency had approved us to adopt Lee, but the "happy call," as the agency referred to it, gave us just a day's notice.

We picked up our baby from the adoption agency in Greensboro. He slept the whole way on the 90-minute drive to our first house in Raleigh. After we got him settled in the crib, one of the first things I did was put a new piece of weather-stripping insulation into the half-moon window in the gable of the nursery. Adding the insulation had been on my list of chores. Closing off that draft, keeping the winter wind off our new baby was the first of many new steps in my life as a father. That day I felt like an adult, maybe for the first time.

Dana joined us five years later, in 1986. Adopting a two and a half year-old went more slowly, with some transition visits with her last foster family. I remember how she carried her little blue chair across the driveway near the bamboo and stream of our second family home, where I'm sitting now. Two kids. A family to raise.

The scene shifts further back in time now, to a conversation with Georgia in 1976, six months before we married. We were on the side porch of the little rented house in the suburbs of Chapel Hill, North Carolina, where we lived.

"I want us both to be involved in raising the children," Georgia said, sitting on the tiny outside porch, surrounded by her electric pottery wheel and an oversized stuffed chair picked up off the street.

"I totally agree. I don't want to be away like my father was. I love kids." The commitment to share the parenting was clear and appealing to both of us.

THE SCENE ON THE WALL GETS BLURRY NOW, as if too many out-of-focus pictures are overlaid in an amateurish collage. My work has lacked a clear trajectory, which my commitment to parenting has seemed to complicate rather than clarify. Since childhood, the single most important decision imbedded in me—and I suspect in most boys—is to decide on a career, to fulfill me and support a family. By the time I graduated from college in 1969, the all-important decision about career began to engage large numbers of women as well men. Betty Friedan and others who launched the modern women's movement had posed challenging questions about gender roles, work, family, and career.

"The times, they were 'a changing." In 1970, when Georgia entered law school, gender roles were getting more complicated and more interesting. I started addressing letters to my parents not to Mr. and Mrs. H.E. Finger—the address on virtually all of their mail—but posting them to "Mamie and Ellis Finger." My mother had her own name, not just her husband's. I decided to emphasize that point. This was a big change at the time for her and for me. When the Equal Rights Amendment required confirmation by state legislatures, a heated battle emerged in North Carolina. Holding little Lee in our arms, Georgia and I joined the large circle of ERA supporters around the legislative building.

Supporting more equality for women felt right, but it complicated my understanding of my role as a man. A calling to career eluded me in adolescence. Through much of my 20s, I moved with fluidity and discontinuity, dealing with the draft and alternative service, exploring my interests through various jobs, slowly making the decision about a life partner, and learning to be a writer. As we began meeting with the adoption agency, I also was able to land a steady job editing the quarterly magazine at a public policy research organization. The creativity of producing each issue with a handful of mostly freelancers and interns carried me for awhile. At least, I was paying my share of the bills.

NOW THE "GOVERNMENT" PERIOD SNAPS into sharp focus on the bare wall. I am looking through the lens of the "involved father" label, which I wore bright and clear on my sleeve, partly out of necessity. I negotiated a half-time writing job during Lee's first year, and Georgia did the same at her legal services job. We were each at home with the baby half the day. Since the small public policy center was strapped for funding, the half-time approach worked for them.

One story I was covering involved a case being heard before the N.C. Supreme Court during the afternoon, when I was keeping watch over our six-month-old. I was confident he would sleep through the heart of the hearing because he was still on a regular nap schedule. I drove to the austere granite building across from the 19th century Capitol in dead-center downtown and carried Lee up to the hearing room in his car seat. I arrived early, long before anyone else, and stationed myself and Lee in the back row. He was asleep like the predictable baby he was. I had my reporter's notebook in hand and an escape route prepared if he started to cry. Just as I planned, Lee slept soundly through the arguments before the highest N.C. justices. I got quotes to add to my policy story on the case. Then I carried the car seat with sleeping baby, briefcase over my shoulder, through the large halls and down the elevator. I was living the dream—being an involved dad, working at a job I liked, and making enough to live on.

But as the years and the issues of the quarterly magazine piled up, the work grew repetitive and laborious. By 1987, after nearly nine years, my attitude toward the work grew stagnant, from initial excitement and curiosity about managing a magazine to feeling trapped. Sometimes I would ride the bus home and see a few regular riders staring out the window. I knew I didn't want to be on that bus for years to come. Something had to change.

SMILING THROUGH THE INVOLVED FATHER PERIOD takes a turn now. Tears gather in the corners of my eyes. I'm remembering the free-lance articles I started writing about subjects closer to my heart, such as adoption and parenting. They landed me mostly in local outlets. I flash now on the last paragraph of my article for an alternative weekly, "What Happened to the Father's Movement?" After going through my own ambivalence about sharing work and parenting and telling stories from other fathers, I ended the article reflecting from my backyard about how much I missed my wife and little son.

"I loved your article," a middle-aged friend not known to be sentimental told me after it was published. "At the end, I even found my eyes watering."

"I cried too, sitting at my computer, when I wrote that paragraph," I told him.

Cracking the national magazines was much harder and less secure. I had to stick with something steady to pay the bills. *Be a man*, I told myself. So I brought work home, got the public policy magazine out, and built a reputation for myself as a well-informed government analyst. My public persona seemed accomplished and presumably happy. And after the fathers article, colleagues expressed admiration about how involved I was as a father.

But I felt it was a lie. I loved being a father but I couldn't work it all out. On Fridays, Dana and I went to story time at the library. I was always the only dad, which the librarian noticed. I felt good external-ly. But at home I felt conflicted. When Georgia decided to quit being a lawyer and pursue her passion for art in a Masters program, we had to re-juggle the work and child-care schedules. She had always been an art-ist, from pursuing fiber and photography projects to building a pottery kiln and joining an artist cooperative. She had enough money saved to cover her share of the family expenses. I knew it was right for her and supported her decision. Plus, responsibilities were growing at the public policy center, so I worked more and enjoyed bigger tasks as an editor.

Juggling time with the kids got harder. And, I had high expectations for being a father. I wanted to be there for my kids in ways my father had not been for me, and to keep the shared parenting contract that Georgia and I made before we married.

I'M GETTING SLEEPY STARING AT THE BLANK WALL, now without Georgia's art. The family memories scroll slowly to a halt. One more scene with Lee pops up and I nod awake, half dreaming.

Bedtime. Reading books. I was tired and wanted to leave. But he wanted more. Finally, I snapped. "Get in that bed and stay there." I sounded mean and left without another word. Georgia was out. My shoulders were stooped on what seemed like a long walk down the stairs. In the back family room, I flopped onto the sofa facing the fireplace and closed my eyes—angry, exhausted, discouraged. No hope for the future. No job. Just a few freelance assignments, little money.

Swish. Swish. Swish. I opened my eyes, sensing something at the back of the sofa. I turned and there was little Lee. He handed me a note and ran back upstairs.

I unfolded the crumpled piece of notebook paper from the tiny square. Finally, the five words were clear, carefully printed across the top lines, with the "little letters" exactly touching the appropriate line on the paper. "Y are you so mad."

The note took me by surprise. I felt worse at first, having taken out my restlessness and confusion on him. But the note also energized me. I felt needed and less self-absorbed. I went back upstairs, no longer tired. I had a purpose.

Lee was in bed, nearly asleep now. "I'm not mad at you. It was just a long day. I'm sorry I yelled."

"O.K. I'm going to sleep now."

I AM EXHAUSTED, SITTING IN FRONT of the blank wall—the long day at the men's conference filtering through my memories. This internal demand to be good at life often leaves me spent, feeling like a failure. My expectations are anchored in circumstances from years ago, which I don't yet understand. But I will. I have to. There are challenges to meet—to figure out my work and job, to meet that vow to share the parenting. For a man struggling with work and money, six months without a steady job magnifies the half-empty glass. At times of transition, the dark hand often pulls me down. Right now, at least I have a blank wall, like a fresh canvas. I fall into bed smiling, but wondering how I'm going to get fed like the dragon and crawl out of that ditch.

The next morning, I tiptoe down the carpeted stairs, grab breakfast, and think I'll make it out the door.

"What happened in the living room?" Georgia says with a cold look, coming into the kitchen as I'm about to leave.

"I took your art down last night."

"I can see that. But why?"

I'm opening the back door now. "I'll talk about it soon. I promise." Georgia's words pound inside me, calling out like another mouth to feed. Driving to the conference, I manage to put her needs aside, at least for now. Today, I vow, I will focus on the meeting and whatever feelings come up there.

NEAR THE END OF THE HALF-DAY SUNDAY session at the conference, I'm at the right side of the room, working with a small group about any closing issues we want to discuss. Across the room, I hear a loud sobbing and look over. A group of men are gathering around a man in the middle, forming a large circle, their arms around him as he sobs. I have never heard such wails from a man.

"Give him some breathing room," Meade says, moving close. Meade sits down next to the man, as the crowd of 15 men or so back up.

"Are you afraid of going back out in the world?" Meade asks him. The young man nods.

I look at another man and whisper, "Going back out?"

The man next to me, who has been in the small group explains, "He has just gotten out of a stay at a mental hospital."

Everyone in the room has gathered around now. A few men hold the weeping friend, his crying now quieted to soft tears. "Transitions back into the world may be the most difficult part," says Meade. "We're all about to leave a safe and sacred space." Gradually, the man settles down more and the scene breaks up.

Slowly, we all gather back in rows of chairs in the semicircle facing Meade. As he talks more about departure, I feel some of the young man's sadness. I don't want to go home and have to discuss the wall with Georgia or juggle freelance writing jobs with raising kids. I don't want to go back into the world.

I do know, as I leave the community center that Sunday afternoon, that I will not be going to a mental hospital. I may not even be going back down into that ditch. I feel stronger. I feel movement somehow. I don't know exactly what to make of fairy tales and gatherings of men. But I do know a little better how to pay attention. How to look for flowers on the wall. I feel like I am waking up.

Waking up to more of the real world—beyond bathroom pictures— seems pretty scary as I reach our driveway. No more safe, sacred space with Meade and the men. The walls of our house are my new container, with wife and kids and work and chores—and with love anchoring it all. I am home with a flood of feelings. I need to take responsibility for my actions regarding her sacred space and her art, even as I felt new and positive energy in seeking my own place in the house. I will find the courage to apologize and seek ways to support our separate and our shared worlds.

CHAPTER 5. A Good Word for Darkness

IN BLACK ROBES AND WHITE STOLES, two men enter the chancel by a side door beneath organ pipes that stretch to the ceiling. Before joining his colleague against the wall, the senior minister retrieves his glasses, lying on a table between the open Bible and a single rose. The organist finishes the prelude. Two girls, maybe six and eight, are walking down the center aisle now, holding brass candle-lighters. With nervous smiles and their flames aloft, the girls walk through the parishioners. They move up five steps, past the pulpits, and finally to opposite ends of the table where the eyeglasses rested just minutes before.

The service at this large liberal Baptist church in Raleigh marches through the Sunday morning liturgy—scripture, prayer, song, offering, and meditation. As the sermon nears, I watch the senior minister, Mahan Siler. He has wavy, silver hair and a restless energy that seems to spread across his face, even as he sits serene and still. I sit in the back row, taking notes for the profile of Siler I'm doing for a local weekly. I'm feeling engaged by the assignment, the second in a series of profiles I started about the time of the Michael Meade workshop. I've been reading about Siler's social action leadership in the area, but this is my first time to see him.

"I want to put in a good word for darkness," Siler says as he moves toward the end of his sermon, which focuses on a dark episode in the life of Jesus. "Just think about some of the awesome mysteries at work in darkness. Let's start with our bodies." My pencil lifts from my note pad, the theme taking me beyond reporting. Siler reminds his congregation how our hearts and livers and intestines work.

"Our bodies literally function in the dark." He then speaks of the vitality under the earth, the seeds knowing when to sprout, and in which direction. "There is our own origin out of the darkness," he says, "We were likely conceived in a dark night of our parents' lovemaking." Siler preaches about economic and ethical darkness, about our dark frustration as a nation and our broken relationships. Siler's words draw me into the story. His message of darkness offers an entry point.

"In your darkness, there will come light," he says, racing to the end. "So with some confidence we can face our darkness." And the source of the light, he says, is the life of Jesus.

I wince at what seems to me a simplistic end to the darkness. From growing up in a Methodist church, I am used to the Jesus message coming in at the end of sermons. But after my year in India, these endings seem too tidy to me for the spiritual complexities raised by Muslims and Hindus and others. I resist his guidance towards the light and keep focusing on his images of darkness.

The sermon over, the final hymn draws the service to a close as the two young acolytes return. The younger one, on the left, relights the wick of her candle-lighter and snuffs out the candle. The taller girl waits for her to finish. The organ bursts into its postlude as the older girl, stepping down from the chancel, shakes her head, embarrassed. She realizes she forgot to relight her candle. The younger girl holds her candle high, walking down the aisle and taking the light into the world. Beside her, the taller one keeps pace.

As they walk past, my eyes fill with tears and then pour down my face as the ministers follow the girls out. I reach for my handkerchief to hide any evidence of emotion. The congregation begins to flood out of the sanctuary, but I sit there, crying for that girl. She is so cute, and the error so inconsequential. But it upset her, carrying her unlit, dark candle out of the sanctuary. She wanted to do it right and had not.

The day after the service, I interview Siler in his church office, a modest room with a large desk, bookshelves, and chairs for visitors. "There are two really strong Biblical themes that I think are important," Siler says from a swivel chair behind his desk. "One is the theme of grace, and one is the theme of liberation." He talks of grace as being "totally accepted and loved and capable of loving as a gift of creation." Accepting this concept of grace counters what Siler calls "our natural propensity to feel we need to earn our sense of worth, by what we do, by what we have."

Grace is his favorite word. It keeps popping up as he talks about his personal story and his vision of blending pastoral care with political witness. I file this word away, knowing I want to come back to it sometime for myself. What does it really mean for me? For now, keeping up with Siler's thinking and making my deadline is challenge enough. Even so, I find myself drawn into Siler's story at key entry points—the objective journalist vulnerable to personal issues—just as Meade described the way a mythological story can grab us.

In the next weeks, as I write the magazine story, I ponder not only the power of the word *grace* but also my resistance to the light. My tears at the end of the service when the acolyte walked out with the dark candle—what sparked that emotion? And, what was the feeling? My children come to mind first, what my role as a father will be in helping them learn and move forward. Perhaps the tears came from my feelings of vulnerability about being a good dad. But then more thoughts peek through as I remember my own acolyte days, nearly forgotten.

At about age 12, I walked down the aisle of the little chapel with a candlestick just like the ones the girls carried. Another young lad and I, also in robes, lit the candles at the early morning communion service at the large downtown Methodist Church near the state Capitol in Jackson. I felt like I was contributing somehow, like the choirboys in European cathedrals I saw on television during Christmas. I felt a part of some great global ritual of peace and hope.

Sitting through the communion service week after week, the liturgy became familiar until I could say it from memory. Several parts had a magical sound, especially sections with words I never heard elsewhere. I felt serenity in this ceremony. For a few moments each Sunday morning I had no worries or preoccupations—no segregated schools, no fishbowl of a family, no grades, no basketball opponent. I was just there, letting that strange word *oblation* roll off my tongue in a quiet ritual, surrounded by the beauty of worship.

AFTER THE SILER ASSIGNMENT COMES a story on a leading advocate for the mentally ill. As part of my research I visit the local mental hospital, which revives images I have from the path-breaking movie about a decade earlier, *One Flew over the Cuckoo's Nest*.

The guide at the mental hospital walks with me through four wards, two for men and two for women, each with twelve to sixteen single rooms, a bathing area, and a living room. Several men and women are sprawled on their beds in a deep, motionless sleep. As I move through the hospital and ask questions for my profile, I keep returning to the image of those patients asleep on their beds. Back in my modest second-floor office, which I share with another writer, I begin to review my notes. Suddenly, all I can think of is Uncle Bill. The memories begin to roll across my mind, taking me back in time.

For a few years when I was a young boy, we had a Christmas-time celebration with my mother's side of the family in Jackson. As we drove to the little house, my mother would say something like, "Uncle Bill is out of the hospital for a few days. He will probably be asleep the whole time we're there." I don't remember her giving us more details about her older brother. I knew only that he lived in a mental hospital.

In the living room with the decorated tree and presents, I would visit with my cousins and then drift toward the kitchen. The wonderful smells of turkey and dressing and sweet potatoes signaled that the feast was nearly ready. In the kitchen, I remember looking through another door, away from the living room, into a small bedroom where Uncle Bill was asleep. I must have been about eight or nine. His thin body arched in a kind of fetal position, the large hump on his back facing toward me. Anticipation of Christmas dinner drifted away as I was pulled toward his world for a moment. No one seemed to notice me at the door. No one explained Uncle Bill, but even then, I knew that his sleeping was different from an afternoon nap.

I learned later of his breakdown and how he came to live at Whitfield, the Mississippi state mental hospital. Not long after World

War II was over, about when I was born, my grandmother boarded a train in Memphis, several hours from her home in the Mississippi Delta, and rode an all-night Pullman to New York City, where Uncle Bill had locked himself in his rented room. While my grandfather had other strengths, he could not stomach this job, and so some reservoir of maternal strength rose to the task.

Nan, our name for my mother's mother, brought Uncle Bill home. He was a young, brilliant electrical engineer who would never hold a long-term job again. His MIT graduate degree had led to secret work for the Defense Department as part of the war effort. The tension of the assignment must have overloaded his fragile circuits. Nan had taken Bill to see a doctor when he was young, in the 1930s, but the mental health options were few. He managed through his college years at Georgia Tech. But after he left the structured life at MIT, Uncle Bill gradually became more and more isolated in the first of many apartments he had, until my grandmother got the call that she had to come.

She took Uncle Bill to Whitfield, where he stayed for a while before he came back to live with his parents. After efforts to sort out his condition in the late 1940s, Uncle Bill gradually drifted into his deep sleep. For many years, he mostly lay there at Whitfield in a fetal position, hardly functioning, with his occasional visits at Christmas when I saw him. Then the pharmacological revolution of the 1960s and 1970s kicked in and woke Uncle Bill up. He began to function again.

I, William Ratliff Finger, only spoke with my uncle, William Ratliff, on two occasions.

On a visit to Jackson in 1972, I was exploring work options. I was ready to leave Boston and thought I might go back to Mississippi. When I had a free afternoon, I decided to make an unplanned side trip to nearby Whitfield. Driving up to the main administration building, I saw that the facility looked run-down, needing fresh paint and undoubtedly, more funding from the Mississippi legislature. The receptionist at the main building directed me to where Uncle Bill lived. I was on my own, no escort or doctor, entering a strange world. It was my first time in a mental hospital.

Inside, a receptionist led me into a large common area. Men were hanging onto rails on the side of the room rocking back and forth. Others sat on couches, staring at the television. One was repeating a phrase that I couldn't understand, over and over to the wall. Several greeted me with voices that did not sound like an everyday greeting.

"Hey, hey, come over and talk to me."

I stood there for what seemed like a very long time but was probably less than a minute.

"Can I help you?" asked an attendant who arrived to help me.

"I've come to see Bill Ratliff. I'm his nephew."

He pointed down the hall. "You'll see him at the end of the hall. He's in his room. You'll be fine."

I wondered what I was getting into as I passed more patients in the hall. I knocked on the open door, and Uncle Bill looked up from his desk. He was fidgeting with his short-wave radio.

"Hi, I'm Bill. I hope you were expecting me."

"Come in. Yes, Mamie said you would be coming sometime this week."

I paused, hearing my mother's name from her brother. I hadn't seen him since I looked through the eyes of a young boy when he was asleep on those Christmas visits so many years ago.

"I'm glad you're here." He offered an engaging smile, his gray hair parted neatly, a bit of sparkle showing through his glasses. He extended his hand, and we shook warmly. He looked normal except for the camel-like hump in his back, from lying in his curved way for so many years.

The compact order of the room made the first impression, bed carefully made, simple desk with his radio, and cards with contact names and signals. What kept Uncle Bill going now was his short-wave radio hobby. He talked to people throughout the western hemisphere on his ham-radio set, a hobby begun as a boy. Only a few clothes hung in an open closet, like those in an inexpensive motel room.

We visited for about an hour, talking about his radio mostly. I was drawn to the visit more by curiosity than for any organized purpose. Not yet a journalist in 1972 or particularly interested in this mysterious uncle, I had only decided to stop by at the last minute. I was not prepared or even aware of the unspoken questions that no doubt engaged us both. What was his illness like? How did he see the world? Was it a scary place?

What was it like growing up? What prompted his breakdown? The experience of going down the corridor of that ward and seeing my uncle was too overwhelming to move to such discussions. But at least I went.

I saw him one other time, when he was on a leave from the hospital and visited my mother in Tennessee. We took a short hike in the mountains. I noticed a limp, as he compensated for the curvature of the spine, but he could still walk up the hill. We talked about the outdoors, the great sunshine. Neither of us edged up to the subjects that by then I wanted to discuss.

Soon after, he moved out of the hospital into his own apartment. Just weeks later, he had a massive heart attack and died. "It was just too much change," my mother said. "After all those years in the hospital, it just overdid his system. The doctors don't know, but that's my theory."

AS I WORK ON THE MAGAZINE ASSIGNMENT, memories of Uncle Bill pop into my head from time to time. Finally, on a Sunday night, working late at my little office, I put the final touches to the story and go home. That night, I have a dream.

I am leaving my office, the magazine story done. I'm pleased with myself, a smile on my face as I lock the door. As I turn left towards the stairs, I notice a door on the right side of the corridor, slightly ajar.

That's strange, I think. *I've never noticed a door there before.*

I take a step to the door and push it open with my foot. Before me is Uncle Bill, sitting on the bed from that Christmas house in Jackson.

Uncle Bill doesn't say a thing to me. But he is awake with a look in his eye that I've never seen from anyone before. As I start to look toward his eyes, I recoil. Panic rushes through me, and my impulse is to run for the stairs and my car. But I stay at the door and take a small step inside.

He is still looking at me with such intensity his eyes seem to be talking. But he does not speak. He seems friendly enough, but as I begin to lock eyes with him, I feel a magnetic-like quality. The fear returns. He seems to be sending a message, a kind of invitation to come into his world, to spend my life as he has spent his.

I feel a tremendous urge to leave yet a fascination to stay. I fidget at the door, not sure what to do. But then, I draw myself up, tall and straight, take a deep breath and look him straight in the eye. His sockets are like dark liquid pools, deep in the earth. I see them and stay there, eye to eye. Then I have the strength to pull my eyes and my body away, like breaking free from quicksand. I turn from him, close the door, and head down the corridor. I look back and the door is gone. Then I wake up.

I lie still a long time, feeling both sad and peaceful, thinking, *I am ready to go into the darkness. I know it will not destroy me.*

CHAPTER 6. Quick as a Flash

THE MAGAZINE ASSIGNMENTS THAT SPRING bring up unresolved issues about my father, religion, and growing up in Mississippi. Even as I write about grace and remember the magic of *oblation*, an invitation provides an opportunity to bring such themes into focus. My father is to be honored as alumnus of the year at Millsaps College, part of Founders' Weekend. He and my mother suggest that the three children (without spouses and grand-children) join them for the occasion, our first time back to Jackson as a family since we left in 1964.

In March, I drive in from the slick new airport outside of Jackson, now in 1989 a modern southern city. Heading across the Pearl River, I skirt downtown and exit before the thoroughfare heads out to the booming suburbs to the north. I am scheduled to meet my parents for lunch at the Holiday Inn, built on land that once formed part of the Millsaps College golf course. In four-lane traffic, my eyes dart across familiar landmarks. Pulling into the motel parking lot, I settle in for a long view across the street.

Bailey Junior High sits solid as ever, a gray concrete edifice built by the Public Works Administration in the 1930s. I can still see my civics teacher clacking across her classroom in extra-high heels drilling the names of the U.S. cabinet secretaries into my 14-year-old brain. Not since ninth-grade have I been able to recite the name and duties of each cabinet member.

I can picture my earnest seventh grade social studies teacher in the room next to the front entrance, sitting at her desk piled high with scrapbooks. Many of us competed in the year-long assignment in her Mississippi history class, a tradition well known through older siblings. We sent letters to every corner of the state seeking materials from chambers of commerce and others. The unstated challenge was to compile the thickest book. In 1960 we loaded the pages with brochures on Picayune cucumbers and Natchez antebellum mansions. No one wrote the NAACP asking why our schools were still segregated, six years after *Brown v. Board of Education* and three years after President Eisenhower sent troops to nearby Little Rock.

Finally, I snap the trunk shut and go to meet my parents. As we finish the lunch buffet I say on an impulse, "Come on and go with me to the library, Dad."

"I don't want to go to the campus now, like this," he says, motioning to his open-neck shirt and sweater. "I'll see someone."

"No one will recognize you," I say, knowing he would prefer a coat and tie if identified as a former president of the college. "When I called and talked with a student about going into the archives, she didn't even know who you were."

With encouragement from my mother, who says she'll go, he agrees to join us. We walk up North State Street, which separates Millsaps from the old Jackson neighborhoods where I delivered papers and played touch football. We turn into the campus, up a small hill and then into the library serving the 1,200 students. A library assistant shows us to the modest two-room archive. We settle into the small room where boxes of records fill the floor-to-ceiling shelves.

In the President Finger section, 1952-64, there are 28 boxes. I pull down a box from 1958 marked "Integration" and stack three folders before me. Dad seems frozen by the sight, as if he's not sure he wants to enter the time capsule. I start flipping through the yellowed papers and quickly find in the 1958 stack the letter I most want to read.

The letter is from Ellis Wright, then head of a large Jackson funeral home and identified by the letterhead as president of the Jackson Citizens' Council: "Dedicated to good government, the promotion of peaceful relations and to the maintenance of segregation by all legal and legitimate means." In the 1950s and 1960s, staunch segregationists throughout Mississippi created these councils as a vehicle to intimidate and pressure those who might be sympathetic with the Civil Rights movement.

"I was appalled and shocked by certain events at Millsaps College this week," Wright wrote. The letter summarized recent events at Millsaps, including a symposium where a speaker espoused integration and classes where Millsaps and Tougaloo students met together. A historically black college on the outskirts of Jackson, Tougaloo College was the base for the famous Freedom Summer of 1964, which drew volunteers from throughout the country.

"The Citizens' Councils and patriotic public officials are engaged in a life and death struggle," Wright continued. "It is intolerable for Millsaps College, right here in the heart of Mississippi, to be in the apparent position of undermining everything we are fighting for." He concluded with a personal challenge. "I tell you frankly and without rancor that the time has come for a showdown. Either you and your faculty are for segregation, or you are for integration. In the best interests of the college, will you make known which position you and every member of your faculty support?"

It was a Friday afternoon when Wright hand delivered the letter to Dad's office, going past his secretary and into his office unannounced. Wright insisted Dad read the letter immediately. Instead, Dad told him he would read it on Monday.

"I slid it into the desk and ushered him out. Then I walked home," Dad says as we look together at the letter 31 years later. His face shows no emotion as he remembers the day. Wright sent the letter to the newspapers, but Dad never responded to it.

"I answered to the trustees of the college, not to Mr. Wright," Dad says to me, still showing no anger or sadness, no pride or sentimentality.

President Finger was 41 years old that spring day in 1958 when the segregationist leader barged into his office. I was 10, always wanting Dad to throw more football, basketball, or baseball with me. I would wait for him with the equipment of the season. That afternoon, with Little League tryouts just weeks away, I was no doubt waiting in the driveway when he walked across the street from Murrah Hall and down the steep drive onto our patio. Often, Dad would pitch baseball or football with me after work. He never had a lot of time, and I loved the time I had, when he tossed long throws making me stretch for the ball.

Today, as we read the letter together, I am 41 and he is 72.

We are running out of time in the archives. In two hours, the weekend events at Millsaps begin with a reception and dinner. Mother finds the scrapbook she kept during those years and is absorbed in the press clippings on the Wright-Finger exchange and many other race-related incidents. Dad is reading through the stacks of letters that poured in after Wright leaked his letter to the press.

The notes from rural Mississippi come from towns with names that have a magical ring, names I heard throughout my childhood—Tupelo and Iuka and Pontotoc, some of the towns where Dad would drive and preach every Sunday morning promoting the college, while Mother got us off to church. The Methodist churches throughout the state were the main funding source for the college in that era. "We the undersigned members of the Official Board of the Coffeeville Methodist Church, in our monthly session this night wish to express our confidence in your leadership ability as President of Millsaps College," reads one from the stack I'm flipping through. Twelve scrawling signatures followed.

"Here's a touching one," Dad says, leaning back and reading phrases from a single sheet in a stack before him. "I want to come back here and spend 10 days," he says, pulling his glasses off, tears leaking down his cheeks. "I've been away from it for 30 years. Now I'm ready to come back."

We stay as long as we can, sorting through the archives. As we walk back to the Holiday Inn, I'm sorting through my feelings as well. I'm proud of my father. I feel the toll the job took on him and on me—a father pulled away from his kids by work and a child who coped with his father's emotional and physical absence.

That night at the dinner, Dad is being honored as the Alumnus of the Year. After several short introductory speeches, he takes the podium; we are sitting at a table next to the platform.

"No student was ever more deeply indebted to an institution than this student was to this college," he tells the 350 people packed into the student union cafeteria. "I left as a 16-year-old lad from a small county-seat town in northeast Mississippi, rode all night on the train without benefit of Pullman." Arriving at 5 a.m., he wandered Capitol Street downtown for two hours before hailing a taxi for Millsaps. Dad reminisces about his student years and coming back as president. He closes with one of his favorite stories, about the introduction that he gave to a dignitary visiting our home.

"I laid it on, calling him one of the foremost authorities in his field in the world," Dad says, emphasizing "foremost." Then he pauses, preparing the crowd for the punch line. "Quick as a flash, Bill, our middle child, asked, 'Who were the other three?'" The chuckles in the crowd show Dad still has his timing from his years in the pulpit. He adds his final twist to the story, saying that as far as he was concerned, there were no "other three"—just Millsaps.

He tells more stories, focusing on the stresses during the Civil Rights period. "There were times when I didn't think we would make it. It took 12, 14, 16 hours a day to keep the college afloat in those days of turmoil." Sitting with Mother less than ten feet away, I fidget with my iced tea glass, wondering how my adolescent psyche absorbed those pressures.

THE NEXT MORNING, WE VISIT THE home where we lived from 1952 to 1964. We moved from Oxford, Mississippi, when I was five and left for Nashville when I was 17. The five of us walk to the side door, down the long sidewalk from Murrah Hall. Hardly anyone used the front door when I was little. As we began the tour, memories are bouncing through my head between snippets of conversation.

"And this must've been your room," our hostess is saying as we move back toward the kitchen.

"Yes, I shared it with my brother, but in 1960 they made the garage into a separate room, and we got our own rooms."

I slip away from the group and head out the back door to the patio, where I spent much of my time shooting at the basketball goal. It was my main companion, along with the tennis courts across the football field, in earshot of Mother's dinner bell. When I lived in the college president's house, my neighbors were the science building, football field, and the small grove of pine trees across the field on the hill leading up to the little star observatory.

I look across the football field and see that the pine trees have grown up along with me, no longer offering a small retreat as they did a generation ago. I usually went to the same tree, which had a natural sitting spot under the wings of its young boughs. Over time, I padded the dead pine needles against the rough spots of earth until I could sit or lie down feeling perfectly comfortable and safe. I liked skimming dry pine needles through my teeth and looking through the slivers of branches into patches of sky and drifting clouds. This pine tree was my place away from the expectations of family and the world, a private sanctuary with the trees and birds, the whistle of the wind and the stabs of rain.

The pine tree provided a place for the melancholy of my life to rest in peace, even if I didn't know what these feelings were. I remember feeling sad and disjointed by things I didn't understand, like the trips with Mother to take our maid, Katie, home. The drive took only a few minutes, just blocks away among streets of poor, dilapidated houses. Sitting with Mother in the front seat, I watched Katie get out of the back seat and walk slowly up the worn plank steps onto the front porch of her shotgun house, weary as she opened the door into what looked a lot like the old plantation slave quarters.

Standing on the patio during this trip down memory lane, the others still in the house, I jump from Katie's house to Galloway Church, the largest Methodist church in the state and a stone's throw from the state Capitol downtown. I spent every Sunday morning at Galloway and as a teenager in youth groups and choir, every Sunday evening as well. The memories dart through my brain in rapid succession—the acolyte years, the time Mother called on me in Sunday School class to lead the Lord's prayer when I was little. I suddenly forgot how the iconic prayer started. And, I remember the Easter Sunday when Galloway made national news. I was sitting in the balcony seats where we kids usually sat with our mother, so I never actually saw the white and black Methodist bishops denied entrance into the Easter service. They came up the wide steps to the front door of the sanctuary before ushers greeted them and said that the Negro could not come in; his white colleague remained outside as well. Segregation lived even in the eyes of worship that day in Jackson.

My father carried a picture of Jesus in his wallet, guided by his faith through his life. Some kind of faith seems to touch me as well, I'm thinking, these memories blasting away inside. But what is that faith? The darkness of Katie's ramshackle house roars back through me, along with that Easter Sunday. The segregated church and Katie's neighborhood contradicted the messages in Sunday sermons. Today on this patio I still feel the confusion of my childhood in the church, yet I also feel a spiritual anchor here, with the pine trees and my memories and my family.

Another scene pulls me away from blaming the church for my confusion. During my junior year the high school singers had a concert across the city. We sang at various settings, traveling in students' cars. Another singer named Larry was driving. I was in the back seat, left window. We headed through downtown. He stopped at a red light close to the pedestrian cross walk, in the area where Katie and her neighbors shopped. Throngs of Negroes crossed directly in front of us, inches away from Larry's front bumper. "I wish I could drive through and kill 'em all," he said.

In the backseat, head against the window, I felt something but didn't know what. The light turned green, a few stragglers scampered out of the way, and Larry accelerated into the barely open space. Not one of us five young men in the car spoke. None of us said it was wrong to wish to hurt someone just because of the color of their skin. Today, standing on the patio, I feel buried emotions climbing into my belly—shame, confusion, and guilt.

Back inside the house now, I readjust to the group, picking up on stories of how the college had redone the kitchen. I see that the old breakfast nook has in fact been revamped. I smile, remembering the security of family rituals. I see Dad leading us in a hymn each morning at the breakfast table. Jokes about how many pieces of toast I would eat, if the milk had bubbles in the top (indicating it had just been poured). But the dark side is so near. I recall one of our favorite hymns. "In Christ there is no East or West, in Him no North or South," it began. My psyche could not integrate the fondness of singing such lines in an appealing family ritual with a segregated Easter Sunday at Galloway.

But my mind turns quickly to good memories again as we walk

into the dining room, going now down the other side of the house. Dad presided over fried chicken every Saturday noon, which we called our weekly "Sunday" dinner. On Sundays, he traveled across Mississippi preaching for the college. We ate in the dining room after he returned from his Saturday morning office hours. Moving into the living room, I see the corner where Dad sat at a card table early every morning studying the names of the Millsaps students and sketching out his sermons. Mother had her piano in the other corner. Occasionally, the family would gather around as she played, Dad standing with us kids, wedged between Mother's back and the Korean prints on the living room wall. They were happy, cozy moments. Sometimes, we even went through our favorite song book, from front to back, with styles ranging from "Onward Christian Soldiers" to "Home, Home on the Range."

Finally, we return to the den where the side entrance to the house opens to the long walk toward Murrah Hall. I glance over where our Encyclopedia Britannica filled an entire section on the built-in bookcase, beside the couch where Dad would take his Saturday afternoon naps. One night a neatly dressed young black man appeared at this side door. I was 15 or 16, aware of the protests in the city. In 1961, the Freedom Riders had made their way into the Jackson bus station after beatings in Alabama. Protests in Jackson had swelled so much that the city used the fairgrounds as a makeshift jail, putting children behind high fences until they could be processed and released. The large protests had not reached Millsaps. But that night a group of students had decided to try to integrate the Christian Center, where the college held concerts and other community events.

"Is President Finger home?" the young man said after I opened the door. I stood a foot away in my first direct encounter with a protester. He didn't look like he was trying to destroy my way of life, as the local press depicted the Civil Rights demonstrators. He was nervous, nearly shaking as he stood there, alone.

"No, he's not home. I think he's at the Christian Center." The young man nodded, thanked me and left. I closed the door and tried to go back to watching television. Some deeper impulse, to think about what was really going on with this young man, was too much to deal with, so my feelings remained hidden, as if in a chasm too dark and deep to risk exploring.

Today's visit is nearly over now. We say our thanks and good-byes and head across the street to continue our reminiscing at Murrah Hall. We walk through Dad's old office and admire his portrait, which hangs in the hall along with other past presidents. Good feelings. The sadness, complexities of the church and race, and loneliness on the college campus seem a distant, other life. But I still feel a residual tension.

Dad was gone so much when I was little. I missed him. But he also provided for us in many ways, going well beyond the basics to family rituals that remain deeply important. And what about the letters in the archives? Of course, he was busy. Those were challenging times. He did the best he could, I tell myself. But my childhood side is not listening to this adult voice of reason. It is too much to piece together in the jammed weekend.

I know I need to talk to Dad, to at least to begin to sort it all out. I think he can help. I can't remember ever discussing with him a conflict over how he raised us. Intellectual disagreements, yes. Differences in whether Georgia and I should live together before we got married, certainly. Anger at him for not helping more as I navigated from child to adult—never. Maybe I never really broke away from a child into a man, in some ways. I resolve to take a step in this direction before I leave. And, I know where to begin.

SUNDAY MORNING, BEFORE I HAVE TO LEAVE for my flight, I ask Dad to come up to my room at the Holiday Inn to talk about something. As we settle into two swivel chairs on the fourth floor, which offers a great view across the edge of the campus, we chat a little about the weekend events, but time is pushing on. So I take a big breath and push into new territory.

"I loved your story in the speech Friday night about the foremost authority," I begin.

"You've never heard that story? I've used it in speeches for years. Another college president heard it once and liked it so much that he uses it too."

Anger flashes through me as I realize that things I said as an innocent kid have been on display all these years. But I stuff this anger down and respond without emotion. "I guess I vaguely recall that story. Maybe I heard it once."

"Quick as a flash," Dad says again, smiling at the punch line. "I always say, 'Quick as a flash' when I tell that story."

I like seeing him smile, realizing I'm part of a fond memory. But my anger is moving closer to the surface now. "It's neat to hear myself in a story," I say. "But it's strange to hear that the story has been used for so long, in so many speeches. It seems like you're communicating with me through a speech." My tone is sharp now, like a teenager arguing in ways I never did. "Yeah, that's it. You're talking to me through a speech rather than just talking to me."

Unresolved emotions from my teenage years are taking over now. "I hear you more in a sermon or a speech than right here with me," I snap. A silence settles between us. Even though I feel flustered and not very polite right now, I feel relieved. And I feel closer to my father.

"In Oxford, we tried to have every Saturday afternoon together," Dad finally says. "We would go to Lake Stevens and then that night I would go to my office and get my ducks lined up for Sunday morning. When we came here it was all I could do to keep my head above water. It was an arduous task."

He says "ar-du-oussss," using the kind of emphasis he liked in sermons. The pause in the message helps me absorb his words and the unspoken emotions. Then he continues.

"I had all I could do to keep up with my job. I let our quality time slip away when we came to Jackson and I regret it." A silence settles in. We talk a little about Oxford when I was little. But it's time for me to go to the airport.

We stand up. His angular handsome face seems softer, the public persona put away for now. He holds out his arms and says, "I love you."

Despite the new type of conversation, his words catch me by surprise. I hardly know what to say or do. I lean in, welcoming his embrace. "I love you too, Dad." We hold each other, and I feel his long arms wrapped against my back. Then, as we separate, I see tears in his eyes. When did we ever say that to each other? Maybe back in Oxford, when I was four? I can't remember.

CHAPTER 7. Digging into Numbness

 "WE NEED TO DIG THIS A LITTLE DEEPER," says Hugh, one of my buddies from the men's group.

"Are you sure?" I ask, leaning against the post-hole digger and catching my breath. "Seems like this will hold fine."

"No, let's go a little deeper, to make sure that dog of yours won't get out. And we'll need some more rocks to mix in with the concrete."

I head down the sloping back yard to the stream and fill a bucket with small rocks. Hugh has handled many such projects before. A large, strong man, six or seven years older than me, he picks up the digger and shoots down into the hard clay. David, whose birthday we celebrated on the canoe trip, joins me at the creek. The work moves quickly after the holes are dug. We stretch the wire around the posts and staple it into place. The door takes more time, but Hugh rigs a makeshift latch for today. Rosebud, the name our son picked for his dog, will be fine behind this fence.

At the end of the full Saturday of work, the early June heat burns off in the dusk. Hugh and I sit on the back steps, drinking cold lemonade. "Georgia and I had another dog before we had kids." I take another long swig, my sweat now dry. "We called her Tasha."

"So what happened to Tasha?"

"With a baby, we decided we couldn't handle Tasha too. She was a runner and took a lot of my time. I would throw her a ball for hours and she would never get tired. So we gave her away to a family on a farm."

Hugh nods, calling to his own dog, who is wandering too far into the bamboo.

I sit quietly, memories of dogs starting to trigger my feelings. Hugh looks over and notices that I'm starting to tear up. A former campus minister, he has a gentle way about him.

"Was it hard to give up Tasha?"

"No, we were fine with that. I'm remembering another dog, Rags. I only had Rags for a short time when I was growing up on the college campus. Rags would follow me to school or wander into the college classrooms. One day, they called Dad to come get Rags out of the science building, which was next to our house. He wandered into a lab!"

Hugh laughs in his loud, engaging way. "The President's dog hits the science lab. I can see that might not be cool for your dad."

"So, Dad decided we couldn't keep a dog. It was the only dog we ever had." My voice is getting whiney, like a kid. Then the tears start flowing. "Why couldn't they build a dog pen for Rags?" My words come out in a burst, louder now. "We built a dog pen! My Dad could've gotten the maintenance people to do it—just like he did my basketball goal!"

The tears are streaming down my cheeks now. I'm surprised by my emotions but feel no embarrassment with Hugh after more than a year of weekly support groups together. No need to cover them up. The big back yard absorbs the sounds as effortlessly as the pine trees soaked in my confusion when I lived in Jackson. Georgia and the kids are off doing errands. The wild bamboo and marshy stream remain as anchored as ever. Hugh puts his arm around my shoulder. I feel like a little kid, maybe 10, walking beside my buddy at Lake Junaluska, the place where I felt the comfort of friends growing up.

While Rosebud is slated as Lee's dog, I know this addition to the family will bring me plenty of joy as well.

IN THE SPRING AND SUMMER OF 1989, after returning from the trip to Millsaps and Jackson, the tears appear often, sudden and unexpected. Events trigger unexpressed emotions from days long past, as if a forgotten genie is poking her head out of the bottle. Maybe talking with my father in that motel room began to open me up to more of my own feelings. Or perhaps writing the profiles on Mahan Siler and the mental health leader prompted more feelings to rise to the surface. Or maybe expanding my creative abilities in those profiles, beyond the more analytical type of writing I did for the public policy magazine, led to new ways of expressing myself.

On a trip to Washington an unexpected memory again triggers tears. Georgia and I decide to attend her nephew's high school graduation, which is being held in the historic Constitution Hall near the downtown Washington Mall. Walking into the grand hall feels like a trip back in time to the era when the African American opera singer, Marian Anderson, was refused permission to sing there by the Daughters of the American Revolution.

We are sitting far back from the large graduating class but still have a good view of the student speakers. They give stirring addresses, calling on history and the energy of the new graduates to make things better for the country. As our family's new graduate gets his hard-earned diploma, my eyes are getting moist. I dab at the tears the way people often do at milestone events, remembering their own graduation or marriage. But I sense something more than symbolic tears.

That afternoon, driving back to North Carolina, we leave Interstate 85 for a rural route through the Virginia countryside. With the hammering 18-wheelers no longer at my side, I relax more at the wheel, memories spinning along with the beautiful rolling hills. The tears from Constitution Hall come back and linger. I feel preoccupied with the emotion from the graduation, even though the time for reminiscing and congratulations at the ceremony are hours past.

At a rest stop in rural Virginia I suddenly make the connection with my own graduation. As I walk slowly around the parking lot, some long-buried sadness is surfacing. I realize that I can barely remember my own high school graduation. Did I walk across a stage? Where was my graduation? At the Hillwood High gym I think. Or was it somewhere else? Was there a party afterwards? I can't recall any details.

I felt numb much of my senior year of high school. I was a shadow emotionally, no joy, no relief—no feelings. I walked through that passage as if adding a notch to the resume of life—high school graduation, check. It was my one and only year in that school.

I moved to Nashville the summer of 1964 when Dad was elected bishop in the Methodist Church. We were all happy to leave the heat and racial tensions of Jackson, but I also left a starting role on the basketball team and a familiar high school and church group. So I spent my last year of high school in Nashville, Tennessee, looking for tennis partners and struggling for playing time under a terrible basketball coach. Emotionally, I retreated into a familiar dark place that helped me cope, like the pine tree did in Jackson.

On the ride home from Washington through rural Virginia, even with a loving wife and kids beside me in the car, I understand better how I can feel detached even from those I love. I understand better my retrenchment into silence, reflection, even sullenness. I am taking a step forward, understanding some of the source of my feelings. This understanding doesn't help me be more available when my wife or children request my attention. But it's a start.

The events of the spring are opening me up, ever so slightly, to mourning old losses and to a sense of hope. The tears are cracking the numbness, like a light rain on dry parched ground. From my Uncle Bill dream, I know I can resist the invitation to fall into his chamber of depression. With Hugh, my sadness tumbles out allowing emotions from years before to surface. Mahan Siler offers me grace and darkness and, unexpectedly, a new window into the confusing messages I got from church. I am getting strong enough to begin to feel, but I still lack the vocabulary. I do not know how to share these feelings. They just burst out in unexpected moments. The numbness reappears as quick as a flash at times, taking me over like one of Dad's stories.

Late that spring a local art center is holding a fundraiser. Georgia has a studio there where she displays the modern quilts she is making, part of her transition from being a lawyer to an artist. We join several couples from our old neighborhood, just a few blocks from downtown, for pictures and hors d'oeuvres before heading to the fundraiser.

On our way, everyone seems so gay and happy. But laughing and enjoying myself become an effort. I want to support Georgia and enjoy friends but feel myself withdrawing, getting quiet and pre-occupied. I feel bad about not feeling good, which makes me feel worse.

Georgia introduces me to a few of her friends and I manage polite greetings. In the renovated three-story downtown building, the hallways on the first two floors are packed with people. Her studio is at the end of the second floor. In the crowded corridor, I began to feel more trapped and overwhelmed by the loud conversations, the groups of friends who seem so relaxed. I hang back as she greets more people and begins to mingle on her own. I see her busy and turn to make my way back downstairs and outside to the fresh air and the sidewalk. For no apparent reason, tears start welling up. I have no idea what emotions I am feeling. I walk around the downtown park awhile—am I gone 30 minutes, an hour? I have no idea. Eventually I make my way back to the party.

"Where have you been?" she asks.

"I've been walking outside. The party was just too much for me." She is ready to go, so we head for the door and, thankfully, into the fresh evening air. I mumble something about being tired and don't attempt to explain what I was feeling. I don't know what I am feeling—only that I am tired and want the night to end.

THE ANNUAL SUMMER TRIP TO LAKE JUNALUSKA in western North Carolina is a welcome vacation. At Junaluska, I always get re-anchored in life, renewed and rested. Throughout my childhood, after managing another year of the stresses of Mississippi, my family made the long overnight drive, pre-Interstate, to this hideaway in the Smokey Mountains. Dad had to return to the college after a month, but Mother stayed with us kids for the summer. At Lake Junaluska, I played steal the bacon and hide and seek with other ministers' children, with no under-current of race and no extra burden of being a preacher's kid.

Walking into the log cabin feels like coming home. My parents love having their grandchildren, and I can take jogs around the beautiful lake in the morning, the mist burning off with the mountain haze. The smell of the chestnut logs and the huge hemlocks embrace me as I sit on the big wraparound screened porch, unwinding from issues in Raleigh.

One night during the week, the North Carolina Symphony is playing in the large lake-side auditorium used for preaching, concerts, and other occasions. The building provides an inspiring venue for joyous music and peaceful reflection. Introducing the symphony, the director for the evening, Jackson Parkhurst, reminisces about his years as a boy at nearby Brevard Music Camp and its influence on his musical directions.

"One evening, I was homesick at the camp," Parkhurst says. "I had walked away from the main amphitheater, in a large grassy area. Then, I heard the sound of the music over the hill from the amphitheater. I walked through the wet grass towards the music. It felt like it was calling me home. Music is a way of coming home, of finding joy in life." He shares memories of the mountains and Brevard and how he hopes the music this evening will remind us of the joys in our own lives.

As I sit there, tears start streaming down my face. *I've never had any such moment of joy in my life.* And, as Parkhurst talks, I truly cannot remember being happy. A critical grown-up voice counters: *Of course you have been happy. Remember when your carried Lee into the house, when Dana arrived, when you got married.*

I don't have the energy to fight back at this logic. My rational brain acknowledges the truth to these moments of happiness, but I cannot feel a positive memory. I try to listen to the music but mostly thoughts of lost and forgotten joys wash through me, like the small surf on the lake outside the auditorium windows.

That night, the children in bed, I sit on the porch alone and think about the evening. Was I wallowing in negative thinking or appropriately grieving for past losses? I'm not sure. I have just read *Feeling Good* by David Burns, which is a guide to the power of positive thinking. But his book did not kick-start me in this direction.

I want to feel what I feel, not force myself to feel good. My instinct is that I need to stay with the bad feelings. Being depressed is a familiar place, as comfortable as one of my old pair of Weejuns. I don't want to leave this place of sadness and grief, which seem both addictive and cathartic. I sort the thoughts through the journalist's filter, distancing myself from the material, as if writing an article. And, gradually, as I structure the analysis in my head, feelings put aside, I began to feel better.

As the concert went on that night, I did hear some of the music. I feel validated now by my gut feelings—to allow the dark thoughts rather than fight them with positive thinking. But I also feel worn out from my double life. I am living an external life, listening to the music or laughing with friends. At the same time, I also am managing an active internal life, sorting out ways to manage an array of new feelings, to analyze and understand—but not discuss.

AT THE END OF THE SUMMER, IN OUR SUPPORT group one night, the other Bill in the group tells a long story about his wonderful travels during the summer, camping in the western states, visiting one of our old group members who moved to Montana, and participating in an archeological dig. Hugh, David, and the other guys laugh with Bill about his adventures, enjoying the stories. But I find myself getting sad. All I can think of is how unhappy my summer was. For several months I told myself, "If I can just make it through the summer." With the new school year for the kids, life would be more structured. Maybe I could find a steady job. Growing up, summer was the fun time, the time at Lake Junaluska. But this summer, I felt like I was slogging through a long journey.

Driving home from my support group that night, I vow never again to go through a summer without doing something special for myself. I am beginning to grow tired, even bored, with feeling bad.

I make another resolution in the early fall, shortly after hearing of Bill's wonderful summer. I decide I will not continue to struggle so much with finances. I will quit being a freelancer and find a job. My consultant job at Legal Services of North Carolina has the potential to expand to a staff position, but I wonder if it will be secure. Another job opening appears in the paper, a writing position at a public health research group called Family Health International, which works primarily with family planning in developing countries. The international work catches my eye.

Walking into the four-story building for my interview, masks and weavings from Asia and Africa hang on the corridor walls. I feel excited by the reminders of my time in India. I learn that many of the staff there are ex-Peace Corps volunteers. The writing samples I sent earlier from the public policy magazine convince the head of the information program that I can handle the public health material. We negotiate a half-time position, which includes health insurance. I can keep doing some freelance writing and keep one day free to take care of the kids after school.

The new job offers an adventure, connecting me back to the Peace Corps and offering me stability. This release from financial pressures makes Georgia and me happy. My circumstances change, and my mood lifts. Only a year earlier I lost my job at the legislature. Michael Meade would call the year I had been through an initiation—a time of being pulled away from my familiar place and tested. I lived through it, not without some anguish. But the question now is how I will function having survived this initiation.

Will I fall back into old patterns? Or will the lessons of the past year broaden my imagination? Now firmly in midlife, past my forty-second birthday, I am entering a new passage. The task will be to integrate the deeper, feeling sides of life into my daily awareness, even if it means accepting the dark feelings when they come.

CHAPTER 8. Pools of Grief

"THE FALCON ERUPTS," MICHAEL MEADE says in his crisp, passionate way, hands resting on his drum. Meade is sitting on a 15-foot log bench before a gathering of 110 men in the dining hall of a church camp near Roanoke, Virginia. "The falcon has great style but how does it carry its force without doing damage?"

Meade is discussing the falcon as part of a broader theme for this week-long men's conference—initiation into a more powerful kind of manhood than I have known. The men arrived the night before from Houston and New Orleans, Myrtle Beach and Manitoba, from 15 states and Canada, ages 26 to 67. It is October 1989, just weeks before I begin my new job with a fresh sense of relief and excitement.

Four men have joined forces to guide our week together: Meade, the drummer and teller of ancient tales; Robert Bly, the poet who triggered what many now refer to as the mythopoetic men's movement; James Hillman, the irreverent Jungian psychologist and widely published author; and John Stokes, a tracker, whose grief sent him into the Australian bush for seven years where he bonded with the animals.

Before hauling sleeping bags to the cabins in the woods, all but the cooks and staff assistants passed through a registration ritual. Descriptions of three animals written on a chalkboard at the leaders' cabin posed a choice of clans. Many of the bulky and older men gravitated to this phrase: "The black bear is father, mother, keeper of the forest... As elders, they master and command respect. And hold the power to curse or bless."

The trout in contrast, "dwell in pools of grief, reflect the upper world, seek wisdom in the water, and elusively avoid capture. [Trout] regard fish and fishing as a holy thing, because one fishes for the wound and the wound that can be named can be healed." Some men became falcons, which "burn for what is difficult, beautiful and dangerous. They desire initiatory experience now."

On the kitchen staff, I feel left out of the clan process. I signed up to help in the kitchen to get a cheaper rate for the week. That first afternoon, as the others were joining clans, our nine-person kitchen crew sat in a circle describing our goals for the week. Our task is to feed the bears, trout, and falcons. We have great powers to nurture and great responsibilities. I love this talk of myths, of animals and nurturing and where we might fit in. I feel thrilled to be in the woods with so many men but also a bit intimidated by the focus on this topic of initiation. What does it mean for me?

Each of the clans has its own pieces of fabric in a distinctive color. We take the color of royal blue, calling ourselves "Men Who Feed the Dragons." All the clans together are cast together as dragons, we decide.

Just eight months before, I was one of the heads of the dragon in the story Meade told at the Raleigh weekend workshop. From time to time over the months, I pondered the power of the image, even as I traveled to Jackson, wrote about my Uncle Bill, and listened to my heart beside Lake Junaluska. At that weekend workshop, we talked about dragons and witches, fierceness and feminine energy. By identifying with the dragon's heads, I was beginning to confront in mythological terms the powerful energies demanding attention—my wife and young children.

And now, with a week ahead of me at this new conference, I am one of the Men Who Feed the Dragons. Maybe I can find more strength to know how to be a man in my own home.

The first night as dinner was ending, three men in the falcon clan leapt from the edge of the dining hall, near the 40 or so drums, into the front of the lodge, beside the log bench. With red cloth flying from arms and legs, they mocked the trout, and did the same to a peace banner. Then

THE CRANE DANCE   75

just as suddenly, they swooped back into the night. Throughout the first day of the conference, side conversations festered about the falcons mocking the peace banner. But the conflict remained covert, festering until finally men begin to speak about it late that afternoon. Meade refereed the angry accusations, defenses, and explanations. As the volleys continued, he closed the topic, moving on in the week's program, called "Male Initiation and Isolation."

The falcons' actions in the dining hall represented the mythological level, Meade said, part of a concept he introduced in the morning session. We live in three levels of experience simultaneously—the concrete, psychological, and mythological—each with its own vibrancy and liabilities. The falcons erupted with an impulse to do damage. That's the way initiation can sometimes go.

ON THE SECOND NIGHT, AFTER MEADE transforms the falcon tension into a discussion of initiation, we move to the personal statements. "Initiation involves wounds," Meade says. "Initial statements are risky."

Men begin to stand up and make brief statements to the group about who they are and why they are here. The first night men told moving stories mostly about their grandfathers, lineage, heritage. The second night, the statements take a more risky turn. A man who had spent a week tracking animals with John Stokes speaks about finding his life by noticing close details in the forest. I feel a chill as he talks of tracking himself, of finding out who he is.

Then I rise, even though Michael had asked to hear from the trout. "I'm one of the men who feed the dragons, Michael," I say. "You really didn't say we could speak yet."

"Dragons can speak anytime," he responds quickly in the staccato style that I remembered from the earlier workshop.

Permission granted, I speak about the earlier weekend with Meade, about my place in the story as the head of a dragon. "This time, instead of having to be fed, I'm feeding the dragons. And that's what I've been doing at home more and more—nurturing my children and opening up to my wife, holding her and taking her tension into my body, instead of putting demands on her. But this new nurturing role I'm playing still seems tenuous. I want it to be deeper, more solid for me. I want to know that it's permanent. And I need support for that." Then I sit down.

I feel vibrant, yet shaky, in stating my purpose before so many men. Meade nods, gazing at me in a supportive yet challenging way. He seems to have an instinct that I need to find a new path to a place where nurturing and being nurtured can merge together, where dragons and feeding the dragons can stand in tension but also as one.

After the night session ends I go with Daniel, another cook, to make a mask. I started the day at 5:30 in the morning, plugging in the camp's first pot of coffee. As I stuck with the kitchen duties, I was also opening up my psyche—listening to poetry, participating in the body exercises, listening to a short story Michael told. I was mixing the responsible, provider side with sensual, passionate expressions—nurturing and being nurtured.

That night at the camp craft shop, I lie on my back with wet plaster of paris smothering my face, a small hole for breathing. I feel panicky at first and almost rip the moist pieces from my eyes and mouth. Tom Daly, one of the staff, holds my hand and reminds me to breathe.

"Have you ever had an operation?" he asks. "The covering of the face is a lot like the anesthesia mask. It can bring up old feelings."

"Yeah. I had my appendix out." Feelings of suffocation I felt as a child as the surgery was about to start were in fact coming back. "And I had a more recent operation too." Tom is still there holding my hand. "A urologist operated on the other side of my belly to cut a vein. We were having trouble getting pregnant. It's supposed to help the sperm count." The feelings of smothering are gone. My emotional pores are opening.

Finally, the mask dries enough so I can take it off. I lay it onto a bench to harden. I sit beside Tom, looking at the white mask, as stark as the emotions. It awaits adornment. I don't know what to create on this virgin plaster so I look around for ideas. One of the men is gluing pine needles on his mask. Now at 11 p.m., I walk into the woods and find myself gathering berries and cones and twigs and mosses as if in a dream. In a surreal, exhausted state, the memories of the operation come roaring in, surrounded by the high canopy of pines.

SCRATCH, SCRATCH, SCRATCH. I didn't have the courage to look down as the orderly shaved my pubic hair for the operation. "Why do you have to shave me down there," I asked. "I thought the incision was up near the belly button?"

"Don't know. I'm just doing what they told me," the young man answered. "I'm almost finished. Don't worry. I'm being careful." I heard the old man moaning behind the curtain on the other side of the two-person hospital room. No one had been to see him since I arrived the day before. The nurse said he wasn't doing so well.

I remember the first meeting with the urologist, an efficient man who did not invite questions. "It's a common condition. Two out of five infertility cases are due to the man. A varicocele reduces the sperm count. This operation usually results in the vein shrinking around the testicle and the count increasing." He got up. But I had a few questions. Georgia had helped me prepare for this. She was used to going to a gynecologist and had learned to be assertive with doctors.

As the memory of my operation fades, I stare at the tall trees in the Virginia woods and take a deep breath. The long grasses at my side seem perfect for the mask. I pick some and gather bluish berries, maybe huckleberries, not yet fallen from a nearby bush. I carefully pick up the small twigs, grasses, and berries and head back to start decorating the mask. As I reach the end of a very long day, another hospital scene snaps into clear view.

Georgia's gynecologist has exited the surgical ward, mask in his hand, just like on TV, the news clear on his face. He had completed the diagnostic procedure on her infertility. "There was way too much scar tissue," he said. "I'm virtually sure she can't get pregnant."

It was the latest blow to Georgia from a drug called DES, which doctors prescribed in the 1940s to her mother and other women who had a risk of miscarriage. Over the years, many of these "DES daughters" as they became known had gynecological problems; some died. Georgia knew she might have trouble having children. Somehow as we ploughed through the doctors and read the books and considered our options with infertility, I had my operation first. Not long after mine, Georgia had hers.

Later that day, I brought her home. She sat in my lap, sobbing, cleansing away the sorrow of her loss. I felt strong and present for her and proud that I was a good husband. Needed by my wife, I rose to the occasion. But I didn't cry for me, for her, for us.

THE NEXT DAY, I GO EARLY AND ADD MORE of the forest to my mask, until there are great tears of grasses falling down one cheek, with shades of greens and browns covering my face, acorns and berries, red and blue, frozen in time on cheek and nose and jawbone. It is the first piece of art I have created since I was a boy in Jackson. The images of grief fall onto the mask, and the memories hold less power over me. Still, though, I don't cry. Yet I do see grief on the mask, taking me further along some journey.

Every morning after breakfast the leaders sit on the log and read poems by D.H. Lawrence, William Blake, and others. I have a hard time plugging my head into images so early in the day. I have never been a poetry fan. Memorizing Longfellow or Whittier in high school had not opened me to the grief of living in Jackson. Bly recites his poems with the aura of an Indian holy man, waving his hands and chanting in a high, nasal pitch at times. James Hillman, an intellectual who led studies at the Jung Institute in Switzerland for a decade, joins in the poetry readings. Surprisingly, Hillman rather than Bly is the one who changes my view of poetry forever.

Hillman starts reading "The Race" by Sharon Olds, about a dash to catch a plane to see a dying father. At first I'm just following the story of the poem. But about halfway through, Hillman chokes with emotion, trying to get through the race down the long airport corridor to the gate. Then he stops, sobbing. Michael reaches his hand across James' shoulder and holds him. Hillman, who is in his 60s, resurfaces and finishes the poem. Tears are streaming down my face too, and I know how it feels to have my heart opened at unexpected moments. After that morning's poetry I know I will move with the trout clan during my free time. I feel pulled toward the "pools of grief" in the phrase written on the backboard upon arrival, to "regard fish and fishing as a holy thing, because one fishes for the wound, and the wound that can be named can be healed."

One afternoon late in the conference, I gather with the trout in the leaders' cabin. Men sit cross-legged on the floor and perch on bunks. Sitting on a blanket in front of a fire in the stone fireplace, Bly tells a fairy tale but with a contemporary twist. A man out of the army has to descend again and again to stir a pot, to earn money, which he brings back to the world. Talking of ashes and grief, Bly suddenly reaches back to the edge of the fire and brushes charcoal onto his forehead and cheeks. As we drift back outside after the story he rubs many of us with ash across our face.

The ash ritual over, I sit against an oak, listening to the migrating geese honking across the sky. Then a chorus of human voices echoes from across the lake, where the tracker Stokes is teaching the bear clan to sing in harmonies that sound as ancient as a Gregorian chant. Chills run deep through me.

DURING THE CONFERENCE MEADE TELLS A LONG STORY in each of the main morning gatherings over four days. As he did in the Raleigh workshop, he asks men to watch for the opening to the story that is unique to them. "A story is like a forest," he says. "You walk around it and find the right door. Look for a door you've not seen. Look for a facet of your psyche you haven't noticed for a long time."

The fairy tale begins with a young man who is watching his pigs in the forest when he discovers a tall tree whose branches disappear into the clouds. Curious, the man begins climbing and after two nights finds a castle where a princess is held prisoner by a wicked magician. The pig herder can stay but must not enter one room.

"He could not resist and so he opened the door," Meade says, striking hard on his drum. A silence lands across the hall as he stills the vibrations from the drum. Now in a normal voice, he asks, "What do you see in that room? Stay with the image that is filling your mind."

He asks men to throw out images that they see. After maybe 10 responses, he guides us into groups that have similar themes. Fear is the common element for about 15 of us, who move from the main hall and sit outside by the lake and discuss our images. If I hadn't been to the earlier workshop in Raleigh, this talk of imagining a room in a fairy tale might seem silly. It might sound like story-time at one of my kid's kindergarten classes. Instead, I stand feeling the warm sun bouncing off the water, pulling me into a sacred circle of sorts. I sit with the other men and sense that we are all somehow joined in some serious quest for truth through the fairy tale.

"I saw a high stack of books on the left when the pig herder opened the door," I say when my turn comes. "On the lower right side of the room, I saw a group of men like a chorus in a cathedral. The men were singing, encouraging me to cross the threshold behind them into a dark forest that was spiraling away in three dimensions."

Other men share their images. As we talk on this warm Indian summer day, my fear becomes more approachable. The group seems to become the men's chorus inside the forbidden room where I just walked. The men are my trusted allies.

Sitting with them, I remember the dream I had of Uncle Bill, especially the look in his eye as I confronted the power of those black pools. Like those pools, the image of the spiraling staircase feels like a seduction downward from which I would never return. But today, on this warm earth, I know that I can manage this challenge somehow, that I don't have to fear stepping into the dark forest. The chorus is with me. I am not overwhelmed.

Later, Meade continues with the fairy tale. We learn that behind the door was a raven, nailed to a wall. The raven complains of being thirsty, and the man gives him water. The nails fall out and the raven escapes. When the princess hears, she is dismayed. "That was the devil who enchanted me!" Meade says with an extra energy on the drum. "He will come back for me." Soon after, she vanishes from the castle.

After the pig herder comes down from the castle, his pigs have disappeared and he wanders through the forest aimlessly. One at a time, he encounters a wolf, a bear, and a lion. They all give him a few hairs from their hides and say he can use the hairs in a time of distress.

The pig herder's journey into the forest involves many twists: the wicked hunter who had been the raven, a witch who breeds magical horses in a corral with skulls on the posts, and the allure of getting one of these magical horses to escape the forest. The wicked hunter, who has one of the horses, also has the captured princess. The only way the pig herder can rescue her is to secure a magical horse himself.

"'You must tend my foals for three days,' the witch says." Meade uses a shrill falsetto, bringing the witch to life. I smile, remembering how I enjoyed watching the witch in Hansel and Gretel with my kids but also remembering moments when they were young and afraid of her.

If the pig herder can return the horses to the corral each night, he can make his choice. "Of course, it's not that easy," Meade says, back to his narrator tone. "The witch gives him brandy after the bargain is sealed, and the young man sleeps late the next morning. The witch, meanwhile, rises well before dawn and tells the foals to go to the deepest corners of the forest and not to return no matter what the pig herder does or says."

When the young man finally makes it to the corral, he sees the horses are all gone and hears they are far away with orders not to return. He wanders in the forest and begins to cry.

"He weeps and weeps at a big stone for hours. And then he hears the sound of a wolf." Meade's hands speed across the goatskin of his drum signaling a new voice.

"Why do you cry so much?" Meade says as if he's a wolf. "Do not worry. Do you remember the hairs I gave you? You can use them. Call on all the wolves in the forest to go and get the horses." Meade pauses, lifts his hands off the drum, stares into our crowd of men, and speaks as the wolf. "Now you must stop your crying. Too many tears will turn your heart to stone." The next two days, the pig herder cries and cries as he faces the same dilemma of corraling all the horses. And, once again, he hears from his allies, the bear and the lion. He uses the magical hairs again each day and returns the horses to the corral, completing his deal with the witch.

"Too many tears will turn your heart to stone." This line from the story bounces about as I move from kitchen to main gathering, from small groups with the trout back to the kitchen. How can tears be a bad thing? I keep thinking I need to cry. I need to grieve. And, I keep soaking in the images from the week, expecting one day that I will understand why that detail looms so large in my heart.

DURING THE CONFERENCE, THE LEADERS discuss themes in the morning general sessions, before the clans work on tracking or drumming or mask-making in the afternoon. During one session, Hillman helps me think of fathers in an entirely new way. "As long as you complain about negative fathers," he says, "you remain a son. Use the negative in your psyche as an initiator." The concept appeals to me.

"Souls choose their parents," Hillman says. "Mythologically, you choose your parents." The first step is to feel the misery, the wound, the victim, he says. Blame your father. But then go to the second step and use the scar tissue. "He should not have been any different."

As the conference winds down, Meade and Bly advise against talking about the inner journey undertaken in the safety of the gathering. "Don't name it," says John Stokes. "If you ask someone the name of a tree and get a quick answer, you quit looking at that tree." I know exactly what he means and have done that many times. "Instead of naming it, look deep into the colors of the bark, the textures of the wood, the curves of the leaves, the patterns of the veins."

But there is a time for naming, which Stokes and the others also discuss during the week. "The wound that can be named can be healed," read the description of the trout.

The final night, after an elaborate meal cooked in a camp kitchen, the clans decorate themselves and the hall for a spirited ceremony and dance. At the carnival, I join the trout and wear my mask. The last night, Michael finishes the pig herder story, and the party continues with drumming and dancing, just as native men have done for centuries. At the banquet, I raise my glass to the Raleigh Men's Center founders, who are there to receive my blessing. "Thank you for giving me the chance to open my heart."

This conference can help to change my life, but it means nothing unless I find the courage to follow the new paths deeper. From the banquet decorations, I bring home grasses and sticks, placed in a rusty can I found in the woods. The rough brown metal seems like an elegant vase. I put these grasses in the bamboo where I go to think alone, along with some waxed autumn leaves from the flower arrangement I gave my wife before I left.

Into a mug decorated with unicorns, I stuff the blue sliver of cloth I had tied around my body as I joined the trout. I add two acorns gathered for my mask, the verse I memorized for the poetry night, and one of my kid's whistles, which is like the one Michael used to direct the drumming.

To take my new energy into my family and life, I need a reentry ritual. The Men's Center monthly drumming sessions, scheduled just three days after my return, serves that purpose. Several of us cooks brought fruit from the conference kitchen. At the drumming, eight of us who were at the gathering stand in the center of the circle and offer the fruit to nourish other dragons.

As we chew slices of tart grapefruit and sweet oranges, we read poems and talk about our return. The men who stayed in Raleigh talk of their lives as well. I drum that day and remember Michael's advice, "When you're in trouble, remember the dances." And, that afternoon, among those men, I read the poem I wrote upon returning, called "Homecoming."

A week with one hundred men…

The images pound against my sleep, push into my consciousness

Faces, colors, touching, dancing and hitting the drum
until I fall into the timeless wonder of rhythms,

My hands moving without instruction

The cacophony bursts as silently as the infinite sounds of the forest,
waiting to be heard.

The memories flap with the swooping wingspan of the woodpecker
that soared away from the hardwood between the back of the kitchen
and the magical den of masks,

Its red feathers bristling like the mane of a horse snorting
instructions to the herd.

With the birds, I fly deeper into the woods,

Trusting my images but knowing they can vanish with the ashes—

Unless they are buried and tilled and sown,

For the forest of the seasons is at hand!

Such a cutting is before me now, the last smell of mown grass for the fall,
reminding me that I am home again.

My daughter snacks inside, happily alone.

My wife swims, bathing her bones—weary from nurturing alone,

While I suspended myself in time.

And my son, at his friend's party, is enjoying a magician.

I am home, with new spirits to guide me deep into the forest.

BOOK 3. ACCEPTANCE
(1990–1993)

CHAPTER 9. Gargoyles Become My Friends

THE CRISP JANUARY DAY HERALDS the arrival of the 1990 spring semester on the Duke University campus. I feel excited and nervous as I walk past the gargoyles gawking from corners of the gothic buildings. The bustle of students going to afternoon classes adds to my eagerness for my first day of teaching. I feel prepared yet intimidated. A lack of confidence stems less from the teaching role than from being back in a Duke classroom.

I pause on the heavy stones of the walkway that passes through the north walls of a small quadrangle of dormitories. Looking up at the concrete ceiling, I picture the study cubicles on the top floor, where I agonized through my first English essay on irony as a freshman in 1965. Picking up my pace again into the next long quadrangle, I take a deep breath. I remind myself that I'm a 42-year-old journalist with more than 60 magazine and newspaper articles under my belt, not an 18-year-old trying to make sense of a new life away from home. While I can feel the memories of my student years demanding attention, I have no time for unresolved issues about my self-confidence from those years.

Heading past the Chapel, which towers over the school like a European cathedral, I push my mind into the present. I review my plans for the first class, a weekly seminar with about 18 bright young men and women. Just weeks before, the instructor expected to teach the writing course in the public policy department dropped out, and a journalist colleague recommended me. I could manage the time around my new half-time position at Family Health International. I needed the extra money and welcomed the opportunity to return to Duke in a different status.

Moving past the impressive library that opened when I was a student, I see the language lab where I tried to learn French from audio tapes. The quadrangle ends in what used to be one of the main entrances to the Duke Hospital, which has now sprawled into a massive collection of buildings with entrances on other parts of the campus. At the end on the left is the public policy department now in the process of planning a new modern building off the main quad. But for this semester, my class will try to bring to life a rather stale room steeped in Duke history.

I unpack my papers at the small, elevated lectern area. The students drift in and find a seat in a room too large for a seminar. Just before the class is to begin, a middle-aged man rushes in and comes to the front to introduce himself.

"I called you a few days ago," he says. "Remember, from *Time* magazine. You said it would be fine for me to visit one of your classes."

"Oh yes. But I didn't realize you were coming today." The department chair said that I might have an occasional guest from the department's visiting journalists program, where top national reporters study on a sabbatical. But I expected more notice so that I could integrate the guests into the class plan.

"Yes. Sorry for this last minute thing. But it worked out in my schedule."

"Okay. Well, it's our first day. So, bear with us."

The bell rings, and we begin. To introduce ourselves, I have the students pair up and tell each other their expectations for the course, why they took this course, and anything else they want their classmates to know. Then everyone will introduce their partners, as if reporting from a news source. The students start their work, and I turn to my visitor. Without thinking the idea through, I suggest that he and I partner and introduce each other.

He tells me the basic information on his career and why he's at Duke—quick, simple, straightforward. His arrogant and detached telling reinforces for me the stereotype of a hardened and weary, yet highly successful reporter. My lack of confidence bubbles up closer to the surface as I feel my grip slipping away from the cozy classroom sharing that I envisioned.

As I relate the basic facts of my career, he begins to probe, like a good reporter. With experiences like the week-long men's conference still fresh, I feel confident in revealing more of myself than might appear on a resume. As he pushes for details, I let my boundaries down too far, losing my role as the teacher of this class. I realize he's doing what I actually hope the students will do.

He's a real reporter, and you're not. A dark message flashes through my mind, but I try to push it aside. *It's my first day as the teacher,* I remind the committee of voices that lurks inside looking for an opportunity to speak.

"So, it sounds like you've only worked at magazines, right?" The writer for *Time* is charging into the dark side. "What about newspapers?"

"I've actually never worked at a newspaper. I've written freelance pieces for papers but have worked at quarterly magazines, covering lots of kinds of stories." I feel my palms getting sweaty but don't take this signal to stop exposing myself. "I'm a little nervous about not having the newspaper experience for this class. Some of the students might expect that from me."

We finish at the front, and I turn back to the class, asking them to wind things up. The introductions of the students go well; then the journalist and I conclude the exercise. I go through his high-powered, national credentials, feeling somewhat second rate. Then it's his turn to introduce me.

"The most interesting thing about Mr. Finger is that he's never worked at a newspaper."

I hardly hear the rest of what he says as a mixture of emotions rise up. I trusted this guy as a colleague, yet he has revealed my weakness, simply in approaching the exercise as a serious journalist. That's what I want these students to learn, I tell myself, as he finishes.

Before you even get through the first class, these students think you don't know what you're doing. I stuff the dark voice in my head down and focus. I can do this. Just like I can stand in front of Michael Meade and 110 men and state my intention to nurture my family and grow into a more initiated man. I can lead this class. As I sum up the exercise, I decide to recognize my vulnerability and step further out of my comfort zone. Rather than ignoring the issue of my inexperience at newspapers, I address it directly.

"I feel a little awkward now, a bit exposed, regarding my lack of experience at newspapers," I say to these eager young faces. "But of course I have a lot of experience at magazines. When you study the syllabus, you'll see that I want us to move toward the process of writing the kind of longer pieces I usually do. I hope that experience will benefit you as you move past straight reporting. But first we have to learn to write short pieces."

I prepared well for the class, so the basic sequence of activities over the afternoon goes fine. We are ready for the next week, with plenty of rigorous work ahead. If the students have any doubts about me, they don't show it.

As I walk to the car, I feel a complicated mixture of relief and embarrassment, pride and resentment. I want to blame the cocky journalist for getting me started on the wrong step, for revealing my shortcoming. Yet, the snafu opened me up as human, and I acknowledged that to the students. This is a tiny step toward integrating two dimensions—my external and internal personas. For so long, my vulnerable, emotional feelings lay either totally buried, or available only in a safe, away-from-daily-life setting, like a therapist's office or a men's gathering.

Today, the probing of the *Time* magazine reporter pushed me into a situation where I chose to accept the two sides of myself as best I could, in front of 18 students. As I return to the car, the exaggerated medieval faces of the gargoyles seem to reflect back my complicated feelings. Maybe these contorted faces are reminding me that growth comes from unexpected visitors.

AS THE WINTER MONTHS MOVE TOWARD SPRING, my walks past the gargoyles feel like a retracing of my steps through Duke as a student. The stone faces seem to vary their looks depending on the scene or buried emotion that arises during my mile or so walk from the distant parking lot to the public policy building. I realize how lost I often felt on those same stone walkways going to class or the dining hall, to the library or language lab.

As a student, I never had a professor take a close interest in me, talk to me about my future or potential. No professor guided me. I needed that and never got it. A few offered a listening ear at times, but I lacked the structure or confidence to confide in them. As I prepared to teach my writing class, I thought about ways teachers can work with students. I realized that I had never eaten lunch with a professor my entire four years at Duke.

I decided that I would include in the class assignments a lunchtime meeting to talk informally about journalism or whatever else the student might want to discuss. At least, every student in my class could eat lunch with one of their teachers once during their college career. Even if the assignment stemmed from a need to counter my own sense of loss, I knew it would help some of them and at least force everyone to talk about journalism in more depth than discussing a single assignment.

The number of weeks in the schedule matches exactly the number of students who stick with the class. Most of them decide to eat lunch at the dining hall next to the Chapel. A few meet with me in my makeshift office in the public policy building. One young man, an editor at the highly regarded Duke student newspaper, aspires to a career as a national journalist. He has a quiet seriousness about him, and a gentleness that I encourage him to keep. I tell him he would make a good investigative reporter on complex topics.

"I'm looking forward to the magazine assignment," he says. "It will be a new challenge compared to the short pieces I do for *The Chronicle*."

The most touching story comes from a young woman with the least journalistic experience in the class. As we settle into a corner table in the crowded student cafeteria, away from easy earshot of others, she takes a deep breath and tells me she has an aggressive kind of cancer. She may not even finish her college years, she says, but there is some hope. She doesn't go into details, and I decide not to probe on that topic.

"Given such news, why did you take this course?"

"I've just decided that I will keep learning new things. That's helping to keep me going."

"And how are you finding it?"

"It's hard, getting the stories, interviewing people. But I'm getting better, I think. That's what you say in your long comments, at least."

We laugh. I tend to write long comments on all the students' papers, I tell her, not just hers. "And you really are getting the knack of it much better."

After lunch, I head to the office where I will grade some more papers and keep my door open in case students come during the hour before the seminar begins. As I settle in for the afternoon, I feel her courage moving through me. Just as she is trying to get the story, to interview people, I feel myself trying to get my own story. What did happen to me at Duke, some 20 years ago?

MANY STORIES BOUNCE AROUND IN my head as I walk through the campus that semester. One story from the winter months stands out. Snowstorms are rare in Durham, North Carolina. But after a storm produced six inches my sophomore year, many students were playing in the snow, enjoying themselves. I was plodding up the walk from lunch, my classes over for the day, almost to that overhang that connected the York and Lancaster dorms. My head was down. I felt a familiar numbness, lack of energy—not exactly sadness, but more like a yoke around my neck, a weight to carry.

The snowball came hard and true, sudden, unexpected—a stinger, right against my bare left cheek. Anchored into this walk, slogging along, I hardly flinched or shifted my stride. But the packed snow burned me into awareness. I stopped and looked across the mall at three guys having fun. They stopped laughing as they saw my stare, wondering if they had hurt me, I suppose. I managed a feeble wave, and they went back to their antics with others. I hunkered down against the cold and ploughed back to my single room on the top floor of the fraternity section where I lived.

I lay on the bed and wondered why I couldn't have fun like the others. Next to the bed was the dream diary that my psychology professor required us to keep. I started reading at random. Maybe my unconscious self, recorded in my dreams, might tell me something. I bounced through a few entries and saw the common theme of a jumble of people entering scenes, mixing Lake Junaluska with Jackson. I was left with a feeling that I had a lot to work out at some point but didn't know what.

After teaching my class that spring of 1990, my walks past the Chapel remind me of the dramatic spring of 1968. After Martin Luther King was assassinated, a vigil arose in front of the Chapel, a sea of tents where many students and some professors lived for a few weeks even in the rain and mud. The students were boycotting the cafeteria in solidarity with the mostly black employees seeking better wages and working conditions, a campaign that escalated in the wake of the King assassination. The protests attracted national attention, with Joan Baez and other notables making appearances. I felt conflicted by the event, not sure whether to boycott the cafeteria or not. I had rarely discussed my feelings about the Civil Rights movement in Mississippi, but the drama at Duke was forcing me to notice events and at least think about them.

One afternoon, standing in the back of the tents, near the circle where the buses took students to and from the separate East Campus, an earnest leader of the boycott came up to me breathless. I barely knew him.

"Bill, will you call your father to get his support for the vigil?" he asked, urgently, with no preliminary greeting. "It would be great to have a Methodist bishop join our list of supporters." He stared at me, waiting for my answer.

Caught totally off guard, I looked back at him for a second and blurted out. "No, I'm not going to call my father. You can call him yourself if you want his endorsement." I turned and walked away.

Now, 22 years later as I walk past the Chapel after teaching, I realize what I was feeling that day. The student organizer had no interest in me, what I felt, how I was struggling to figure out how to respond to the vigil. He was only interested in using me to get to my father. I was a tactical pawn. And I feel angry even now, a delayed response never really felt or understood so many years ago.

Through the spring, as my teaching races to a close, I notice more couples flirting, holding hands, kissing, sending me back to 1969. I met Georgia my last semester at Duke, in a fourth period class on religion and contemporary literature on East Campus.

We sat in old benches that had movable desk tops you could lift up for writing notes, like the hidden tray in airplane seats. We sat in our rows, discussing Flannery O'Connor, William Golding, and others. By my senior year in the spring of 1969, I was engaged in the kind of existential and political issues prompted by these books. Not only had the vigil started to wake me up, but Duke had another major upheaval early in 1969 when the black student group took over part of the administration building. Classes were again disrupted. There was plenty to talk about, and I was finally ready. I just needed the right person.

"What did you think of class today?" I'd ask the bouncy, energetic young woman who usually sat in front of me.

"Oh, it was good, keeps me thinking," she'd say.

My conversations with Georgia gradually expanded into suggestions for lunch. Conveniently, our class ended at 12:30, and we began eating together every Tuesday and Thursday. The conversations quickly moved from class assignments and the Allen Building takeover to our families and other interests.

"Lake Junaluska was an escape from the attention in Jackson," I told her one day. "In Jackson, we were always the college president's kids. But at the Lake, all of my friends were preachers' kids. And, then when Dad was elected bishop, it was no big deal for my buddies at the Lake."

She listened and then told her own story of having a father working in the public domain. As we got to know each other more, the sparks began to grow well past our common interest in books and similarities in our backgrounds. She started coming to my home varsity tennis matches. One Saturday, we played the University of Virginia in Charlottesville. Match and showers over, we headed back to Duke, about a four hour drive.

As soon as we hit campus, I jumped into my little red VW bug, inherited from my brother, and drove to downtown Durham. A big dance was going on at a large old tobacco warehouse, and I had told Georgia I would meet her there late, as soon as I got back. On the crowded dance floor, bodies pulsated in pairs to the music that blared from the stage. Spilt beer competed with the aromas of past tobacco harvests. Then, across the huge crowd, I spotted her and that magical smile. As we walked towards each other, no one else seemed to exist.

TEACHING AT DUKE PRESENTS numerous challenges, beyond that first day with the visiting hot-shot journalist. I plod through the various issues, from blown assignments by the students to challenging questions I can't answer. I give a lot of attention to the students and their writing and add a bit of the wisdom I have accumulated as a journalist. Uneven evaluations from the students reflect the somewhat rocky semester, but I feel good about my effort—and even better about allowing the memories of my student days to bubble up.

As a student, I also plodded through Duke, relying on the tools I had. Sports kept my endorphins going, and good study habits kept me focused on school. My dream journal opened me to themes in psychology and internal reflections; I learned from the highly charged campus events how to pay attention to world affairs. And, I met a woman who saw something special in me, as I did in her. When I finished my undergrad years, I was confident enough to join the Peace Corps. But incorporating all these experiences into a balanced life would take time.

By the end of teaching my course, now in the spring of 1990, I feel positive enough to take new risks, past the complexities of Duke. With the semester at Duke barely over, I lead the service at our church for Father's Day, working with several men who have also attended events with Michael Meade.

I have become increasingly involved in the Unitarian Universalist Fellowship of Raleigh or UUFR as we call it. Since living in India with the Raza family, I had found the Christian message of salvation limiting. But much about theology and the sacredness of worship had remained comforting. Words like *oblation* conjured up feelings of peacefulness, not anger. Soon after returning from India, I happened onto a UU church on the Boston Commons one Sunday morning. African dancers came down the middle aisle in the worship service that morning, and I felt I had found a place I could call home.

Gradually, I became acquainted with the ecumenical theology of the Unitarian Universalist Association and such denominational for-bearers as Ralph Waldo Emerson. Then with Georgia, we found UUFR and began attending regularly, helping with services and the religious education program.

About 100 people arrive for the UUFR Father's Day service, held in a large room with a cathedral ceiling, functioning as an informal sanctuary and a fellowship hall. We direct all the men to go outside and the women and children to sit in the back rows. I explain that we are going to honor all the men on this Father's Day with a procession.

We open the service with the men walking from the side yard into the sanctuary, led by the oldest—the elders of our community. We recognize all the men as nurturers—of their own children, of this religious community's children, and of the next generation on earth. The service includes some readings on male nurturing and a segment of a fairy tale recorded in a pamphlet by Robert Bly. Then I tell a short African folk tale called "The Cow-Tail Switch."

"A father goes hunting in the jungle and does not return," I say. "His name was Ogaloussa. At first no one asks about Ogaloussa. The days and weeks and months go by, and even though the community is worried, no one dares to speak.

"But the youngest child, who couldn't talk when his father had left, starts to grow up. He wonders where his father is."

On cue, a young boy in the congregation comes up and stands beside me in front of the congregation. He delivers his line perfectly: "Where is my father?"

I proceed with the story. After the youngest dared to ask that question, the older brothers decide to go find their father. Deep in the woods, they discover his bones. As each son encourages his father to return, his body magically takes shape again. Finally, the father has reappeared entirely. The village prepares a feast to celebrate his return, with a special ornament made with the tail of a cow, at Ogaloussa's request. After the feast and the dancing and the toasts, Ogaloussa asks for silence. He wants to give away the cow-tail switch as a symbol of hope and endurance.

"Who do you think should get the cow-tail switch," I ask the congregation. "In the story, people suggest the eldest and wisest, his wife, and various sons. But each time, Ogaloussa says, 'No.'" Finally, I turn to the young boy in the congregation who played the youngest son and present him with the makeshift "cow-tail switch."

"It was the youngest, who asked, 'Where is my father?'"

In a ritual near the end of the service, each person writes a Father's Day blessing and brings it to the burning flame in the chalice at the front. Some choose to read their blessings.

"Today, I remember the birth fathers of my two children," I read. "Those men must feel some sadness without these children. I hope they have peace in their lives. I will do my best to help raise these children."

CHAPTER 10. Carrying My Mother's Depression

MY MOTHER IS SITTING ALONE on the back screened porch at the Lake Junaluska house. She still has on her sweater from the mountain chill that lingers on summer mornings. But the sun is starting to warm the long porch that sweeps around two sides of the cabin.

"What's your project today?" I ask, coming out from the small kitchen, steam rising from my coffee.

"Come sit down. I want to show you." The morning sun slants across her face as I walk toward the big round table in the corner where Mother loves to spread out her summer projects. Now 72, she has beautiful silver hair that she keeps cut short and occasionally manicured at the beauty parlor for church occasions. I pull up one of the rockers and see copies of a small booklet. She holds one up so I can see a hand-written title, *Dear Mamie.*

"What is it?"

"I put this little book together several years ago, but I've been hesitant to share it with you. It's hard for Dad."

"What do you mean, hard for Dad?" I glance outside to see if he's in sight. He's pulling briars from the bushes in the lower part of the property, far from earshot, working next to our portion of the 99 steps that lead down past other cabins to the lane below.

Mother pauses, takes a deep breath. Her eyes dash back and forth nervously. "I re-read the packet of letters Dad wrote when he went to the

World Methodist Conference in England in 1951. Do you remember stories about that meeting?"

I nod tentatively, family stories and memories of Methodist conferences zipping through my mind. I only remember a few things from those years in Oxford. I was four years old in 1951 and mostly played with my older brother. I barely remember my baby sister arriving. Besides being at home with three young children, Mother also functioned as the minister's wife at the prestigious University Methodist Church, attended by many of the most liberal professors from the University of Mississippi.

"I remember hearing about Dad being on a boat. The Queen Elizabeth maybe? I don't remember much from the time though."

"Yes, it was the Queen Elizabeth." She pauses and takes a deep breath. "I felt it was time to tell you children about what happened then. So I wrote down my memories and put them with Dad's letters to me from the trip."

She pauses. I sense something stronger coming. "You see, I had severe postpartum depression—a kind of nervous breakdown. I describe it here." She pats the little photocopied pages. "Dad felt really bad about being gone while I was in the hospital. When he got back, he vowed never to go to one of these meetings without taking me."

I sit back, stunned by both pieces of news—the depression and the decision about taking Mother with him on trips. The second piece about the trips to the big Methodist Church meetings lands the first blow to the belly, taking my breath away. Feelings stored away like stacks of unused cordwood now seem within grasp. *So that's why we were by ourselves so many times. Dad made that vow in 1951.*

For nearly two years now, I've been sorting through feelings about my father—at the men's conferences, on the trip back to Jackson in 1989, and just a month ago, 1990, at the Father's Day service with the tale about Ogaloussa. Now, hearing this news, I'm cataloguing the years of having various babysitters move into the house every several years—young couples, a dorm housemother at the college. I flash through the three weeks when I decided to run for student body president, ran, and lost—all while they were gone. They hardly knew it happened. Old anger is bubbling up. But Mother interrupts the feeling.

"I wrote this down about four years ago, but only recently gave a copy to Skip. I haven't given it to Betsy yet. It might be harder on her. She might feel guilty. I'll give it to her soon."

We hear Dad coming in from the back yard now. "I've told him that I'm giving these to you children," she says quickly, gathering up the books. "But I think you might wait a while before you discuss it with him. It's a painful memory for him and for me."

THAT NIGHT, ALONE IN THE FRONT BEDROOM of the two-bedroom cabin, I turn to Mother's 20-page booklet. Georgia and the children are still in Illinois with her parents. I drove back for work, stopping over at Junaluska for a brief visit. Now, as the details of mother's story jump off the page like headlines, I feel like I'm entering her life in 1951, and maybe a little of mine too. But the tears that are coming up seem linked to the many years that followed, with feeling upon feeling piled into my life, waiting to be recognized and opened up to the sunlight.

"My young husband was feeling great uncertainty about going on this trip, but I was strongly insistent that he should go," Mother wrote in the three-page prologue. Excerpts from the 28 letters and cards Dad sent to her on the trip follow, interspersed by Mother's memories, which she wrote in 1986.

"We both felt distinct doubts that I could care for seven- and four-year-old boys, and an eight-month-old daughter while dealing with my fragile health situation…. The health problem came from an early false pregnancy, precarious health after the delayed delivery, postpartum depression, and the demands of these three children as well as community involvements."

As a gift to her children, and I suspect as a way to reach some closure for herself, Mother recorded her memories of her 1951 emotional breakdown. Lying in bed that night, I'm trying to imagine the early 1950s—what it would be like as a primary caregiver of three young children in the parsonage. Now, when Georgia goes out for her women's group or another meeting, just getting our two children to bed in the evening is hard. How did Mother do it?

Her pages continue: "Beyond the devastating fatigue, I was consumed by general panic, lack of stability, total ineptness which now I know as a chemical imbalance." She began to feel herself losing her balance with life during the spring of 1951, with severe postpartum depression.

"Once during several days' bed rest during the spring attempting recovery, I remember the distinct whirring in my head as if that too-tight spring had sprung. The panic led me to believe that my husband and my children would be better off without me."

In June of 1951, Dad's church hosted the annual North Mississippi Annual Conference. "It demanded all of Ellis' time... to the exclusion of almost everything else.... I was trying to pull myself together, with the added tension of knowing I would have to do it alone by August 13." The conference had chosen Dad to be a delegate to the World Methodist Conference and, as a bonus, to take greetings from Oxford, Mississippi, to Oxford, England, the meeting site.

The first postcard came from New York City:

"Dear Mamie, It's hard to realize that I am in New York! I still get scared at such a city—particularly when I am all alone! I wish you were with me and that you would be going all the way.... I know you're going to be fine. Otherwise I would never have left."

Dear Mamie summarizes her memory of the first round of postcards Dad wrote on the Queen Elizabeth, about the delicious food, tours of the ship, and movies. They "must not have impressed me at all as I was trying to deal with sleepless nights, frustrating days of ineptness with the children, inability to find clothes in dresser drawers because my illness was limiting my vision."

The booklet also tells a little about where we lived when Dad went on the trip. First, she took us to Dad's parents, in the little North Mississippi town of Ripley. There, things got worse. "One morning at daybreak, I heard the train that went through downtown Ripley. I toyed with the notion of slipping out of the house the next morning and letting the train run me down and all of my problems with it." She resisted that notion, thinking about what it would do to Dad's parents. She talked to them about going to Memphis for some treatment, but they advised her to wait until Dad returned.

She went on to her parents' house in Sherard, a tiny little Delta farm community on the Mississippi River near Clarksdale. My grandmother had already taken her eldest child, my Uncle Bill, to a mental hospital. She was a tough woman, a world traveler who also met with integrated church groups in the 1940s in Mississippi. "Seeing how my health condition was, my parents took me to Gartley-Ramsey Hospital in Memphis," Mother says simply in her little memoir.

I don't know what to feel that night, as I fold the book on my chest and close my eyes, lying in bed. I'm seeing my mother in an entirely new way—not only admitting weaknesses but acknowledging that she was totally out of control. My mother was raised as a performer—on the piano and in the classroom. She then performed briefly in the career world before becoming a prominent minister's wife. I smile, remembering her playing the piano at my wedding and sometimes on Christmas Eve at Dad's request, the complicated version of "The Lord's Prayer."

She was a Phi Beta Kappa English major, proud of her education at Agnes Scott, a women's college on the edge of Atlanta. I smile again, picturing her in cap and gown, representing Agnes Scott at the Millsaps College occasion. The college inaugurated the first Phi Beta Kappa chapter in Mississippi the same weekend I visited the Millsaps archives to read about my dad and the white Citizens' Council.

After graduation, she held various duties at the Agnes Scott Alumni Affairs office, including hosting guest speakers such as Robert Frost, a story she loved to tell. After a brief journey into the professional world as an aspiring writer in New York, in 1942 she returned to Mississippi to marry and raise a family.

In *Dear Mamie*, Mother wrote that her father told her she could do anything she set her mind to. "And I had always thought so, too. Perhaps this developed posture of performance for perfection had pushed me into my present state."

I look up from the book and out at the street light on Littleton Road in front of the cabin. Mother could be describing me as well. A performer—at sports, studies, student offices as a kid, then in a competitive writing career, and as a part-time, stay-at-home dad. I couldn't handle all of this. Maybe this "posture of performance" had pushed me into my present state.

The excerpts from Dad's postcards and letters pile together on the pages, the literary tone providing a painful window into the past.

> CUNARD LINE, RMS QUEEN ELIZABETH, AUGUST 19
> DEAR MAMIE [all the salutations were in all capital letters]: I've almost forgotten to report on food today: lamb chops for lunch a Bordeaux pigeon for dinner.

> KENSINGTON PALACE MANSIONS LTD. DE VERE GARDENS, LONDON, W.S., AUGUST 22
> DEAR MAMIE: Tomorrow you go to Sherard. The first lap of our separation is over.... I feel terrible describing all these wonderful experiences. But I want to share them and I would feel more guilty if I did not tell you everything…

> When I arrived, I found your letters of Thursday and Friday. I can't describe how happy I was to find two pages on both sides. You sound like your old self; though you didn't say you were feeling good I know you will be. You're courageous to be fighting so bravely.

By August 25, Dad's letters were being forwarded to Mother at the Memphis hospital. Then by September, they came straight to the hospital. The letters tell of a ride to Edinburgh on third class, the opera, a trip to Paris, a chance meeting with a Mississippi preacher in front of the Café de Paris, and finally onto Oxford and his room in Christ Church College.

> OXFORD, AUGUST 30:
> DEAR MAMIE: You are going to be well again! And we will both work hard to keep you well!… I promise to be a better husband and a better Daddy! … I have walked so much that there is now a hole in one black one and a hole in one brown one! I change shoes often, so my feet won't stay wet.

The notes from Dad cascade down the page and touch many topics: the Oxford conference, messages to the children, Methodist history, teacakes and rain, a dream about Betsy talking, hopes for the future, and always Mother's health.

"As I read all of this now," Mother wrote in 1986 as she put the post-cards together into a story, "it is as if I never had read it before. Because by this time I was experiencing several insulin shock treatments a week." This was a common treatment in the early 1950s.

By the time she was ready to leave the hospital and Dad was home from the month-long trip to England, the Ratliff family faced another crisis. My grandmother had to take my grandfather to the same hospital in Memphis, before Mother was discharged.

We affectionately called Mother's father Big Daddy, for his ample stomach I suppose. For me, the name fit in my early childhood memory of sitting on this substantial lap. I recall a dream-like setting, as four-year-olds remember, the large den where Big Daddy would hold huge conch shells to my ear and ask, "Do you hear the ocean?" The magic sounded through my little ears and I giggled with glee. I also recall the telltale pipe holder on the same big table beside his easy chair, and one of the pipes always in his mouth.

Big Daddy had a malignant lump removed from his throat, which presumably came as a legacy of his pipe. He never recovered. Mother stayed at the hospital with her father. She left the hospital and went straight to Sherard for the funeral. She wrote, "Finally by the beginning of October, Ellis, our three children, and I were all settled into a regular routine of life in the parsonage for a stabilizing winter and spring together."

Writing in 1986, after the feminist movement became part of the cultural mainstream, Mother concluded her memoir, "At the time, I was totally in the non-feminist, housewife syndrome: Any professional acclaim which came to Ellis was also good luck for me. Any upward mobility for me would of necessity come through him. That was my stance—to be a good mother, wife, hostess—whatever would help him on our way in his profession. And I did very well! Better than I would do now? Perhaps. A different way, no doubt."

ON MY TRIP BACK TO RALEIGH, and during the rest of the summer and into the fall, I carry mother's depression story with me like a psychological talisman. I don't want it for protection like a good luck charm but as a reminder that this thing called depression has struck before in my family—and Mother survived it. I begin to think, probably for the first time, that my periods of depression were not my fault. Reading that depression can be genetic, carried within families, I see a broader picture. I thought of Uncle Bill as outside the mainstream of the family. But maybe the Ratliff genes make me more susceptible to depression.

What interests me even more as the months pass is how Mother's depression affected me at age four, what that trauma did to me and how mother raised me coming out of that illness. I read a book by a German psychiatrist, Alice Miller, called *The Drama of the Gifted Child*. The book's thesis jumps out at me, as if watching my mother labor through her years of childrearing. The primary caregiver of young children—usually the mother—often lacks full satisfaction as a person and thus seeks emotional support *from her children*, rather than meeting the emotional needs *of the* children.

During the fall, I think about my life through the lens of my mother's experience. Her nurturing came more through supporting her children's activities than our emotions—our sports, our clubs at schools, our theater practices. No bedtime stories or playful baths with us as young children. Dad did that emotional care work. Ironically, I start to think of Dad as the nurturer and Mother as the career builder for the children. Mother may not have gotten "emotional support from her children," as Alice Miller posits, but my mother did have to get some of her strong needs as a professional woman met through the type of support she gave to her children.

I'm not sure what to make of my reflections about my mother. After we children started our own families, Mother did blossom as a professional, including a prominent role raising millions of dollars for the large Methodist-supported Ewha University in South Korea.

Regardless of what she did in the 1980s, her life in the 1950s affected me greatly. Alice Miller explains that children raised by an emotionally needy parent admit only those feelings that are accepted and approved by their inner censor. "Depression and a sense of inner emptiness" are the prices children pay for this inner control. Such a child develops intellectual capacities undisturbed, "but not the world of his emotions, and this will have far-reaching consequences for his well-being," Miller writes. "Now his intellect will assume a supportive function of enormous value in strengthening his defense mechanism."

I feel like Miller has seen into my drama. Her conclusion rivets my attention: this gifted child leans toward a narcissistic disturbance, which manifests as grandiosity or depression, two sides of the same coin.

ONE WEEKEND AFTERNOON, LATE IN THE FALL of 1990, I'm sitting in the back room of the Dixie Trail house, where I've moved my desk next to the fireplace. I can spread papers on the hearth and look out the sliding doors across the patio, to the large back yard. And most importantly, together Georgia and I have configured a study and wall space where I can put up my own photos and momentos.

On the wall, a handsome, erect Uncle Bill looks down at me in coat and tie, from his college years before the breakdown. Beside that picture is another black-and-white shot of Arthur Raper, a teacher at Agnes Scott. During my twenties when I was questioning my career, Mother suggested I visit Dr. Raper. He became my friend and mentor. He looks down from my photo wall, comforting me with his full white beard and dignified face.

That afternoon, sorting through other options for my wall, I pull out from a box of family papers a copy of the family Christmas card my parents sent in 1951. My mother suggested in *Dear Mamie* that all was well after she returned to the Oxford parsonage, for "a stabilizing winter and spring together." My instinct reading that phrase was that she was glossing over the impact of that summer in the Memphis hospital. Now, I find my evidence—in the photo of myself as a four-year-old. I know immediately I must blow up this photo and give it a central place among the images I am putting on the wall above my desk. I need to see that four-year-old self looking down at me. I'm not sure why. Maybe I can give that little boy back some care and love. This four-year-old needs attention, as if to help him find the sunshine that he lost in 1951.

In that 1951 Christmas card photo, my eyes have a hardened look, like those of a man steeling himself for another day at a dreary job. Perhaps the narrow gaze is only to protect against the sun—a shadow angles across the left eye and down the nose, covering the right cheek. Sitting on the front porch of the Oxford parsonage, I am a little boy posing dutifully for the adult in charge. I stare off center from the camera's eye, perhaps looking for an anchor I lost that year. The boy seems to want to cry but doesn't know how or why. But I sense more, as if a grip has taken hold of my heart, a hold that will take many years to untangle.

The three sets of hands draw my eye to the strong horizontal line they form in the composition of the black-and-white shot. Little Betsy sits in the middle with open mouth and parted hands held up as if about to clap. A cute baby somewhere between an infant and a toddler, she must be about ten months. Skipper and I each have our fingers interlaced, and he lets his hands fall naturally between his legs, the fingers pointing to the porch step. His hands carry a confidence and strength, it seems, perhaps reflecting a core self, established before the shuffling among caretakers occurred in 1951. In contrast, my right hand falls into my left hand, appearing to be turned at a sharp, unnatural angle at the wrist. As I stare more at the wrist, it looks like a physical handicap.

As a kid, I played a lot of ping pong at Lake Junaluska. One opponent had a hand badly deformed with a wrist angled back toward his forearm. But he played a pretty good game of table tennis. He dropped the ball awkwardly with one hand and served and smashed away with the other. He had compensated for his weakness. Playing this man in ping pong was somehow comforting, as if I was facing a vaguely familiar side of myself. Now, I am beginning to understand that feeling.

Thoughts of ping pong and of Alice Miller jump around my head as I stare at the Christmas card. Maybe that's what happened to me. I compensated with my intellect. I played out the drama of the gifted child, performing as my mother had, unaware of my feelings much of the time. But where does it leave me as a middle-aged man? Where is my joy? I look around for the right page from Miller's book: "The true opposite of depression is not gaiety or absence of pain, but vitality; the freedom to experience spontaneous feelings."

I cannot say almost 40 years later what kind of parenting my mother gave me those early years in Oxford. I do not know how closely our household fit the Alice Miller paradigm when we moved to Jackson in 1952. Mother became a college president's wife at age 34, without her own career but with a lot of childrearing ahead as well as those trips to Methodist conferences. What I do know is the feeling from the eyes of that four-year-old—a steely resolve. That sense of perseverance has stayed with me, a gift from those years. But it came at a price.

Looking at the 1951 Christmas card, I feel gratitude for my mother's coming forth with her story after so many years. While grandparents and other relatives knew about Mother's insulin shock treatments, no one ever told the children. My hunch is that the relatives never made a bond to keep it a secret, but that people simply did not discuss such topics as depression. Why dredge up the pain? Whatever the reason, the news appeared as a long-lost piece to the puzzle I am working out about my own life. When my mother broke the silence in 1990, she offered me clues to the complex riddle I'm trying to unravel. And, from her speaking up, I am gaining confidence to give a voice—at least to myself—about the power of depression. But it's a slow process, and I am not there yet.

CHAPTER 11. Rage Erupts but Roots Remain

TEN-YEAR-OLD LEE IS COAXING a simple melody from the reed flute he picked out just hours ago at the Atlanta Cyclorama, a Civil War museum. Hearing Lee's haunting, hollow tunes now, as I drive down a large thoroughfare near downtown Atlanta, I feel pride in passing down a bit of generational memory.

A fascination with the Union and Confederate soldiers at the Cyclorama has stayed with me since my parents took me to Atlanta at about his age, more than 30 years earlier. The life-size figures nearest the viewing area seem as evocative now, the day before Easter in March of 1991. The models further from the viewers are smaller and smaller, blending seamlessly into a circular mural with vast armies, horses, cannons, and dead men sprawling on the canvas.

"How about pizza for dinner," I say. Lee is absorbed in the tune and doesn't respond. I turn left and head to the neon sign I spotted where a few cars are parked.

While the memories are comforting, Lee's tunes are fading, and I feel a heavy cloak descending over me, bringing not warmth but isolation. I tell myself I've been happy the last two days, celebrating Lee's tenth birthday with this journey to a big city. We've had fun riding the subway, touring the Coca-Cola center, seeing Martin Luther King's boyhood home. But reminding myself of the good things I'm doing as a father with his son, and the real fun we've had, does not alter my mood. The bare café booths now visible through large windows do not help as I fight the sinking feeling.

The stop at the pizza place falls into the difficult transition time between the structured day's work, in this case sightseeing, and the less-defined evening. I sit together with one of the people I love most in the world but without a structure or agenda. The mood I'm feeling is a familiar one, where a dark shadow seems to hold joy apart, as if outside a locked door. I have learned to will myself to stay connected, and I tell myself to make an effort for Lee's sake. Only a few other customers are there. The linoleum-topped table near the window offers little hope to lift my mood, but the pizza arrives quicker than I expect, hot and tasty.

"What did you think of Martin Luther King's room?" I ask, trying to call up some of the fun from the day.

"It was neat. Like a regular kid's room."

"It reminded me of Grandpa's room in Mississippi, where he grew up. Maybe we'll go there someday. He and Martin Luther King grew up about the same time."

We talk a little around the pizza and head back to the bed-and-breakfast several miles away. Lee loves the adventure. He explores his adjoining room with its own television. After a little time in his separate space, he joins me to watch the Duke basketball team upset the undefeated, top-ranked UNLV in the NCAA basketball tournament semifinals. We cheer as our home team pulls off the surprise win.

Before leaving the Atlanta area on Monday, I take Lee to see Agnes Scott College, where my mother got her college degree. Nestled in the suburb of Decatur, the small women's school has maintained a strong reputation as a leading liberal arts institution. Among the handsome mix of architectures, we find the old music building where Mother played piano and the academic halls where she studied with sociologist Arthur Raper, whose photo is over my desk at home. Then we head into the new library. The reading room near the front entrance has tall windows looking out onto the quadrangle. Books climb the other walls. Few students are here on this quiet holiday weekend. Lee is happy looking through large picture books, playing with a toy we got at the gift shop.

Sitting at a large table in the reading room, I pick an old book of Southern maps at random and flip through them. Then, I close my eyes and just sit. While the book sits untouched on the table, other images dart through my mind and then seep down into my body, as if through a hidden passage. A series of memories compete for space.

THE CHRONOLOGY BEGINS WHEN I was very young, before we left Oxford, with Mother putting antiseptic on my red bug bites at the Mississippi coast. Next comes a typical Sunday morning scene after we moved to Jackson. Dad was out somewhere in Mississippi preaching for Millsaps College, and Mother often had to separate Skipper and me from arguing. She gathered up Betsy and got us into the station wagon for the ride downtown to Galloway Church.

Mother often taught Sunday school, putting her private persona on hold for her public role. I flash on the Sunday when Mother called on me at the end of the class to start the Lord's Prayer. I hated being picked. I must've been about 10 or so, about Lee's age. Suddenly my little mind went blank. I couldn't think of the first words. So, Mother picked up the role and led it herself without embarrassing me further. I felt relieved she found a way out but resentful that she chose me in the first place.

The memories zoom through—the Cub Scout troop in Elbert Bivens' garage where Mother helped organize boys starting to make sense of things in life. At Lake Junaluska, she often played a kind of den mother's role, along with other mothers on the street. The long evenings of hide-and-seek and steal-the-bacon that lasted well into the late dusk of early summer now take center stage in my daydreams. Mother was there, holding down the cabin while we played with the abandon of children on a summer night.

The times at the Lake were happier than in Jackson, where I now see myself in high school, getting ready for a basketball game. On game nights, Mother was always willing to make me a pre-game, afternoon meal of minute steak with mashed potatoes, separately from the rest of the family. I took it for granted then. Now, I wonder what she would have rather been doing. Rearing children seemed a task for her more than a passion. She was at her best when intellectually challenged.

In the tenth grade, in the early 1960s, I had an excellent world history teacher who encouraged us to think ambitiously. As the topic for my semester-long project, I decided on the new European Common Market. Mother encouraged me to send letters to the European addresses I found in the library. I see myself sitting with piles of papers, brochures, and letters spread across the den floor in our Jackson house, compiling my report. Mother is there at a card table typing my handwritten paper.

Synthesizing information into papers became the bread and butter of my career, helping to pay for this trip to Atlanta. The encouragement from Mother on that high-school paper feels now like a defining moment in my life. She helped me realize that such work always offered an anchor, even if other things made no sense.

I see Mother standing behind me in these practical ways. The typing, the support for the basketball games. But I do not remember her talking to me about feelings—mine or hers. Maybe she did, but I have a hunch she was too busy with her public role as a college president's wife and the practical demands of raising three children. Or maybe she had sublimated her feelings to this supportive role of wife and mother. But she stood with me as best she could and never judged me. In my 20s, when I felt lost after the Peace Corps, I never told Mother about the really dark feelings I had in Boston, but she sensed things were not good.

These memories send me into a kind of trance, as if my mother is actually sitting in this reading room, not me. A strange feeling ripples through me, as if I am seeing the world through her eyes. In fact, finding my own vision of life seems to be the challenge, to break away from her. Then, a fiery scene flashes into focus, summer of 1976, just months before Georgia and I got married.

"I'M SORRY IF THIS IS HARD FOR YOU, DAD." My voice is loud with anger and self-righteousness. We are standing under the large hemlock tree at Lake Junaluska. Never did we talk like this, especially outside next to Littleton Road, where people walk by regularly during the busy summer season. "But this is what Georgia and I have to do, to figure out if we want to get married."

Georgia and I have been living together in North Carolina for the last year. Only now has my father's situation brought this cultural taboo to the fore. By 1976, protests over Viet Nam and other issues have led to vast cultural changes. While couples living together openly before marriage is becoming more common, it is not yet an acceptable norm to my parents' generation.

The Southeastern Conference of the Methodist Church is meeting at Lake Junaluska, and Dad is about to receive a new assignment after serving 12 years as bishop. Charlotte, N.C., appears to be a possible opening, a prestigious position that he would love, given our ties to North Carolina through our Lake house. Mother wants to go to Charlotte too. But Dad feels it would be awkward if his son is living "in sin" in the same state.

My flushed face is inches from his. "I won't change my mind. It's not your call." I have never been so mad at my father, ever. Dad dips his face toward the hemlock needles and cones beneath, hiding his pain. He's a gentle man who speaks quietly and thoughtfully, never in anger or with rancor. I feel guilty that apparently my life with Georgia might affect where he goes for the next 12 years. But I'm not budging. I storm back into the house, onto the side porch and into the little kitchen. Mother is there and tries to talk to me.

"Can't you see how good it would be for Dad to go –"

"Don't try to convince me!" I interrupt. "I've already discussed this with Dad. What you really mean is that it's where YOU want to go. Why don't you go and tell Dad that yourself." The cruel tone in my voice startles me. But it's true. Mother has trouble standing up to Dad. Her role has been to support his career, not pursue her own desires.

Mother is quiet, but her eyes open wider. She is unprepared for this outburst, as if we're back in those stormy times when I fought with my brother in Jackson. She starts to put her hand on my arm to calm me. I knock it away with my forearm.

The dishtowel she was holding falls to the floor. The physical contact scares me. Never have I pushed against my mother, even verbally, and certainly not physically. Rage is boiling up in me. I bolt out the screen porch and outside, striding up Littleton Road. I have to rein in this anger. But I'm not giving in.

After walking off the rage, I slowly amble back down Littleton Road to the cabin. I feel settled with my father, even cathartic, having stood up to him. That conflict seemed pure and straightforward. But the encounter with my mother leaves me feeling unresolved. I'm trying to break away from her patterns in a more complex way. While I stick to my decision to keep living with Georgia, the tension between Mother and me dangles unresolved, burying itself somewhere in my body and psyche.

I FEEL RESOLVED WITH MY MOTHER these days, but not with the side of my mother I've incorporated into myself. Just as Mother struggled to find her role in life beyond a minister's wife and mother—which included standing up to my father—I can neither sort out my roles as father and breadwinner nor figure out my life as a journalist. Part of this quandary is learning to stand up for what I need while also listening to Georgia's needs and working with her to figure out what is best for the family. I find this balance hard to navigate. Since I lost my job at the legislature in 1988, approaching three years now, I have worked hard at sorting through the conundrum of balancing family, work, career, and money. As I seek to solve the puzzle, I am communicating more directly with Georgia, this strong and wise woman whom I love and who loves me.

Even so, I'm waking up in the middle of the night and not able to go back to sleep. Sometimes, I lie there restless, worrying. Others, I get up and try to make sense of what I'm feeling. At 4:30 a.m. one night, I write in my journal. "Depression the last two months… I've been absorbed by it yet working on it."

Then I re-read one of Georgia's notes: "I am sorry for your illness but you must take aggressive clear responsibility for changing your behavior when it occurs and only you can do that. But it is totally unacceptable for you to blame me or the children for the problems it creates. We have enough of our own."

I wince, hearing her saying that I blame them. I feel like she's blaming me. But I feel she's right too. Why do I have to worry about blame? At a gut level, I feel I'm being a good father but I hear from this woman I basically trust that my depression is hurting them.

I try hard to be a good father. The special times like the Atlanta trip with Lee are milestone events, but the day-to-day schedules are more challenging. When I am working at my office near downtown Raleigh, which I still share with another freelance writer, I can get to the kids' school in less than 10 minutes. I often eat lunch with one of them and play on the playground with them and their friends. The school encourages such parental involvement, although more moms than dads are there regularly. At the school or volunteering on field trips, I often feel more alive than at work.

But the evenings are often stark, especially the one night a week when Georgia's out. Far too often that spring, I am dragging in from either my half-time job at Family Health International or my freelance work at the Raleigh office. In either place, I sometimes allow myself to feel some kind of sadness I don't understand, but more often, I stay emotionally numb so I can keep my mind sharp.

Georgia continues to support my involvement in my men's group and the occasional weekends sponsored by the Men's Center. When an opportunity arises for me to join the Men's Center Council, she agrees. I look forward to deeper involvement in this group, where I seem to find ways to notice the beauty in life more easily, away from the many negotiations at home and the demands at work.

During the spring, I attend a weekend retreat at a center called Recompense, located on the Rocky River about an hour from Raleigh. This is the second meeting of the young Men's Center Council at this location. At the end of the retreat, a poem forms in my mind. I race for a pencil and scribble it down just before the departure circle, where I read "Recompense II":

We circle among the elements, men together
Alive to the mist and the frost and the stars
Celebrating beginnings and endings
Passing of time and marking of accomplishments.

We bless the earth who gave us the chance
We respect the fire, its warmth and power,

The air, whistling into our nostrils
And the water tumbling by us
The Rocky River, the sweet drinks of our days.

Forks are ahead, decaying logs regenerate
Moss hugs the branches as we step forward
Leading, with the powers we have to regenerate
Men's souls.... And our own.

We have come far, alone and together
Our small band circling out and in
Deep into grief, and skyward, as warriors.

Our energy takes us forward
Into the next stage of our journey
Now, in our new year, it is good.

A FEW WEEKS LATER, I'M AT MY office near downtown Raleigh trying to work on one of the few consulting jobs that I still have. This place gets me away from family worries. Above my computer is a quote from J.B. Priestley, the English author who lived in my grandfather's era. "To show a child what has once delighted you, to find the child's delight added to your own, so that there is now a double delight seen in the glow of trust and affection, this is happiness."

Today, as I read the Priestley quote, for no apparent reason I begin weeping. I wonder why and begin to think, *I do not remember a single thing that has ever delighted me. How then can I impart anything to my children and achieve a double delight? How can I be anything but a failure?*

That day I write in my journal: "I feel I will never know the kind of happiness that Priestley identifies, despite my many years of working to be a good father. The reason for my conclusion: I'm depressed."

Several days later, again at my freelance office, I go to the nearby Chinese restaurant and eat lunch outside alone. I decide to write Dad a letter. Since the visit to Millsaps two years earlier, we have continued to talk to each other more, and have even gone on trips together—a first for us. We went to New York, visiting some of his favorite places at Union Theological Seminary where he studied after returning from World War II. We went to the New York Public Library, where he saw with pride my name in the card catalogue. When working for the public policy center in the 1980s, I had edited a book, *The Tobacco Industry in Transition*, which got national distribution, all the way to this famous library.

I have just returned from taking Dad to the large, multi-generational Finger family reunion, our first time to this annual event. I start my letter by telling Dad what a great time I had with him at the reunion. Then I continue. "Enclosed is an interview with John Bradshaw whom you might've heard of or seen on a talk show. Several things about it are what I wanted to talk with you about."

I remind him of the family stories he was beginning to tell me as we parted at the reunion. Bradshaw calls such stories a "psychic archaeology," I write, "which speaks to me a lot regarding how I've been feeling with you in our last several visits. In my writing and thinking about my childhood and my visits and conversations with you, I've done a lot of healing. I had a very lonely childhood in many ways and missed not having more of you."

Sitting on the picnic table in the warm June sunshine, my thoughts are flowing faster than I can write. I glance up and see the lunch crowd is thinning. I'm the only one left outside the restaurant.

"I've had a rough time the last several years, trying to sort through the many cycles of depression I've had for most of my adult life. Not that I've always been depressed and never, thank God, clinically like Uncle Bill, but I have coped with many periods of unhappiness. There are many reasons and I am exploring them all. The work and parenting styles that Georgia and I have chosen have been very stressful. The family history of mental instability in the Ratliff family, especially Mother's hospitalization when I was four—an important developmental stage for boys with their mothers—has a part."

The tears are pouring down my cheek now. I've never written my father anything like this before. Sharing my problems. Opening up to him like so many parishioners have with him over the years. Maybe these are the types of things I needed to say as a boy when I was lonely or scared. But I never knew how. And, I don't know how now either, but I keep on writing anyway.

"The stresses on me as a child also played a role—the fishbowl life, dual life in Jackson and North Carolina, your workaholism. I've incorporated all of that of course in fundamental ways, along with the many blessings I received from the same circumstances—the integrity, discipline, resolve, high standards, etc."

Next, I return to safe territory, an analytical, even sociological tone. "I feel very fortunate to have come along at a time when there is a reassessment of gender roles and a revolution in knowledge and resources re: mental health and family issues. But this same opportunity has been stressful. Carving out my home and family life with my vocational goals has been for me what the Civil Rights Movement was for you, I think. In fact, remembering how you handled the 1958 crisis—learning about that with you—inspires me to hang tough with my own struggles. But the struggles are much more inward and focused on feelings, a strange terrain for me."

At the bottom on the third page, I get to the heart of my message, I realize now as I'm sobbing. I blow my nose and see no one is left at the little take-out restaurant with the two outside picnic tables. I'm here alone, cars whizzing by on the four-lane street.

"I've come to a point in my life where I no longer want to run from depression, or contain its symptoms (mood swings, workaholism, anger, rage) but to understand it so that I no longer fear it."

CHAPTER 12. Dancing with Allies

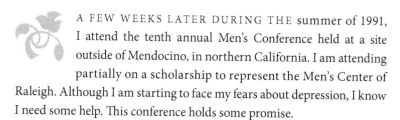

A FEW WEEKS LATER DURING THE summer of 1991, I attend the tenth annual Men's Conference held at a site outside of Mendocino, in northern California. I am attending partially on a scholarship to represent the Men's Center of Raleigh. Although I am starting to face my fears about depression, I know I need some help. This conference holds some promise.

I fly to San Francisco and get a ride to the conference up the rocky northern California coastline with eye-boggling sheer drops to the Pacific Ocean. At this conference, I do not have to work in the kitchen, as I did in Virginia nearly two years earlier. When I register, I get to choose a clan. The descriptions Michael Meade has written on a big board make my selection easy.

"The salmon investigates the waters of grief, of mother's longing and father's disappointments," one begins. "The salmon's isolation comes from depression." The D-word jumps out like a neon sign. I know where I belong this week.

"The depression comes from not being protected, from the sense of being kicked out of the family, from years spent in latency and evasion." I wonder about those phrases, how to look at my latency and place in the family—both mine of origin and now, with my wife and kids. But I feel my heart drawn to the closing sentences, which hit me cold and true, with no mental clutter to soften the impact.

"Salmon regard fishing as a holy thing. They fish for the wound...."

Only the wound that can be honored can be healed. The salmon aims at personality, genuine personality, well grounded in sorrow, in water, and in truth."

The first day, the salmon clan is working with Ricardo Morrison, who leads movement exercises at the conference. We are spread out across the wooden floor of the large dining hall, heavy tables shoved to the side. It is late afternoon in a dark room with heavy beam rafters and wooden siding.

"Think of something painful in your family, something you can make physical," Morrison says, as he starts crouching in a ball. He slowly unfolds his body, and we gradually begin to see his face. It's cocked at a funny angle, with his lip pulled out in a jarring, grotesque way. He finishes his unwinding and then relaxes, standing normal again.

"My uncle had a disfigured face, and I was always ashamed of that," he explains. "This is a way to manifest that feeling I held inside, to bring it out." He looks around at the 35 or so men, checking for questions, comments. "Use your body to show some kind of grief that you've carried for too long. Now, you go try it."

Standing here with men from across the country and overseas, wondering what kind of movement to create, Uncle Bill comes to mind. I start in a ball on the floor and slowly unfold, leaving my back with a big hump, like the one he developed lying in the mental hospital for so many years. At first I feel nothing except awkwardness in my body, no sense of catharsis for any grief about Uncle Bill and how I might be like him in some ways.

Morrison gives us the next step in the exercise: get a partner and have one of us shine our flashlight on the flaw of the person who is doing the movement. The spheres of light splash across the room as the afternoon sun fades. This time, as I unfold, with my partner's light bright on my humpback, I began to feel that I am carrying some kind of heavy load. My body even seems to resist standing up, as if my back is in fact deformed. I feel no clear emotion, no tears, no catharsis, but I do feel my body carrying something I did not know was there.

Over the week, the salmon clan meets with Morrison several times and gradually puts together a fully choreographed presentation—he calls it a dance—for the closing night's feast and celebration. He teaches us how to turn a somersault across the back of another man, landing without hitting our spine on the hard wooden planks, a modified Aikido move, he explains. Even overweight and non-athletic men manage the move.

ONE OF THE MOST POWERFUL MOMENTS of the week comes one morning when Meade and Robert Bly are discussing how grief is expressed in various cultures. Suddenly, without warning, eight men in the front row stand up.

"We want to interrupt you here," one man says. "We need to express our grief about Vietnam, to honor the men we knew who were killed there." Meade and Bly stare at the men, uncharacteristically lost for words for a few seconds. Then their faces soften as they remain quiet, waiting for the group to proceed with their presentation about Vietnam.

With no more explanation, one man steps forward and says a man's name loud enough to be heard across the 110 men filling the hall. He then bows his head. Then the man to his left steps forward and says another name. They go down the line until all eight have said a name. Then, they start again and go down their line. And again. And again. They go on and on. Finally, after what seems an eternity, names echoing through the hall and images bouncing through our minds, they stop. The silence does not go on for long.

A man in the crowd stands up and continues the ritual, calling out a man's name. Then, another in the room stands and another, each announcing another man killed in the War. "Jerry Huneycutt," I say, adding the name of a young man I knew at Lake Junaluska, who preceded me to Duke.

Tears start quietly in one part of the room as the names accumulate. Some sob, and others burst out with sudden wails. I've never seen so many men crying at once. The burden of Vietnam rises up in a palpable way across the entire gathering. Long buried thoughts about the War rise to the surface, but my feelings remain still deeper, like anther vein of untouched ore. I feel no tears.

As I hear the names of the dead, memories fill my mind. I remember presenting my case for the Conscientious Objector status among skeptical, middle-aged men. Grinding my wingtips into the snow, returning to the car, sitting beside my father who waited for me. Two days later, jumping for joy in the driveway when I tore open the letter with the surprising news. Joining the Methodist Church agency that supported alternative service in social change agencies. As the images overlap like a collage, feelings seem to be trying to break through the data, the thinking, the scenes. I realize some buried, unresolved feeling remains. Perhaps it is guilt I feel for not having gone to war. I believed in the course I took, but I never faced the risk of having my name called here, 20 years after that pivotal appearance before my draft board in 1971. But the feeling seems too buried even to arise today.

After about 30 minutes, Meade steps in and offers an idea to bring this ritual of names and tears to a close. First, he describes a chant from a West African ritual of honoring dead warriors and then teaches it to us. Called "Ah wei" (pronounced "ah way"), the chant has a slow, mournful tone, ending in a quicker pace that brings some resolution, "ai la, ai la, ai la." After we sing the chant through a few times, he tells us about a trail at the edge of the woods, and he guides us outside the hall.

We walk across the clearing in front and to a trailhead that leads up through tall redwoods. We move single file into the trees, as we continue to sing, "Ah wei, ah wei, ah wei, ah wei." The raw grief from the room seems to flow into the trees, absorbed by the hundreds of years of fibers circling the trunks and shooting high into the sky. As I walk with the others up the steep path, I don't know what the singing is doing, but I do feel better. Smelling the damp forest while I sing the chant brings a feeling of acceptance of this grieving today. Perhaps another day, thoughts about Vietnam may uncover some hidden passageway to my heart.

The final night of the week, at our feast and celebration, each clan performs. The salmon dance starts with the bodies unfolding with the flaw and flashlights—"the wound that can be honored can be healed." I had never thought of honoring Uncle Bill's disease, manifested as it was in his back. But I am doing just that. With my hump exposed by the flashlight, I feel something. Perhaps it is a burden, a weariness of still dealing with grief, but also I feel the dancing making it better. Juices are flowing through me.

Then we add the moves Morrison taught us through the week. We lie flat on the hard floor, our arms extended. We roll down what becomes, in our imagery, a broad stream like the ones salmon use for spawning. Sometimes, men roll on top and over another, as salmon do crowding for positions on the upstream swim. As we all roll, a man gets up on all fours, his back level across, and another turns the somersault across the flat back, then two and three and four others, and it is as if the salmon are jumping upstream toward their spawning ground.

Energy, joy, and pain are merging as I turn my body in unexpected ways, first humping my back, then rolling and somersaulting—all with other men who also feel grief and pain from their own histories. As we dance, some of us move about the hall and encourage the entire group to sing with us as we begin the "Ah wei" chant.

Hearing more than 100 men singing loud through the hall heightens the heaviness I feel. Maybe it is something of what Uncle Bill felt. Maybe something of what my mother felt in the hospital. What my grandmother must have felt for her two children. At the same time, I feel a resurgent energy. What of my grief? What parts of that do I feel? I wonder as we all sing the haunting, somber chant.

"Ah wei, ah wei," the voices sing, strong and deep, sounding like heavy footsteps of soldiers returning from a painful battle. Then, down to a lower register. "Ah wei, ah wei." Another pause, and back up. "Ah wei, ah wei,"—then a quicker tempo—"ai la," pause, "ai la," pause, "ai la."

THE WEEK IN THE SALMON CLAN provides another opportunity for me to approach some deep sadness, but some feelings nevertheless remain tucked away from tears and catharsis. At the same time, throughout that week, I feel more power as I chant, dance, and learn, and deepen my resolve to be a good father in a strong marriage and to keep growing my writing career. A few days after I return from California, Georgia and I go on a camping trip to the N.C. mountains. Standing in the misty morning outside our tent, my arm around her, I feel content, happy, even blissful. A cool breeze flows through the trees that hover over us. I smile deeply.

I take the children to Sliding Rock near Lake Junaluska, where I introduce them to a pastime that gave me great pleasure as a kid. We slide down a huge rock in a mountain stream into an icy pool at the bottom. My little daughter, skinny as a rail, turns almost blue but goes down again and again. I sit happily on the side, well past my limit of trips down the rock, watching my kids embrace the magic of childhood and nature.

As summer turns to fall, as getaways and weeks in the woods turn to daily routines and homework, old emotional patterns return—with a twist. This time, I allow myself to start feeling some of the sadness, some of the dark feelings. I'm feeling less afraid of them. Still, I struggle with lethargy, lack of vitality, and plodding through the day.

I turn to tricks to get me through the workday. My job at Family Health International is routine, predictable, for now, important but often uninspiring work. My job basically is to decipher findings from scientific articles, interview the researchers, and explain the topic in our magazine clearly enough for health providers in a developing country, where English is often their second language. I hunker down in my office, trying to concentrate, reminding myself that I'm lucky to have this job. I get through the day, but it takes all the energy I can muster.

Then, I return to my other job, at home—cooking dinner once a week, staying engaged with the kids, keeping up with the homework systems that Georgia monitors, the bedtime routine, parenting rules. I try to stay consistent, but sometimes it all seems like a foreign language. While my men's group and the conference have opened new doors and given me a core group of friends, I still feel locked up inside somehow. Managing a job and home life seems overwhelming. Getting away to men's gatherings to drum and chant and dance seems like real life. Daily routines seem like a series of chores.

In the fall, I grow increasingly restless. I love my family and kids, but I'm beginning to feel like I will explode if something doesn't change. I'm 44 years old and well aware of the frequent articles appearing on midlife crises. Men buy a red sports car, run off with a woman 20 years younger, or quit their job and pursue a long-held dream—or so the stereotype goes. None of those grab my attention, but I do feel that compulsion to break away.

I think about one of my favorite books from years before, *All the King's Men*, the novel about Huey Long, the populist governor of Louisiana. The protagonist of the novel, an idealistic journalist, captivated me. Named Jack Burden, he became Long's right-hand man. I remember feeling his burden through the story. Now, as I make my way through the fall routine, a scene from the book grabs me, like a segment of a fairy tale. Near the end of the book, as the Huey Long character self-destructs, Burden feels the weight of the collapse. I remember him jumping in his car and bolting. He drives and drives, leaving it all behind—but finally returns to face his fears and his own future.

I need a way to bolt. I don't know what it is. One option arises during my morning jog with Rosebud, our little white dog. Before the children have to get ready for school, I hook her on the leash, then run across Dixie Trail, the busy street in front of the house. I head toward the stream and greenway that go by the playground where I sometimes take the kids. One morning, I feel like Jack Burden, tempted to leave his life behind.

"Apartment for rent," the sign says on the little street between Dixie Trail and the stream. *What would it be like to move in*, I think as I jog by. Instead of noticing the stream and early morning stillness, my mind kicks into gear, imagining a fresh start. Morning after morning, I pass that sign, for maybe a month. I think about a new place where I can just rest.

At the stream, the apartment two blocks behind me, I notice the large boulder-like stones that form the bottom of the stream bed. I breathe the morning air and for a moment feel connected with the same beauty that reminds me of the cascading, crashing waters racing down mountain streams in places like Sliding Rock.

I breathe deeper and smile as I remember all the time spent with the kids on this little side street, helping them to learn to ride their bikes, races down to the playground. The kids' stories crowd into my own tale now. The morning when Dana tried to join me on the run with Rosebud jumps into memory. Tears dash into my eyes now, as I remember her telling me the story.

"I wanted to ride my bike with you and Rosebud, so I got up early," she told me one day. "But you and Rosebud were already across the street. So I was going to catch up."

Despite the strict rule that she was not to cross Dixie Trail alone at age seven, traffic was very light that early, and she headed across alone. About where the apartment sign for rent is standing, she fell off the bike on the edge of the street.

"I wasn't hurt but knew I couldn't catch you. So I walked home with my bike."

She didn't tell me the story for a long time, because she broke the rule about crossing Dixie Trail. But it came out finally, along with her punch line. "I didn't get hurt, but I was so sad not to go with you and Rosebud."

On my morning run now, I wipe tears away and smile at Dana's story, thoughts of the vacant apartment gone. Now, I reach the playground where I've spent so many hours with the kids, and I circle back down the other side of the stream.

I think of the men in my support group and how they have all managed in one way or another to raise their children. I picture these men running beside me, with their experience, perseverance, and support. Sometimes, their faces appear as I run. And, sometimes I say their names out loud: "Lester, Tierney, Stohler." The names enter this little forest with me, with the water and trees. Like allies in a battle, they move with me, readying me for the action ahead in the day. I can call on these allies when things get discouraging. They are still standing, with humor, grown children, long marriages, enjoying life.

Through the autumn months, especially heading into the holidays, the hardest time is often the early morning hours, when I awaken too soon. At least now, I am willing to put my darkest thoughts down on paper. I see this as progress, as strength. But my thoughts keep me from sleeping, and they compete for attention during my waking hours. My journal entries tell the story:

> DECEMBER 12, 1991: Been awake since 4 spiraling into deep depression… Get up to keep from falling deeper. … can't do the science at work. Parenting seems to be a mess, along with the house. Christmas is here and I'm not looking forward to anything except not traveling. But then we'll be here and I'll be more depressed. So I get up to read *Learned Optimism*.
>
> DECEMBER 26, 2 A.M.: Very depressed last two days, struggling not to spin deeper.
>
> JANUARY 8, 1992, 4:20 AM.: Wake up depressed. Went to sleep depressed and with tears. Tears come back when I make the association. I'm depressed at my mother's house. I'm depressed

at my wife's house—our house. My readings of infantile pre-Oedipal regression… of blissful vision with the Mother. An escape from manhood. The fear of that regression motivates men to act. Dreams have feces in them. Toilet training period. Question: Did I regress in toilet training when mother was in the hospital?… Feel better having written this. Seem to be getting at it.

JANUARY 23: Woke up at 4, very depressed. It was really time to give up, with family and with work. Tears—but I stayed in bed, went to sleep and dreamed. Many details. The men's group went on a picnic at a lake. Nobody called me but I showed up. It was a celebration. I had fruit to share, but it didn't work out quite right. The celebration was inside a closed door, for a select group. Michael Meade was presiding. We went around the group and said what we were doing in this work. An Asian man from Sesame Street played guitar. He was leaving the show. A few more were let in, hangers on. Was I invited?

Then I spoke, said I was working on a book but felt inadequate with family. I was looking up a pure white stairway, looking up, but no one was there to hear me. I felt terror, as if—who cared about me at all? Then I said, "Doesn't anyone want to hear me? Are you all too tired of this story?"

I'm talking to myself, tired of hearing about how hard it is. A few men come into a side view. It's a vivid scene, but I knew none of them, shadowy…. I'm going home now. People step out of closets, old friends. I keep leaving pieces of my knapsack. Someone is watching. But I made it.

I NEED TO BOLT, LIKE JACK BURDEN. Or if not escape, make some major shift in my life. The apartment sign seduces me, but I resist. The right opportunity for change arises unexpectedly, in late January, as I'm struggling to keep my dark thoughts from immobilizing me.

I'm standing with the six members of my men's group in David's front yard. It's about 10:30 Tuesday night. David leaves the living room last, after checking to be sure his son is fast asleep. For four years, we have met once a week, with occasional outings like the canoe trip and a beach weekend. Mostly, though, week after week, we have gathered on a school night and talked about what was going on in our lives. Generally, I have felt better when I went home.

Tonight, I move slowly to the middle of the front yard, as the others begin assembling into a circle. I have been restless in the group in recent months. The conversations seem to be cycling over the same territory. I throw my arms around two guys' shoulders, completing the circle. We huddle there, grown men in our 30s and 40s, just as I used to circle up to call the plays in grade school football.

Over the years, I have talked about my difficulties but sharing with these men has not helped enough. I need to probe the dark layers in a different way, and I need more help—beyond this group, beyond my journals and books like *Learned Optimism*, and beyond the therapist I've been seeing. I need something else, but I don't know what it is yet. This closing ritual evolved without design. We circle into our huddle and instead of saying final words, we just began making sounds, which becomes a slow growl. We start low and quiet and build up gradually into something like: "gggggggggrrrrrrrrrrrrooooooowwwwwwwwlllllllllllllll."

Tonight, just before the growl begins, I blurt out, "I've got to leave." Everyone looks up from the huddle and stares. "This is going to be my last night in the group. I need to do something different. I don't know what it is. I know this is sudden but this is what I've got to do." I'm surprised at how clear the words are, how definitive. I had not planned to say this. It was instinct.

Hugh looks startled, as do the others. I don't like the long silence. "I know I've said I was restless in the group. Maybe I should've said more. I just didn't realize how much until this very moment."

Silence competes with the few insects that brave the winter night. Finally, Hugh speaks up, the man who sat with me after building the dog pen and held my shoulder as I remembered my childhood dog. "You've been great for me, for all of us, from the beginning," he says. "If this is what you need, then I wish you well. I'll certainly miss you in the group, but we'll be okay." More silence.

Then the other Bill in the group with his honesty and grit gives the other perspective. "For me, I feel abandoned, with you leaving so suddenly. I would've liked some time to prepare for this."

A few others add short words of surprise and appreciation. I listen as best I can and wonder where I am headed. I've just walked across a bridge away from my primary support outside my family. And then at last, we growl. It is smaller than many of them, but a solid enough growl. We all turn for our cars and leave.

Bolting from my support group provides the relief valve I need and keeps me from pursuing the apartment. They are close like family, but abandoning them has a lot fewer consequences and involves less pain than leaving my family.

But I need more than a relief valve. Where are more allies in this dance through my darkness? Later that week, I am flipping through the area's weekly newsmagazine and see an advertisement for an adult creative movement class for the spring session. I sit up straight, recalling the dance at the California conference. I remember Arts Together fondly, when Dana took a creative movement class for preschoolers. The woman who started this arts center, Lemma Mackie, is teaching the adult class advertised. Before I lose my nerve, I call the number in the ad. A female answers right away, and I tell her what I'm calling about.

"Is the class only for women or can men attend?" Later that day she calls back to confirm that men are welcome.

The following Tuesday, at the same time my men's group is meeting, I go instead to the new Arts Together building. It is a restored carriage house near downtown Raleigh, with a beautiful dance floor and high ceilings. I'm nervous, virtually certain that I'll be the only man there. Some kind of karma is in the air, I'm thinking, with this class on the same night of my support group.

Five middle-aged women are sitting around waiting for the class to start as I arrive just before 7:30. Lemma is chatting, her eyes sparkling with energy. I met her many years before but don't know her well. Her slight frame seems slowed down by both age and illness. But when she turns her head or raises an arm, the authority in each movement carries purpose and power.

"Welcome, Bill. I'm delighted you're here." She talks a little about the structure of the class and then takes out a book.

"I'll generally read something at the beginning of class to give us an idea for moving or reflection. Or just for fun." She has a twinkle in her eye. "Or maybe I'll sing!" She laughs. "I'll have fun and want you to do the same. We'll create some beauty together." Another laugh. She doesn't seem to take herself too seriously, but she does seem to be serious about the class.

I feel strangely relaxed, as if the dancing at Mendocino with the salmon is about to continue. But I'm still too nervous to settle in with women, just one week after leaving the safety and familiarly of the men's group.

Then Lemma starts to read. I hear the call to move our bodies, to dance, to explore our feelings and make art with movement. It's an inspiring call to dance, with an emphasis on men. "It's by Ted Shawn, one of the men who helped start modern dance," she says. "He created a male dance company at a farm in western Massachusetts. It's known now as Jacob's Pillow, a modern dance center. Maybe some of you know it." Then she turns to me again, looking straight in my eyes. "Welcome, Bill. We are really glad you're here."

DEPARTING FROM MY MEN'S GROUP LED to an unexpected opening, but even after my first creative movement class, I have an instinct that dancing alone cannot reach this darkness. Another shock has to come. I need more help.

Late that January, in a session with my therapist, she says, "I've been trying to help you for three years now." We both acknowledge that our sessions have grown stagnant. "I've been reading more about the new generation of antidepressants, including Prozac. I think it's time for you to try medication. It's been hard for you to turn the corner."

"I think of medication as what my uncle took, as something for mentally ill people."

"More and more people are using antidepressants now. They're not just for those with serious mental illness. I've not been in favor of it myself, but I've recently changed my mind. You should explore it."

I have been reading more and more about depression, mostly in books like *Learned Optimism* and *Feeling Good*, which don't focus on medication. But, I've seen more about antidepressants for many types of people, not just for those in mental hospitals. Articles on Prozac in particular are beginning to appear in newspapers and *Newsweek*.

Clearly, antidepressants are something I need to learn about. I realize they are more easily available, and many now take them.

Still, instinctively, I am against taking medication. I don't even like to take aspirin, much less a drug that would alter my mind. Even after learning about my mother, taking antidepressants seems like a weakness. I feel like I ought to be able to sort this out for myself. But I know I need help.

A week after my therapist visit, I call my friend Stacy, a physician's assistant whom I know from men's conferences and drumming gatherings. I go out to his apartment and we sit down over tea. "What do you think about my taking antidepressants?" I ask.

"I prescribe a lot of them these days," he says. "They are becoming more and more widely used. They help a lot of people. I don't know if that's what you need, but they are certainly a tool that can help many people."

I didn't even know a physician's assistant could prescribe antidepressants. That makes the whole enterprise less intimidating. Still, I'm not quite ready to take the leap. Another two weeks pass.

Georgia has found a couples therapist that she likes. I agree to an introductory appointment. We go together but the therapist sees us separately. Georgia goes first. In the waiting room, I feel exhausted by the thought of more therapy. But I also have a feeling that this might be good for us as a couple. Then I go in. For about 15 minutes, I try to describe what is going on with me and our marriage.

Then she sits back, looks me in the eye and says, "I'll be willing to work with you but you'll have to start taking medication first."

I feel like she's landed a blow in the stomach. But strangely, I feel like it's one I need. The messages are clear, like a choreographed dance linking old therapist, friend, and now new therapist.

My new therapist adds, "Until you have more energy to work, then it won't be worth it."

The importance of work in my life showed up early. Here, about age 10 (1957), I focus at the desk in the bedroom I shared with my brother in Jackson, Mississippi.

I left this desk at the N.C. Center for Public Policy Research, where I edited their magazine, to work as a consultant at the N.C. Legislature in 1988.

My son delivered this note to me downstairs after a rocky bedtime routine in 1987.

26A   Asheville Citizen-Times, Sun., Aug. 14, 1988

Democrats Fire Consultant Wh[

The Associated Press

RALEIGH — Democratic lawmakers fired a consultant to a legislative study panel despite his warning that to do so could damage Lt. Gov. Bob Jordan's bid for governor.

Bill Finger had angered some lawmakers by writing that Republican Gov. Jim Martin had urged the General Assembly to consider new proposals for the elderly.

"Hell, we're politicians," said Sen. Jim Richardson, D-Mecklenburg, co-chairman of the Legislative Study Commission on Aging. "Everything we do is political."

But other lawmakers said they fired Finger as part of a new policy to use the Legislature's full-time staff of attorneys, instead of private consultants, to advise study commission.

"We're cutting back on consultants," said House Speaker Liston Ramsey, D-Madison. "We will use our own staff wherever we possibly can."

But Finger, a free-lance writer and consultant from Raleigh, said aging legislation passed in July included $50,000 for a consultant to the commission this year.

Finger was paid $250 a day and, under his contract, was to work no more than 100 days during the 13-month contract. He had served as a consultant to the panel since January.

He said he was terminated because Democrats perceived an article he wrote for the Independent newspaper of Durham as favoring aging program proposed by Martin, Jordan's November opponent.

"Apparently, some Democrats see me as a problem because of an article I wrote about Great Aunt Bess.' Rather than creating any problems for the Democrats, I view the article as a way to keep the aging issue visible — an issue that should help Jordan

and Democrats amo are elderly," Finger sey and state Sen. Ke

The article said: the N.C. Study Com urged the state legisl have made specific tion during the curre

Richardson said widely respected fo issues, was not fired but because of the tempt to limit the use

But he said the Democratic lawmake

"I'm not person said. "But there wer were concerned abou him to mix the gover on aging.

"I don't think th

The 1988 Associated Press article on my firing as a legislative consultant triggered my concerns about money and the future.

William Ratliff,
my mother's older
brother and my
Uncle Bill.

CREDIT: TEENY RATLIFF

In 1942, my mother (back row, far left) left a fledgling writing career in New York to return to Mississippi and marry my father. This nuptial event occurred at the top of the Peabody Hotel in Memphis.

My dad (4th from right) looks out from the deck of the Queen Elizabeth en route to the World Methodist Conference in 1951.

This 1951 family Christmas card, months after my mother's hospitalization while Dad was in England at a Methodist conference: 7-year-old brother, baby sister, and me, age 4.

The men's support group before I left in 1992: David, David, Bill, myself, Hugh, and Frank.

(L to R): Hugh, myself, Stacy, and Mike at a weekend retreat of the Raleigh Men's Center Council.

Jim Hunt (with glasses), one of my mentors at the 1993 initiation performance, prepares for the final phase of the ceremony.

Posing on the porch of Roshan Raza's house in 1970, with
her sons holding the goat, Moin (left) and Taqi (right).

On my return to Jabalpur in 2003 (L to R): Roshan Raza, younger son Moin,
Kehkashan (Taqi's wife), and Taqi.

Feeding the ducks at Lake Junaluska,
shortly after we adopted Dana at age 2.

Having fun with Georgia
before children.

With my mother and father in the Lake Junaluska living room, about 2000.

*The family at Recompense retreat center on one of our
Thanksgiving holidays there, about 1990.*

Having fun with Georgia after the children have become adults.

CHAPTER 13. Teflon Drug Goes to Work

"IMAGINE A SAFE PLACE TO GO. A place that gives you comfort," says Dr. Roger Perilstein, the psychiatrist I started to see in the early months of 1992. A short man wearing a tie, he sits casually apart from his desk, looking over at me on the edge of a small couch. "If you can't think of a real place, make one up. Make it a place of beauty."

About a month earlier, I took the Prozac prescription from Perilstein to the pharmacy and began taking the little green and white pill every morning. He suggested that we continue with hour-long therapy sessions as well. We have talked about depression and my life, the style of "talk therapy" that I'm used to. But this is the first time he suggests that I relax and close my eyes for a different approach, one that is new to me.

Perilstein's instruction to think of a place of beauty bounces through my mind as I stretch my feet halfway across the space between us. I lean my head back in a relaxed, almost sleeping posture. I have already come to trust his Yoda-like counsel. He has the intellectual content that I expected from a psychiatrist—I had never sought help from one before. He feels like a friend, guiding me along with some extra knowledge about life and the mind.

Gradually an image appears. I am at the river at Recompense, the retreat center an hour away from this modern office building. I'm with the other guys on the Men's Center Council, mostly middle-aged, white men. We are playing like boys. I feel the coolness of sitting in the river naked, the water around my armpits on a 90 degree summer day. Someone splashes water across my face, and a cold taste washes over my lips.

On this Saturday morning, we have just finished a ritual honoring the men leaving the board and welcoming the newcomers. We chanted, recited poems, and offered blessings. Hot from beating drums and singing, we knelt spontaneously onto the cool earth in the large teepee, around the fire pit. Then we left the teepee and went down the hill to the river, stripped and lounged naked in shoulder-deep water.

I can't remember skinny-dipping as a kid. I smile, sitting on Perilstein's couch, letting this regret of childhood melt away into the memory of the Recompense moment—that memory of beauty.

Perilstein's voice sounds again. "Have you got a place?" I nod. "So, totally immerse yourself in the beauty of that place."

Time is standing still. Eight of us are playing in the water. I move to avoid a heavy splash of water coming from someone and then wince as a pain shoots up my leg from stubbing my toe on a rock. But the pain is short-lived as I breathe in the pleasure of the morning, of the laughing and conversations. The smell of dew sinks into my lungs, burning off the field across the small river. The heat of the day is rising.

"Now, I want you to prepare to leave that place," he says. "But bring the feelings with you, the comfort with you."

I picture myself coming out of the water, leaving the guys behind. I put on my clothes and prepare to go back into the world.

"Now, I want you to start walking away from that place and see where you go. There's no hurry. Watch yourself, see where you go. What do you look like? What is around you?"

For a few seconds, the voice sounds very distant. I don't realize that it is directed at me. Vaguely, I realize I'm on this couch in a therapy session, just off the Raleigh beltline. But my sensations remain at Recompense, on the hot walk up the river, past the teepee, and up toward the farmhouse.

"I'm walking up from a river into a house," I say quietly, my first words since the exercise began. "There are a bunch of my friends still playing in the river. It's a lot of fun."

"Now, keep your eyes closed," the voice says softly, "and tell me what you see."

"I'm walking into the little house and toward the kitchen." Silence. "I'm very small, smaller than a midget. It's like that movie where the kids got shrunk."

"What else do you notice?"

Silence. I don't notice anything except being very, very small. But I hear words coming out of my mouth anyway. "My arms and legs don't work very well. I see a huge chair and some cereal on the counter. I'm very hungry. But I can't get up onto the chair to eat." In fact, I'm suddenly ravenous in this doctor's office in the middle of the afternoon, away from work, my kids in school, my life as a 45-year-old man on hold.

"So, what happens then?"

"I need help but no one is there to help me. The other guys will be at the river a long time. I don't expect them to ever come help me. I'm by myself."

"So, what are you going to do?"

Silence. More silence. The doctor doesn't offer advice. "I don't know what to do. I'm so tiny." More silence. I get no guidance from Perilstein. But again, I hear words from my own mouth. "I start to climb up the legs of the chair." Silence. "Somehow, I'm able to shimmy up the leg. I finally get to the seat and flop over, exhausted. The back of the chair has those little rods up from the seat to the top. I'm leaning against one of the rods. That's how little I am." I pause, exhausted as well as hungry in my adult body. But more words are coming. "I climb onto the top of the counter and push over the cereal box. I eat a meal from several pieces of cereal."

Perilstein and I talk about this image over several weeks. I tell him about my room in Jackson where I grew up, which I shared with my brother. My bed was adjacent to the kitchen. At breakfast, we would usually eat together as a family. Mother and Dad liked to read the daily Methodist Church devotional, *The Upper Room*. My father often tucked his tie into his shirt and put a napkin over it, in case juice squirted up as he cut into his grapefruit half. A series of pictures of plantation home kitchens surrounded the table in the little nook, which was just large enough for our simple kitchen table.

Now, decades later, I see another image of this breakfast scene. I see a tiny little boy, maybe 4 inches tall, handicapped with braces on his legs and arms. Oddly, as if turning the end of a kaleidoscope, I also see a vibrant young boy, a wiry frame full of athleticism and a shock of red-dish hair covering his bright ideas. This young boy carries seriously his responsibilities in the sixth grade as captain of the patrol boys for the elementary school and as a class leader in junior high.

But with another turn of this visual dial back in time, the little shack-led child appears again, even as the other boy grows older and stronger and more capable. A side of me is frozen in that chair, handicapped and tiny, never reaching the cereal box at all growing up. The larger personality is well nourished, eating fried eggs and four pieces of toast for breakfast, one of those family stories that we like to tell now, how I carefully put grape jelly on every piece of toast and spread them around my plate.

EVERY MORNING, AS THE WINTER ROLLS INTO SPRING, I stand in front of the downstairs bathroom mirror, just before shaving, and take the 20 milligrams of Prozac. Some mornings, I think no more of the action than squeezing toothpaste onto my toothbrush. Other days, I hold the pill for a moment in my hand and wonder what it is doing to me. Then I look into the mirror, my glasses off, and stare deeply into that face. Who am I—the guy who took the pill or the guy who lived without Prozac for so many years?

I ponder the question as I begin this Prozac journey: As these man-made chemicals alter my brain, are they changing my basic personality? Are they re-aligning who I am? My core self? Do I want this to happen? I turn to books to help me through this dilemma.

Peter Matthiessen, an environmental writer and novelist, offered one perspective on my question in his book *Snow Leopard*. After living deep in the Himalayas for two months, he looked at himself differently: "In the gaunt, brown face in the mirror—unseen since last September—the blue eyes in a monkish skull seem eerily clear, but his is the face of a man I do not know." The transformation in that face came from a source other than antidepressants. I wonder if I am taking a shortcut.

"I think of Prozac like Teflon," Perilstein says in one of our early sessions. "Prozac can keep things from sticking."

This un-sticking takes various forms. Most obvious, I find myself drawn to the new therapist that Georgia found. And, I find it easy to stop seeing my old therapist. I agree that I need to work with Perilstein and in couple's therapy instead.

AT A WEEKEND WORKSHOP with men from around the area, we are focusing on female energy in our lives. The leader is Tom Daly, the man who comforted me when I was making a mask at my first week-long men's conference. When I started feeling a suffocating feeling, lying on the bench with plaster drying on my face, it was Tom who held my hand and asked me whether I had ever had anesthesia for an operation. Then I told him about my varicocele operation.

During this weekend, he directs us to draw a timeline of our lives, marking key events related to feminine energy—positive events above a line drawn across the center of a long sheet of paper, negative events below the line. Then, we work with a partner, sharing the ones that jump out at us as significant. My mother's breakdown goes below the line at age four, meeting Georgia above the line, along with the arrival of this wonderful daughter we were privileged to adopt.

We also break several times into small groups of about eight to share themes that come up. My time comes, and I share the data, various pieces of information. At first, there is no feeling, but then an unexpected subject comes up. "I realize that I didn't put infertility on the chart, it didn't fit in exactly. But as I'm thinking….."

I begin to choke up and the words don't come. I try to continue, talking over the first tears now. "Georgia came home from the hospital and I …" a sob interrupts the words. "I held her, comforted her. We couldn't…." More sobs, louder. "… have children. But I never…" Sobs are louder. "I never cried my…." Louder and steady sobs now. I manage the last word, gasping for air, inside a deep cry that is taking me over. "Myself." Then, the wails are loud, reaching into the trees. Several men lean over and comfort me, arms about my shoulders. And, I just keep crying, deep, long, loud.

Gradually, I come back to regular breathing. The last sobs have left now, accepted by the men and then carried with the wind across the landscape of grief we humans visit from time to time. I did not find this land easily but I am there now. I am feeling my own grief. And my breath goes deeper into the belly, the raging fire gone with the wind.

WALKING ACROSS A FIELD OF GRIEF often leads to other paths. With a sense of curiosity and adventure, new roads can lead to unexpected beauty. On a sunny Saturday later that spring of 1992, Lee and I drive to nearby Meredith College with our dog Rosebud. We go to the large hills that climb up from a lovely pond and amphitheater. Lee runs with Rosie, leash off and racing around in circles among the knolls.

I practice over and over a simple rhythm on the little Middle Eastern drum hung on a strap around my neck. After some time, I break onto a new plateau as one does in learning an instrument and find that I can play and chant together. "Fanga Alafia, Ashee, Ashee," I sing, in perfect rhythm with the beats: dum, da-da, da-da, dum, dum, da-da. "Fanga Alafia, Ashee, Ashee." The beat stays the same on the next line. "Aki wa illeh wa, Ashee, Ashee. Aki wa illeh wa, Ashee, Ashee."

I learned the chant at a community gathering led by the African American Dance Ensemble. When we used it at the ritual in the teepee at Recompense, welcoming the new Men's Center Council members, I was still learning the drum rhythms.

Lee turns his head toward me from the next small hill and begins running excitedly towards me, little Rosebud sprinting at his side. "I heard that same thing at school," he says, gasping for breath as he reaches me. "It was one of those guest artists." I smile, happy that this chant has reached into mainstream elementary school life.

"Do you want to try the drum?" I ask. He enjoys beating on my big red Cuban conga drum at home in the living room and knows the basic hand motions. He slides the little dumbek around his neck and begins beating in his familiar motions. I show him the simple rhythm, and it grabs him like a magnet. He already knows the first line of the chant from school, and we start to put the phrase together with the beats. And then, slowly, we move past "Fanga" to the harder "Aki wa illeh wa," chanting at the top of our lungs, taking turns on the drum, loud with precise syncopation.

And so, that afternoon, Prozac flowing through my brain, feelings soaring through my heart, my 11-year-old son and I relish this moment, each in our own way. The bright sunlight on a Saturday afternoon in the South smiles across us in a timeless rhythm of joy. And the hours race by with glee.

CHAPTER 14. An Old Pair of Loafers

THAT WINTER AND SPRING of 1992, I work on memories and feelings, alone with Perilstein and in couples therapy. I also rediscover my body, a long-neglected side of this unfolding riddle. Lemma Mackie knows her body and how it has responded to dance, song, movement, and expression beyond words and conscious thought. Using dance to heal herself and singing to explore the beauty of her life, she also offered her wisdom to the community by creating Arts Together, a center mostly for children's theater, dance, and arts programs. Now in an emeritus role, she teaches only rarely.

From the beginning, I never feel awkward in her class. Any uncertainties of being the only man dancing with women quickly shift to an eagerly awaited evening each week. She introduces us to a basic movement vocabulary—like teaching a foreign language.

Shapes function like words, which we can connect into phrases, and with work and experience, sentences and paragraphs. She shows us how to craft this language using what I think of as strong verbs—the angle of the body, the level in space (full height, middle height, or on the floor), and the degree of shifts in time and space. Too many adjectives and the phrase can lose power, but a few can evoke more meaning. Unnecessary flourishes of the hands distract both the viewer and the creator, like excessive use of adverbs.

"Move as if it were winter," she says one night. I hold my body close together, arms across my chest, moving slowly across the floor. "Do you feel cold? Is it dark?" Gradually, her instructions push us along. "But spring is coming now, begin to open up. How does the unfolding feel inside?"

With a growing vocabulary, I begin to move past straight panto-mime, past trying to match an unfolding flower literally by opening my arms wide to mimic the petals. I sense a deeper springtime that needs expression emanating from the belly, from the center of the self. Then, my body begins to move as if with its own memories and bold new ways of seeking, without cerebral instructions. The torso shifts more gradu-ally, rib cage leading a more solid opening, like the tenacious day lilies that have begun to poke their heads out of the ditches along the North Carolina country roads.

She has us dance as individuals, spread across the floor, sometimes forming duets or working together as an ensemble. She plays background music or sometimes sings. I am transported in these moments, beyond cares and callings of the week, simply into the sounds and the space, feeling my body move with grace and beauty.

One night, I move with a partner into a fluid improvisation, the others watching on the edge of the floor. With extended arms and dip-ping shoulders almost as one, color and emotion seem to fill the room as tangibly as if we are moving through a rose garden. We sense an ending pose, arched into the middle level of the space, torsos almost parallel to the floor. We hold the final shape as if a curtain is dropping before us and finally stand. One of the other students says quickly, "I'd pay to see that!" We all smile and clap together like gleeful schoolchildren.

"Spread across the floor," Lemma instructs us another night. "Now, curve yourself up into a ball." The six of us respond in kind. A memory dashes through me of the ball that I formed at Mendocino, in that exercise when Ricardo Morrison instructed us to show some kind of grief. "Now, as you hear the music, I want you to break out of the ball, like a chick breaks out of a shell, into a new life. See what kind of life you find."

The music starts, and I float into my body with the gentle sounds, as if *in utero* listening to my mother sing a lullaby. An elbow finally emerges, and I feel the complementary side of Morrison's exercise. My skinny, angled arms unfold into graceful arcs exploring high into space. A crouching, powerful young man takes shape, neither obsessed with responsibility nor strapped down into a tiny handicapped morsel of a self. The music practically catapults me across the floor, into a new life, broken free from the egg and fully present on this dance floor, this night.

PROZAC, PERILSTEIN, AND DANCE WORK—not necessarily in that order—provide the strength I need in 1992 to make a hard decision. When I started working half-time at Family Health International in late 1989, I kept open my little office about three miles from my house in a small two-story brick building. I had a place to focus on freelance jobs, writing as much as I could about fathers, hoping it could become a book. The scramble of freelance assignments and my FHI job left little energy for the book. But I did manage to get a coherent proposal into the hands of an agent, with whom I had a hopeful meeting in New York.

Several months later, she called. "This is hard," she said. "There is a lot of good material here, but it just isn't quite right for us. I'm sorry."

The call solidified the feeling I already sensed: my energy has shifted from writing about fathers to understanding myself, to peeling back the layers that have made me who I am as a man and a father.

Standing in my freelance office that spring, I know it is time to move on—to close this place and the energy it takes to keep going here, while increasing my hours (with the much-needed increased salary) at FHI, an option that fortunately is available. The three bookshelves on the side wall are crammed with volumes and files that carry memories from the last 20 years, boxed again and again as I settled into various spaces. To the left sits the large desk my grandfather used in his dry goods business in North Mississippi, now with my computer as the centerpiece instead of his little black records book. A long folding table, like those used at church picnics, holds my printer and stacks of papers. I see myself sitting there, drawing on the discipline I learned from Dad, hammering out the draft for legislation that netted more than $1.9 million for new, innovative projects for elders. Other days, pages poured out of the same computer, of memories, commentary, and reporting about fathers—my dad, myself, men around me, and a few from around the country.

I turn and look out the door, across the hall, remembering the dream of Uncle Bill, luring me into his life of illness with dark eye sockets from behind that wall. Tears begin to trickle down my face. In my dream, something in me resisted Uncle Bill's invitation, a sense of self still unearthed from beneath layers of biochemistry, culture, family, coping, and grief.

The closing of the office offers a signal to wean myself from times past. Turning to pack now, I pull books off the shelves. I sit cross-legged on the oak flooring, watching as the books fall into clear stacks as if in a dance. The men in my support group, whom I left suddenly just a few months earlier, seem to be with me as I sort through the paperbacks, pamphlets, and hard backs. My sudden departure was not the way I wanted to end the ritual gatherings of four years, when we sat in dens and beside campfires. This group anchored me, and certain books are resisting being packed, forming stacks like personal totems. I will use these in a gesture of appreciation, to help heal the way I left.

A book by Tracy Kidder about building a house clearly belongs to Frank, the architect in our group. My camping books will go to the other Bill, who shared long stories of hikes and the woods. The children's stories will be well cared for by David, an editor, who loves books and his children. Hugh, the former minister and talented Renaissance man with the beach house we visited, lays claim to an eclectic stack including a slim booklet on seashells and a Bonheoffer paperback.

My office stands bare and empty now. My friend Sam has come with me for the final goodbye. He helps me take the sorted boxes downstairs to my old station wagon and his truck. Then we return to the empty space for the final goodbye. I have learned to avoid isolation at important passages. Looking now at the long bare wall where my bookcases stood, Sam stands with me as I say a poem of grief and sorrow for leaving what I have not finished. Then, I thank this space for allowing me to move through it, allowing me to write down a bit of myself as best I could. Sam heads down the hall, and I close the door to my office for the last time.

The next week, the five guys in my support group come to my house for a final goodbye. Five lawn chairs stand in a semicircle at the left edge of the yard. My friends settle into place, looking down the sloping backyard, past the black walnut and persimmon trees that hold the family hammock, through the old grape arbor, and finally across the little stream to the huge stand of bamboo between us and our neighbor. In front of the chairs, long sticks of bamboo lie on the grass. They frame a stage with the open side to my five-person audience. Ideas from Lemma and others, including the dance books I've begun reading, shape this, my first choreographed dance. Stacks of books covered in fabric lie ready on stage, key props for my performance.

I begin with a set of simple gestures and then twirl back to the first piece of cloth, a bit like the Rumi dervishes I've begun to read about. I pick the first stack up. Holding it like a precious earthen vessel, I dance up to Frank, who is sitting nearest the holly hedge, stage right. I pull off the cloth and offer the books, with Tracy Kidder's *House* on top, in a slight bow from the waist, lower back stiff. No words, only this gesture of connections between our stories shared and years passed together. Frank smiles faintly in his understated way, which I know from our years together signals his understanding of my book choices and his deep appreciation.

I repeat the routine for the other four until the stacks are gone—the reactions reflecting the men, large crinkled smiles, warmth spreading across hard faces, humility at being noticed with details of specific books. I bow to them all now, and the dance is over. This ritual deepens my apology, with bonds noted concretely through this art of choreography—however elementary the composition and design. The stars are out now, and we join around our backyard campfire spot for one last growl together.

SOME EVENINGS, LEMMA WOULD encourage us to develop simple dances around emotional themes, suggesting different types of memories or parts of our bodies as a focus. Late in the spring, near the last session of the class, I find myself unexpectedly walking through a movement sequence where I'm moving sideways across the floor, my feet crossing one in front of the other, like a folk dance from Eastern Europe. Feelings start to rise that suggest some added urgency, perhaps loss or anger or sadness. My knees bend now, back straight but slanted forward, and I am looking directly across, as if in conversation. The angles of my body and the freedom of this dance floor combine into the kind of magic that occurs in unforeseen moments. Suddenly, I feel transported back to my teenage years.

"Maggie!" someone called out, so clear in my memory that it might as well be coming from our class music. "Are you going to Maggie?" I hear the call again mixed within Lemma's directions. And I go back to my teenage years, even as I move in the old carriage house in Raleigh.

"Of course," I yelled across the athletic field. The late summer afternoon signaled the time to return to my job serving food at the cafeteria. Nearly every Saturday night in my teenage years during those summer months, I did go to the evening of square dancing in nearby Maggie Valley.

My mind now dances from Lake Junaluska and Maggie Valley to the old pair of loafers at the back of a seldom-used drawer at home. I run across them occasionally, but I haven't worn my clogging shoes for decades. These are not the kind of tap shoes designed for Fred Astaire or Gregory Hines. These clogging shoes emerged in the Blue Ridge Mountains along with world class clogging teams. On the front third of the shoe sole is a metal plate, with a small ball-bearing loose in the middle of the metal. The shoe stores in the mountains of western North Carolina call it a "click tap." At least they did in the late 1950s and early 1960s, when I wore out several sets. A large solid tap covers the entire heel.

I used my click taps in Maggie Valley, on the edge of the Great Smokey Mountains National Park. We would pile into cars at Lake Junaluska and drive the eight miles or so down the two-lane highway towards the Cherokee Indian reservation. Some tourists came to the old barn-like structure, but mostly the square dancers were natives of the mountains, plus our group from the Methodist Assembly grounds. From great grandmas to babies, all ages filled the three small bleachers that ran down the long left wall, interrupted by a small elevated band stage. Some nights, an older woman would grab my slender frame and twirl me around as if I were a pair of old overalls. Over the years, Maggie became an institution.

At Maggie, every week the same man would call out on the mike, "Circle up." Wearing overalls, he had a distinguished softness about him, the gray hair cut close around his mostly bald head. People responded quickly to his lead. All sizes and shapes joined in a huge circle for instructions. He would walk around it on the inside, counting the couples off.

"Odd," he said, pointing at a couple who must've been married for 35 years, "even," motioning to the 10-year-olds who were next.

And, on he would go. He managed to get an even number of couples, sometimes as many as 100 or more. In this form of square dancing, we would join into groups of four, doing such routines as "four-leaf clover" and "Georgia rang-tang," quickly demonstrated by the leader with a few of the locals. Then we would swing our opposite and our own before the odd couples would move around the circle to join into a new foursome.

Instructions over, the full group would "circle forward" and then "half back," before the caller called for "odd couples out," and the four-person sections would begin. After about 15 minutes of controlled confusion, as the tourists muddled through with mostly patient locals, the caller finally called, "Promenade."

The experienced couples would take the square dance position, with the man's right hand on the woman's right shoulder, her hand reaching up to meet it. Left hands joined in front. Many couples just held hands. Gradually, though, things got even more casual and chaotic. The lead couple would split, the men peeling off one way, the women the other.

The highlight of the dance would occur during the division of men and women into the long freelance clogging time. The men would go by the bandstand and show their fanciest footwork, called buck dancing. At the bandstand, the guitar, dobro, and bass players would be pounding out "Down Yonder" and other traditional tunes. The caller would be sitting there tapping his foot. I would do my wildest and loudest buck dance. Sometimes, two of us would do a spontaneous duet. More often, we were on our own. A part of what I was doing was to show these mountaineers that an interloper like me could match them on the dance floor. It was competitive and thrilling and exhausting—pure joy, with no overlays of thinking.

IN MAKING THESE SHAPES tonight in the Arts Together studio, the details of the Maggie Valley dance floor coalesce into a message. I received the signals 30 years ago, but the meaning is only now becoming clear. Maybe my crouching body has the same tension that sprung through my tightly wound legs so many years ago. Whatever the sensation, the dancing brings the long-buried message into focus.

The music from Lemma's little boom-box might as well be "Down Yonder." The caller, standing on stage next to the dobro, holds the mike as the buck dancers move across. As I move directly in front of him, he sees me and offers a message. I see his clear blue eyes looking at me, timeless now with kindness and attention. In his overalls and plaid shirt, he looks at peace with his world as if he knows he belongs exactly in this place, running this square dance that is getting a bit wild. He does not know my name but he does know my clogging. Somehow, he senses a bit of desperation in my joyful dancing, as if it holds some promise that often escapes me when I return to the rest of my life.

Clogging in front of the bandstand, I face my silent leader. I slide the click tap on my left foot against the floor in a fraction of a second, creating a crisp rhythm, and quickly cross it into the air in front of my body. I pivot my right heel and foot sideways across the floor, anchoring my body as my clicking left foot provides the auditory and visual magic.

This wise face looks back at me and offers a blessing. "You're doing fine young man. This is the right place for you. Just keep on dancing," his eyes say, as if delivering a father's blessing. I needed such blessings more often from my own father during my teenage years.

TONIGHT IN CLASS, my spirit is joining my body to embrace this message—just keep on dancing. When Lemma ends the dance, I drop to the floor exhausted. As others share their experiences in the exercise, I sit quietly with this recovered message from my past, humble and grateful. The joy of that moment, the old man's blessing, Saturday night after Saturday night had burrowed deep into memory. I moved from Lake Junaluska back to Jackson, year after year, and then through college and into manhood. That message might have been lost forever, but the dancing brought it back.

As the spring semester class comes to a close, I know I need to keep dancing. I also need to be doing it with men. The women's dance class has been supportive, anchoring me just as the men's support group did. But I need to go deeper. Even though I don't know enough to lead a dance class, I write a proposal to the director of Arts Together to coordinate a creative movement class for men. I will call on trained dancers to lead some classes, I explain. Men desperately need to express themselves physically, for their own spirits, which in turn will help them with their families and other relationships, the proposal notes. The director agrees to give it a try.

The advertisement for the fall class appears in the Men's Center newsletter and the Arts Together brochure: "We will stretch, explore how our bodies remind us of particular animals, dance emotions and colors and seasons, learn basic movement techniques, and use poems, drawing, and music as springboards into the space around us." I call my friends in the Men's Center and manage to get eight people, enough for the class to go.

While I don't know exactly how this class will unfold, I do know that I have discovered a new tool in moving through depression, a new path that will lead me back to my true self. I am finding a path back to the joy I experienced those nights in Maggie—not to the fancy footwork but to the creative impulses that lay beneath the dancing. Now I need to keep nurturing this inherent creativity within myself.

Clogging in Maggie Valley helped me hold onto the inherent joy I had as a young child. Discovering dance in midlife was like finding a long forgotten path in the forest. I have been wandering for many years—working, providing, and growing older and wiser in many ways, but longing, often unconsciously, for that part of the forest that had given me much joy and pleasure as a boy.

CHAPTER 15. I'm Not Ashamed

LEADING THE DANCE CLASS that fall of 1992 provides a weekly laboratory to play with poems, to explore the body, and to encourage men to move with emotion rather than athleticism. Creative impulses are jumping from the dance floor into my daily life as well. Watching the Karate Kid movie, I am struck by the crane-like dance his teacher did to gather strength.

I start doing little crane dances to accent my long, thin arms as huge wings, my hands bent at the wrist, fingers pointing down. My lean legs, balancing on one and then the other, complement the picture. Bending my left knee, I pick my right leg up. Then, I raise my forearms up, fingers pointing to the sky. As if flying forward, I shift my weight and land on my right leg, left leg into the air with my arms flapping again. As I practice in the backyard, I feel as though I'm soaring through my imagination.

I begin to read about the whooping crane, how it almost became extinct but has very slowly managed to survive through careful breeding programs and protection of a few habitats. The whooping crane becomes my totem. My kids think I'm ridiculous as I play around in the backyard on one leg, arms stretched out and up. Whenever my mind wanders towards worries of money or family or work, I try to call up the crane within me and remember that survival is possible.

One day, on an outing with my daughter to Charlotte—a train ride and overnights with a friend—she picks shopping as her activity. I

reluctantly agree, since I dragged her to the Charlotte Hornets professional basketball game. At a large department store in a sprawling mall, she
settles into her age section, considering one dress at a time on the rack. I
am getting restless. Away from home where nobody I know will ever see
me, I step between two rows of dresses, well hidden, and slowly move into
my crane stance. Unfortunately, the one person who DOES know me
turns the corner. My daughter is mortified and heads straight for the exit.

"Daddy, how could you do the crane dance HERE!" she says when
we safely reach the rental car. "I will never go shopping with you ever
again. EVER!" This nine-year-old, brown eyes darkened to match her
jet-black hair, looks as steely as a judge handing down a life sentence. I
dutifully apologize for not being more sensitive to her shopping trip, my
straight face full of remorse while holding back my laughter. I loved doing the crane dance in a fount of commercial America, and I love seeing
my daughter so feisty and assertive.

In October, the entire family goes back to Mississippi for an elaborate celebration of my parents' 50th wedding anniversary. The multi-day
affair starts in Memphis, the site of my mother's engagement party at
the legendary Peabody Hotel, and moves through Dad's early parishes in
North Mississippi. The extravaganza ends in Clarksdale, the little town
just a few miles from the River, where they got married in 1942. Amongst
the festivities, we visit the graveyard where Mother's parents and her
brother, my Uncle Bill, are buried. After a time of quiet reflection, an
idea pops into my head as both reverent and celebratory.

"Mother, I'd like to do a crane dance on Uncle Bill's grave—just
a few steps." She's heard about my dancing class, as well as how I have
latched onto the crane as a shape that fits my body and offers an antidote
of creativity to my depression. Over the years, we've talked about how
I feel connected to Uncle Bill, even telling her about the dream where I
walked away from his dark eyes.

"That sounds like a wonderful idea." She beams, always eager to
support creative efforts. My daughter slinks behind a giant oak in the
graveyard, embarrassed beyond belief that Dad would do such a thing,
even though family members are the only ones to hide from. Georgia
and our son have returned to Raleigh and miss this gravesite visit.

The graveyard is sunny and deserted this morning. I feel invigorated and fun-loving, adding this quirky moment to the family stroll through the headstones. Why not honor the life of Uncle Bill with a dance on this small piece of Mississippi soil? I lift my right leg high, tilt my torso slightly, extend my arms parallel to the ground, fingers down. I see myself anchored to the Ratliff's, to Uncle Bill and my grandparents. The reminder comes: I can survive, just as the whooping crane did.

IN DECEMBER, NOT LONG AFTER RETURNING from the Mississippi trip, I am invited to participate in the early morning service at our church. The topic for the lay-led, informal service is the freedoms we have in America, marking Bill of Rights day, December 15. I decide to speak on the freedom I had to be a Conscientious Objector in 1971, at the height of the Vietnam War.

The service goes as expected. Natalie presents an engaging overview of the topic before sharing how in midlife she got career counseling. Women in this country have the freedom to pursue their own life dreams, she says, upbeat and perky.

The next speaker, named Fred, says, "This country offered me and my family the basic freedom of religion and expression." He explains that he was born in the Netherlands, and the Germans invaded his town during World War II. "I was about five or six when we had to flee," he says. I notice his eyes are glistening, moist. As he continues, his words come haltingly as his tears get stronger. Then, he begins to slur his speech, chokes back a sob that catches in his throat.

Fred's voice shifts now to a higher pitch and he starts to speak as if in a trance. The words have a guttural sound, and I realize they must be Dutch. His memories of childhood, in a native tongue long ago stored away, pour out now, between loud sobs no longer contained. He seems unaware of his language and continues with no apparent embarrassment. I am crying now, as are others around me. Finally, he sits down beside me on the front row. I put my arm around his shoulder. He whimpers, the sobs coming under control. He looks up at me, his eyes filled with relief.

I am next and head to the podium wiping tears from my face. I introduce my topic: having the freedom to choose to be a Conscientious

Objector in 1971. I briefly summarize the draft system at the time, where the military met its manpower needs using a lottery that determined the order men would be called.

"I knew I couldn't be part of a military system that was designed to kill Vietnamese. I was a young man, back from the Peace Corps, trying to figure out the best thing to do. When I realized I was about to be drafted, I felt I had three choices: go in and be a medic, go to Canada and live until I could come home, or seek a CO classification."

I describe briefly my learning with the Quakers in Boston, deciding to seek the CO, the session before my draft board, and doing two years of alternative service. "But over the years, I've often felt ambiguous about getting the CO. I've felt pride certainly, but also pangs of guilt, regret, and embarrassment."

Fred's outpouring before me has exposed my vulnerabilities, and now tears trickle down my face again, this time for myself.

"This is the first time I've ever said in public how I have felt guilt about getting the CO status, about the fact that many of my contemporaries died or came home broken—an ordeal I avoided."

Then I tell them about a passage in a book of oral histories from southerners who served in Vietnam, called *Landing Zones* by James R. Wilson. "One of the stories in the book is from a nurse named Brenda Sue Castro. It has really helped me. I want to read to you from her story."

I pick up the hard copy book and start reading the memories and feelings of this nurse whom I've never met. "To be honest with you, I haven't liked myself very much since Vietnam," Brenda Sue Castro says. "I've felt very empty. I think anybody who went to the war left behind an enormous part of his youth and vitality." I choke slightly and then skip to the end of her story.

"Vietnam was such a waste for our country. In some ways, the people who stayed home were victims of the war as much as the veterans were." I look up, hoping people absorb this. "So many people come up to me now and say, 'I protested the war, I'm so ashamed.' I tell them not to be ashamed. I gave a talk at one of the local schools and a kid said he was ashamed of an uncle who ran away to Canada. I told him to be glad his uncle exercised his right as an American citizen. Once I didn't agree with that. But maybe people like his uncle exercised their rights more than I did."

I close the book and look up, the long years of grief I've felt for myself and the soldiers heading towards some resolution in this early Sunday morning service. "This woman's story helped me to realize that we all had hard choices during the War." My tears are flowing steadily now, not the guttural sobs like Fred's or the loud crying I did with the men's group mourning my infertility. The tears feel cleansing and cathartic, marking a time of closure for this event that so much defined my early adult years.

"Now, the losses I have carried since Vietnam are before you, and this makes the pain of my choice years ago easier to bear," I say in conclusion. "Freedom has served us in different ways, for Fred in World War II and for me during Vietnam." I return to my seat, tears flowing, exhausted but also strangely refreshed—a paradox that reflects the interplay of freedom, war, and the power of unexpressed emotions.

In Mendocino, when the men stepped forward honoring all of their friends who died in Vietnam, I did not cry—as most did in the crowded dining hall that afternoon. While I was not yet ready to feel the emotions that day, I did recognize intellectually this grief inside of me. Over the last two years, the Teflon drug, the dancing, and the journeys into my subconscious have helped to set the table that I am ready to join. Now, I feel safe and strong enough to expose to a community of worship a secret that has haunted me. Fred opened the door for me, and I walked through.

ABOUT A MONTH LATER, on a cold night in the early winter of 1993, 12-year-old Lee and I pull our jackets closer against the wind coming off the Atlantic Ocean. Standing on the beach, about three hours from home, we are looking straight overhead on this moonless night, brilliant stars engulfing us.

"First you find Orion, Dad," he says. I have learned that you can hardly miss Orion on a clear night. "See it?"

I nod.

"Now, follow the belt up to that patch of stars. That's the seven sisters. Together, it's Pleiades." And, there it was, clear enough to count the separate seven sisters. Lee picked this weekend after reading about

Pleiades in his astronomy book, which advised a moonless night. He looks a short while then goes scampering down the beach collecting shells. And that was that, his restless energy moving on to other mysteries of the night.

Back home, five days later, a cold blast of Arctic air comes through Raleigh. That night, I stand in the backyard, invigorated, and look for Pleiades. The children are asleep. I am walking the dog and find the sisters by myself—the first time in my 46 years that I have ever looked for them. My high school literary magazine was named "Pleiades," and even when I published a poem once, I never bothered to find out what the name meant. That January night, I inhale deeply through my mouth, tasting the icy air, feeling the sharp sensation go down my throat and inside my lungs. The frigid oxygen molecules seem to knock against my heart, awakening cells and prompting electronic signals in my nervous system that are deeper I think than the pharmacological revolution of the late 20th century.

I smile, remembering now the sunset I saw the day before, pausing as I walked out of my office, heading for rush hour traffic on Interstate 40, absorbing the beauty of the purples and oranges spilling across the winter sky. My memory of yesterday's sunset moves back now to a recent walk with Dana through snow and holding hands. "Dad, look at the sunset," she said, stopping. "Isn't it pretty!" We paused, needing no words.

Looking alone at Pleiades and remembering these sunsets, I turn around in my brain the Priestley quotation, picturing it over my computer at the office I closed. "To show a child what has once delighted you, to find the child's delight added to your own, so that there is now a double delight seen in the glow of trust and affection, this is happiness." The phrase from the English author stood before me as a guide for this world of fatherhood. Now, the quotation is turning itself upside down for me, the chilly night air forgotten for a moment as I stand under Pleiades. The double delight comes not from showing my child what has delighted me but rather by paying attention to their delights.

As I bring our dog Rosebud into her warm spot on the porch for the coldest night of the winter, I smile with gratitude for the crane dance and therapy sessions, for my children and my wife, who has stood by me, patient and resolute in her own goals and dreams. We have found a new rhythm of understanding and listening. A more steady income from my job has also helped. But, there is something else that both comforts me and confounds my understanding: Prozac has played a central role, I know, in taking me from weeping on Father's Day to seeing the double delights from my children.

IN 1993, A NEW BOOK COMES OUT that solidifies my confidence in this medication, now in my bloodstream and brain chemistry for nearly a year. Called *Listening to Prozac,* by Peter Kramer, it traces the development of the new wave of antidepressants increasingly being disbursed by doctors throughout the country. "The medication seemed to flip a switch, to turn black and white into Technicolor," Kramer, a psychiatrist, says in this review of clinical trials and stories from both patients and doctors.

Pen in hand, studying the pages, I stop often, writing notes in the margin, trying to follow his reasoning. Sometimes, I sit up when he describes the kind of brain that has been shown to benefit from Prozac and say aloud: "I know that person—it's me!" This book comforts my dark side. "Perhaps in some people, low self-esteem may be less a result of biography then of genetics: a low serotonin setting in a sense *is* low self-esteem" (his italics). My problems aren't a matter of personal failure but rather a matter of how my brain works.

The science is hard to follow. Even the acronym for these new antidepressants—SSRI's for "selective serotonin re-uptake inhibitors"—seems counterintuitive. Don't I want more serotonin, not inhibited serotonin? I understand better when Kramer talks about the kindling effect. "Psychosocial stressors like pain, isolation, confinement, and lack of control can lead to structural changes in the brain and can kindle progressively more autonomous acute symptoms," he writes. As time goes by, progressive changes in the brain can lead to more frequent, and more severe, depressive episodes, even with less of a causative factor.

I talk about the kindling effect with Perilstein. He's heard many of my stories by now, and we go through some again, now with "kindling" in mind: my senior year in high school after I moved from Jackson to Nashville, periods at Duke, time in India, returning to Boston, losing my job at the legislature, and recent years at my job and raising kids.

As the decades fell one into the next, smaller stresses triggered familiar feelings of isolation and hopelessness. With each of these episodes, I have been fortunate to keep functioning through what I think of as low-grade depression.

"If Prozac works best for lesser degrees of depression, perhaps in some patients it will only 'kick in' when they are already psychologically and neurochemically on the mend," Kramer adds. I smile and look up from the page, flipping through memories at Recompense and the men's groups, with Perilstein and Georgia, and on the dance floor. All of this work has put me "on the mend."

Reading Annie Proulx's novel, *The Shipping News*, I stop cold near the end of her tale of a man building a new life with his children in Newfoundland. Getting out of a hot bath, he sees himself in a full-length mirror. "Middle age not too far ahead, but it didn't frighten him. It was harder to count his errors now, perhaps because they had compounded beyond counting, or had blurred into his general condition. He pulled on the gray nightshirt, which was torn under the arms and clung to his wet back. Again, a bolt of joy passed through him. For no reason."

Since I began taking Prozac, bolts of joy are passing through me with greater frequency. And when I feel no such bolts, I am managing to accept most of the humdrum moments, the gray days, the routines of my job, the boredoms of life, the growing challenges with pre-adolescent children.

TALKING ABOUT DEPRESSION remains difficult. Sometimes I mention the topic to Georgia, but usually only when I'm feeling upbeat, reflecting on how much I enjoy dancing, for example. Georgia, our therapist, and Perilstein are the only ones who know I take Prozac. Despite their support, I feel ashamed—that I'm weak somehow. I'm embarrassed to admit taking it to anyone. Weekly news magazines are devoting more stories to the new generation of antidepressants, and Kramer's book has reached bestseller status. Still, I'm not eager to step out of the closet.

While medication is helping me move through daily tasks, it remains linked for me with shame. Is there some kinship to the range of emotions I felt getting a CO instead of putting on a uniform? What about the image of manhood that I know intellectually is wrong but lies imprinted inside, from John Wayne and General Patton? Is taking medication the same as not being willing to kill? The message rings deep inside me: Men don't take drugs to help them through pain, especially a little melancholy. I'm not sure what shame I feel. But I am clear—I do not feel safe telling people I am taking Prozac. And, meanwhile, this secret forges another layer of resistance to finding my true self.

In early 1993, the Men's Center and local women's groups sponsor a weekend retreat. Tom Daly, who has worked with Men's Center gatherings before (and helped me with my mask at my first week-long men's conference), is leading the event with his wife. About 35 of us gather at a YMCA camp in the woods, men and women. The first night, we break into small groups for individual work and support. The three women and two other men in my small group are new to me.

Saturday morning, our small group goes to the lake, a clear winter day with temperatures in the 50s. Listening to others discuss difficult issues, I feel safe enough to step beyond therapists and men's gatherings. During a small group session in the afternoon, I take a deep breath. "I need to say something." The full attention of the other five is on me. "I haven't admitted this to anyone beyond my wife and therapist." I take a deep breath and push on. "I'm taking Prozac. For about a year now."

I tell a little of my story, about work and family and trying to figure out the role of Prozac. As a competent worker, making deadlines, turning out magazine articles, I often feel like a fraud. But I have been doing so much better the last year. I have more energy at work, cry less often, am more present with my children and wife. Am I able to do this now, to have more energy, because I take Prozac?

"I feel a lot of shame admitting all of this," I say. "Maybe this is the biggest issue—I don't know what being depressed means. Who am I, really? Am I the person without Prozac or the altered personality with this chemical jump-starting the synapses of my brain?" The group listens and that helps a lot. I don't feel embarrassed or ashamed with them. But I feel like I need to go a step further, into some sort of presentation to the full group. I need to push this thing into the open. This secret is starting to spill out, like I need more air or it will suffocate me.

The group breaks from this late afternoon session, and I take a walk alone, surrounded by tall pines and the nippy air near sunset. For some reason—Christians might call it grace—I remember attending a concert with the singer and songwriter Holly Near. In this concert, maybe a decade earlier on the University of North Carolina campus, she led the audience in a song that suddenly becomes very clear again. Stopping now by one of the pines, I see myself sitting near the front of the auditorium with Georgia as Holly Near gave her instructions to the audience.

The next song, she explained, was about gay and lesbian issues. She had come out herself and had become an advocate for these issues. In the song, she said, we will all have a chance to sing out loud, "I am gay." When the line came, she asked that everyone in the entire hall sing the line together. Then, nearly 1,000 people would be saying together, "I am gay." And by doing that, people there who were actually gay would be able to give voice to this fundamental part of their identity, perhaps for the first time in their lives. They would have the safety of 1,000 people saying this together. Georgia and I looked at each other, and when the cue came, we sang, "I am gay" along with others in the auditorium.

I race back as dinner is starting and tell some of my small group I had an idea. That night, the plan begins to take shape. I tell the Holly Near story and say I want to do the same thing with a song about depression. The leader of our small group could explain to the full community that we are going to sing a song—first the six of us, then we would ask the entire group to join in.

When I finish explaining the plan, another man in the group says, "This will help me too. Actually, I'm taking Prozac too and haven't told many people." Already, this ritual is doing more than just helping me, even in the planning. By giving voice to my own pain in this ritualized and protective way, I feel stronger already in picturing the full community deepening and growing stronger.

The next day, late in the morning, the retreat is racing toward a close. In one of the few time slots left, Tom and his wife agree to let our small group lead the full community in a short ritual. First, the six of us form a small circle in the middle, surrounded by the others in a large circle. A brilliant blue sky is overhead, and a circle of pines rings the larger circle.

As our leader explains the ritual to the large group, I am very nervous. I feel like everyone can see that I am the one. But I know that is not true. The structure ensures anonymity. I am safe.

We will sing a simple verse several times and then motion for the whole group to join in, our leader explains. It is about depression, she adds. This will give a feeling of safety to anyone who has never spoken out loud about their own depression or taking medication. Part of me still feels I should be able to solve this problem without Prozac, if I just danced more or beat the drum harder or read enough books about how men can get in touch with their archetypal energy. But here we are, in this large circle. This song feels like a huge risk to me. She goes over the words once, and the crowd seems ready.

So, at last, the explanation finished, my heart pounding as we stand in the mid-day sun, our six voices sing. "I am depressed and I'm not ashamed." We hold the last syllable for several beats. I begin to smile with a release of nervous energy and joy. Again we go from a high pitch down to a lyrical deeper tone. "I am on Prozac, there's no cause for shame." We sing the two lines through three times and then gesture for the full circle to join us. Just as happened with Holly Near a decade earlier, the entire circle begins singing. I look around and see everyone in the larger circle smiling, holding hands, swaying and singing the words, "I am on Prozac and I'm not ashamed."

BOOK 4. ACTION
(1993–2002)

CHAPTER 16. Grace, Grief, and Grandeur

ON A CLEAR MAY EVENING this spring of 1993, the weekend of my 46th birthday, families arrive late in the afternoon with picnic baskets and blankets. Tables are spread out at the left end of our backyard, ready for the feast. The sloping grassy area in the middle of the yard functions as an amphitheater, with ample room for blankets and chairs. The audience will see as a backdrop the grape arbor winding in front of our towering bamboo.

The seven men in my spring dance class help me greet the guests. We are excited and a bit nervous, but confident as well. We hand out the forest-green program folded like a church bulletin. The cover reads:

THE MEN'S CENTER AND ARTS TOGETHER PRESENT
MOVEMENT IMPROVISATION FOR MEN, A CLASS PERFORMANCE
INITIATION FOR AMERICAN MEN

My name appears next, centered above two columns of the other seven names in alphabetical order. Patrick, a teacher, can do a true cartwheel. Lucimba, a musician, can do a flip. Paul, an architect who is dying of prostate cancer, can play the French horn. After his first class, he went home so excited by moving to music that he stood on his bed, which was more comfortable than sitting, and moved about for hours. The others, by day, are a chemist, a yoga teacher, a businessman, and a nursing home worker. But tonight, we leave career labels and take other risks. None of us is a trained dancer. We met for 15 Tuesday night classes, beginning in January, and a dress rehearsal here earlier in the week.

The program describes the four sections of the dance: Prologue, Grace, Grief, and Grandeur. "This performance and gathering are built around the two themes underlying our class this spring: the need for community in our lives and the power of expressing such needs through our bodies. This evening also has the intent of embodying a fundamental element of male initiation, which we generally have missed in our experience as American men."

The notes explain the traditional three-part concept of male initiation: a separation from mother/childhood, a testing and transforming process, and a reincorporating into community as a man. "American men go through many separations and transformations, with varying success. Our modern, technological culture, however, has diminished, if not destroyed, the crucial third step.... Too often, the transformed person eventually dies; isolated, our hearts turn to stone."

The guests are settling in now; parents are feeding young children. Georgia and I move to the top step of the back patio, and the 70 or so people, including the dancers, give us their attention. We welcome them to our home and thank them for coming.

"Thanks especially to Georgia for helping to make this evening possible. And be sure and read the special thanks in the program for the others who helped." I hug her, then look around at friends and some I don't know. "We will start in about five minutes. The dance will last about an hour. And, then we'll eat." The audience settles into yard chairs and on blankets.

I WALK OUT FROM THE OTHER SEVEN MEN, who remain half-hidden by the bushes near the back of the yard. I stop just in front of the row of monkey grass that divides me in our large garden plot from the audience in the sloping backyard. This area has remained fallow for several years now, which works fine for a stage. Behind me, the grapevines cascade to the ground, marking the back of the stage. Standing as the final backdrop is the bamboo, stretching skyward just over the stream.

The audience applauds as I take center stage in black tights, Guatemalan shorts with white and blue Native American patterns, and a dark tank top.

"Welcome children, welcome women, welcome men—our community tonight. I invite you to join with me in forming a container for the surprises that dancing spirits hold for us during this time together." Speaking calms my nervousness, as does the cool earth against my bare feet.

"In this prologue, when I give you this signal"—I hold both arms to the sky, shoulder width apart—"you will offer a call, the single word... GRACE." I step back ready to begin the dance, "Initiation for American Men." I lift my arms.

"GRACE," the crowd responds on cue.

"Gift of creation," the seven other dancers reply, grouped like a Greek chorus, completing the first line of a poem I have written with their help. Then, I begin my first dance segment in the prologue, which combines dialogue with movements. I've modeled my story after "21"—a biographical creation by the modern dancer Bill T. Jones, known as Bill T.

"My arms have always been long and skinny, with veined spidery fingers," I say, holding my thin limbs straight out, accenting the 35-inch sleeve length. "My parents used to buy me new white coats at Easter but the sleeves never covered my wrists. My arms had power though. I could throw a football and hit a tennis ball."

I move my outstretched arms to a football quarterback pose, make a long passing motion. Then, I leap off the ground, as if hitting an overhead shot in tennis. My left arm is stretched straight out for balance, and I cock my right arm back, then swing it down and across my body.

"But in the locker room, my dangly arms always embarrassed me." Today, I feel no embarrassment, only freedom and excitement as I step forward. I move to the monkey grass and raise both arms.

"GRACE," say some 60 voices.

"Totally accepted and loved as we are," the seven men say from the wings.

With this introduction, I begin a series of 14 movements, like Bill T.'s 21. "One," I say as I dangle my arms, exaggerating their length. "Two." I step back as if throwing a football. "Three." I do the motion of hitting a tennis overhead shot.

"Four." I crouch in a sitting position, as if at a desk with my arms typing. I count up to 14, with a shape for each number, then step forward and raise both hands.

"GRACE," echoes through the amphitheater.

"Being loved and being lovable," say my seven dancing buddies.

"I grew up on a college campus—William Ratliff Finger. Balls and rackets and schoolwork were my main companions." Arms up.

"GRACE."

"Capable of loving," responds the Greek chorus.

I go quickly through my life story, making 14 shapes or short movement phrases that symbolize my life. I move at five-year intervals up to age 40, then one shape for each year from age 41 to 46. Back to the monkey grass.

"GRACE."

"Frees us for healing within."

"Sometimes at Christmas, Uncle Bill came out of the mental hospital. But he never opened presents or ate Christmas dinner." I am running in place. "William Ratliff—my Uncle Bill—was a brilliant engineer trained at MIT. In his early 20s, he was working on a top secret science project to help beat the Nazis. Isolated, under pressure, his demons became his reality and overwhelmed him." I drop to the ground, completely prone.

"He locked himself in a hotel room in New York City. My grandmother rode the train from Clarksdale, Mississippi, to Grand Central Station to get her son, William Ratliff." I inch along the ground, the way soldiers do in tall brush. I get back to the monkey grass, stand up and raise my arms.

"GRACE." The audience grows louder, sounding increasingly like a single voice.

"Promotes the healing between people." The chorus responds, taking on a rhythmic quality with the themes that thread through my stories.

I go through the first five motions, counting, "Five, 10, 15…"

"GRACE!"

"Makes healing possible within institutions."

I tell a story for age 20 of going to India with phrases like "Ask not what your country can do for you…" Back to the monkey grass, hands high.

"GRACE" echoes across the yard.

"Takes social action beyond obligation."

Then a story of returning to face the draft, for age 25.

"GRACE!"

"Walks along the hike of responsibility."

At age 40, my stories describe each step of my midlife passage, one year at a time. "Forty." Dive to ground to a new life, quit my job and vow to write a book about fathers, carrying a burden of discipline. Arms rise.

"GRACE."

"Turns the hike into a dance of liberation."

"Forty-one." Circle my arms, as if in a huddle with my support group. "I joined a support group with Hugh and David and Bill and Tom and Frank and David." Then stage front.

"Forty-two." Pound my hands against a make believe drum. Up to "Forty-five," with the lines from the poem ringing when I return to stage front and raise my arms.

"GRACE."

At age 46, I spread my arms, lift my left leg with knee bent toward the sky. I go from my crane pose through the shapes of years 41 to 46 and expand parts of the story.

I form the huddle. Pound the drum. Then, at age 45: "I decided to close my office, to give away my books, and to start dancing again." I do a little clogging.

"One night in my first dance class, my long thin arms spread and I became a crane, a whooping crane. My burden, my skinny, long arms, became my gift—my long wings stretched wide enough to carry my grief. The whooping cranes dwindled to less than 50 on the face of the earth. But they have survived." I hold my arms up high.

"GRACE."

"Our gift today—here and now." The Greek chorus rings loud with their last line.

I say the year and quickly repeat the shapes for years 41 to 46, trying to achieve the power of repeated patterns, like the master, Bill T. Then I move toward the chorus of seven men, doing my crane dance—swooping my arms, raising one knee skyward, then the other, as I move across the grass. I say random phrases from the dance:

"Ask not what your country can do… Long, skinny arms… The crane survived." As I reach the end of the monkey grass, I look across my left shoulder to the audience and say my last line, "And so did I."

MY SON AND DAUGHTER, NOW TWELVE AND NINE, joined by other children, come out to the monkey grass holding pieces of bamboo about five feet tall. They stand together, bamboo held upright in front of them and form a symbolic curtain, closing the prologue. As the children draw the audience's attention, the seven men from the Greek chorus vanish, creeping behind the swing set into the long, dense foliage of the grape arbor. The next segment of the dance begins.

Taped music from Mickey Hart's "birth dance" fades in from the small boom box near the blueberry bushes, stage left. The Grateful Dead drummer, so the story goes, recorded the heartbeat of his child *in utero* and then during the birth, played the music in the delivery room. As this heartbeat spreads across the backyard, men's bodies begin to appear from the grapevine, an arm here, a leg there, then a head. In slow motion, Sam and Judge, Paul and Tom, Lucimba and Patrick and Chris emerge.

The men draw on the class exercise of unfolding from a ball like a chick from an egg. They exaggerate each movement, each limb, as if discovering it for the first time. After about three minutes, men of various sizes are coming forth from the earth. When Hart's music ends, the seven men, still separate, freeze into a single frame.

I am standing on a small mound off stage in a new costume, an African shirt and wide flowing pants brought back from India. A djimbe drum from West African hangs from my neck as I call out, "Dancers, how do you rise?"

"The ground sends us," they respond. A recording of whales sounds from the tape deck, and the seven men begin to make duets and trios. Some are standing, others kneeling, others still on the ground. The seven gradually become a single ensemble, moving closer to the audience, like an organism that has inherent wisdom.

"Dancers, how do you rise?" I ask again.

"Grace suspends us." Breaking their single shape, they form a tunnel, a kind of birth canal, bowing heads against the ground, half on one side, half the other. "Gravity lands us."

I begin a hand drumming pattern with two others, all veterans of Michael Meade's drumming instructions. "Dancers, how do you leap?" I call out over the pounding rhythms. The men are kneeling on the ground facing each other, forming a tunnel.

They rise and say, "The ground spurns us." Lucimba, an athletic man with long dreadlocks, breaks away from the group and moves swiftly back toward the bamboo. The other six men lock arms, hands gripped near the opposite man's elbows, and bend at the knee, preparing for Lucimba's run.

"Dancers, how do you leap?"

The drumming is louder.

"Grace contains us," the men reply.

Lucimba dashes towards them and dives horizontally through the air between the six other men. They deflect his weight, guiding him to the ground the way we practiced. They avoid the temptation to resist the weight and work against gravity.

"Dancers, how do you leap?"

"Gravity returns us." Lucimba joins the group, locking arms across the birth canal, and another man takes his place by the bamboo and begins to run. Each dancer in turn leaps into space, to be guided to earth by gravity and the other men.

The men now form a semicircle with their backs to the bamboo, forming a smaller more contained performing area before the audience. Patrick cartwheels into the center and does a solo dance, twirling and spinning across the old garden area. The others sway in their places. Each man in turn introduces himself with a solo, no words this time. Separate personalities come forward in seven unique presentations. Paul does gentle motions with his head and shoulders, his feet not moving while his face glows as if in heaven.

The drum fades now. The seven men in the semicircle drop to their knees and spread their arms out straight from their side, palms up. They look skyward, as I ask the last question. "Dancers, how do you dance?"

"The ground endows us. Grace allows us. Gravity bows us." The men lean forward, their heads against the earth. The children return with the bamboo, and the audience applauds.

WHILE THE CHILDREN HOLD THE BAMBOO curtain, the seven men exit to the makeshift dressing room where they earlier formed the Greek chorus. I join them as we gather up shrouds of fabric with Middle Eastern designs. Tom and Paul, the elders of our group, prepare the fire starter in the metal base. Our guest demon, his face painted white and wearing an all-black outfit, has disappeared into the bamboo. All is ready. I motion for the curtain to part, and the kids go back to the audience, leaving their bamboo by the hammock. We begin a chant of grief, the West African chant I learned first with the ritual for those fallen in Vietnam: "Ah wei, ah wei." Then the pause and down to a lower register. "Ah wei, ah wei." Pause. "Ah wei, ah wei." Quicker tempo. "Ai la," pause, "ai la," pause, "ai la."

Tom and Paul enter with the portable fire pit, light the flame, and bow down around the fire, shrouds over their heads. The other five dancers and I join them, and the eight of us circle the fire, bowing to the earth, singing "Ah wei, ah wei," the cloths covering our heads. Our singing fades as the fire leaps toward the sky, now turning to dusk.

The boom box suddenly erupts with loud, challenging sounds. And the demon jumps forth from the arbor. Tom and Paul rise to face their own demons. They dance against this dark shadow of a man, a large, animated figure with a black cape. First Tom or Paul challenges him alone. Then they go together as allies. And, after symbolic combat, they return, exhausted, to the fire circle. Two by two, we take our turn fighting against this shadow, this dark presence from the underworld, from our own psyche, from our past, from the unknown.

The dance stays heated. As two of us collapse back to our circle, two more rise. The demon never tires. He maintains his swooping presence across the stage, luring us into the vines and back again before the audience. Each pair dances for one, two, or three minutes. The fire flickers with the leaps through the space.

THE CHILDREN BRING THE CURTAIN to the front for the last time. The fire is burning still, and the sky has darkened. The eight of us form a single-file line. We take our pieces of fabric and use them as blindfolds.

In this ceremony of American men, in our 30s to late 50s, our initiation depends on an entire community. We left home and parents

THE CRANE DANCE   *173*

many years ago, but sides of our childhood live in our psyches in non-productive ways. We need the full community of women and men to honor us and to recognize our efforts as we resolve the discord of our psychological committees and move into full adulthood.

Two friends from our church, Jim and Jane Hunt, play the role of the elders tonight. They stand at the front of our line. Jim, a scholar, has written several books on Gandhi and looks a bit like him. A small man with a bristly mustache, Jim leans over to hear my instructions. Jane, his wife of many years, raised their four children and then taught school. She speaks her mind in causes of social justice and asks individuals to stand up for what they say they believe. I finish telling Jim and Jane the details of the next steps and tighten my blindfold into place.

The audience is now on its feet, and ten drummers have formed a corridor for us. Grandeur begins, our integration into the community. The rhythmic beat crescendos. Leading us between the drummers, Jane and Jim hold lighted torches. The audience awaits us at the end of this final birth canal, honoring us as transformed men. I am first and have my right hand on Jim's shoulder. Paul, Tom, Sam, Lucimba, Judge, Chris, and Patrick follow, all of us joined hand to shoulder as we move forward through the drums.

As we reach the middle of the backyard, where the audience is now standing, Jane and Jim guide the eight of us into a circle. The community gathers close behind us. Jim asks the audience to untie our blindfolds and drape the fabric across our shoulders. The eight of us and the Hunts link arms behind each other's back. The audience forms around our smaller circle, a full and safe container, as if welcoming its men home from a distant journey. It is time for blessings.

"We will offer blessings on these men now, calling on many ancient traditions," says Jim. "I will begin and end the blessing and call on the community—women, children and men—to add others if you wish." The assemblage takes on a sacred quality, insects whistling in the grasses around the edge of the yard.

"First, we offer the blessings from the East," Jim says. "The mystery of a rising sun, the gusting wind blowing through us all, the ancient call of the whooping crane. Are there other blessings from the East?"

People shout out their words. Eyes closed, I feel these blessings moving back in time, reaching Uncle Bill and his father, and his father's father, and beyond. And when the last blessing is over, Jim says, "Nama Shiva!"

"We offer blessings from the South," says Jim. "The heat of noontime, the spark of fire within us, the howl of the coyote. Are there other blessings from the South?" And, when the words have ended, he says, "Ho!"

"We offer blessings from the West," says Jane. "The spectacular beauty of the purple sunsets, the wisdom of deep waters, the majestic music of the whale. Are there other blessings from the West?" After the community has spoken, Jane adds, "So be it!"

"We offer blessings on these men from the North," says Jane. "The unexpected allies of the forest, the resiliency and fertility of the earth, the stately roar of the lion. Are there other blessings from the North?" And, when they have finished, she says, "Amen."

"We ask all of these blessings to be within the hearts and souls of these men as they spiral into the next circle of their manhood," Jim says, concluding the ceremony. "And we ask the drummers to take these blessings now into the rhythms of sound and dance!"

The drumming begins. We form a dancing line, expanding our circle to include the audience now, and we are all dancing, one community. There is fire in the air, as the community seems to explode into joyous celebration.

The feast is at hand. The children are tired, and we are all hungry for nourishment. We are a community to be fed, to be reborn, to die, and to live again. People speak to me of their own renewal and sense of hope and energy. The evening has accomplished its purpose, as our program notes envisioned: "We hope that in our embodiment of the three stages of initiation, all of us can benefit at whatever stage of our journeys we find ourselves."

CHAPTER 17. Prozac and the Real Me

 ON A MILD SUMMER EVENING, I sit on the deck of a small café at the Omega Conference Center in upstate New York. A bright sliver of moon stares down. The long day winds to a close as I reflect on the dancing, conversations, quiet time in the vegetable garden, and walks about the grounds. This holistic health center, once a large Jewish family camp for escapes from New York City, has offered workshops for adults and families for some 20 years. Georgia and I are spending a week here. I'm focusing on the basics of Afro-Cuban dance and she on advanced drawing. The initiation dance in my backyard a few months ago emboldened me to seek out new dance experiences.

At the large Omega dining hall, along with some 200 people that week, we eat piles of salad, tofu, couscous, and vegetables. I begin to think more about diet, and I stop drinking caffeinated coffee. For years in my various offices, I have relied on caffeine and sugar to roll me through the day, perking up and then when the inevitable valley occurs, pouring in more caffeine or a snack to keep going.

Structured meditation is a new experience. My acolyte days in the chapel in downtown Jackson certainly had a meditative quality. Hearing words like *oblation* sounding in the silence offered some emotional relief, even safety, from the civil rights revolution outside the doors. But until this summer of 1993, I have never sat in an upright posture on a big pillow on the floor, focusing on my breathing, body, and mind in a structured way.

About 20 people show up each morning during the week, to sit with Bantu, a Burmese monk with shaved head and black, mysterious eyes. His voice melts across the little room. "Let your breath come in slowly," he says, like balm to a burn. "Feel your breath as it goes into your body." He talks a little, helps us settle into our breathing patterns, and mostly sits in silence, ringing a bell to signal the ending. Any mystique to the word *meditation* dissolves as I discover the peacefulness and challenge of simply sitting still for 30 minutes.

The crowd on the café deck is thinning. Georgia has returned to our little room with the shared bath. Thinking about Bantu and my dance class, I look again at the moon. Some shift occurs, almost palpably, as if a charge of energy is re-aligning a set of muscles. The bright curve of light draws me in, rather than the dark side of the moon. For years, I have heard and read of the value of focusing on the positive. Tom from my men's support group used to talk about Norman Vincent Peale and the power of positive thinking. And more recently, in the psychological and self-help literature, David Burns' *Feeling Good* and Martin Seligman's *Learned Optimism* made the case logically and forcefully. But I could not will this shift of attitude into my system or learn it from reading.

For some reason, tonight, I see this light now in a new way, on a quiet evening alone with my thoughts, hundreds of miles from home. The setting and stimuli at the conference center have contributed to this epiphany. But I wonder about another factor: How has 18 months of my Prozac regimen affected my view of the world?

SIX MONTHS LATER, ON JANUARY 1, 1994, I'm at an annual New Year's Day party at a friend's house. My conversation with a doctor from the Duke University Medical Center lengthens as the two of us finish with shrimp and sweets, sitting in a far corner of the room where some kids are playing pool. "What do you think about depression and antidepressants?" I ask, well into a far-ranging discussion of disease and public health. Not a psychiatrist or mental health specialist, he nevertheless has clear views.

"Depression is like diabetes," he says. "We know now that taking antidepressants is just like taking insulin. It's just a matter of regulating the brain's chemistry."

His comment hangs in the air as I notice my conflicting feelings of relief and anger. Hearing a doctor talk about the brain as an organ, like other body parts, that can be adjusted with medicine does help me feel like I am not a flawed person. But I also resent the simplistic suggestion that medicine is all that a person needs to move beyond depression. His arrogant style also unsettles me, as if he knows more from a casual view than I know after several years of living with this issue.

"Seems a little more complicated to me," I finally manage, holding back amidst the laughter at the pool table from a full-fledged counter argument.

"Well, maybe, but the antidepressants are the new key to this disease."

This view seems to be sinking deeper into the culture, reinforced by *Newsweek* cover stories on breakthroughs in brain chemistry research and new books on depression that emphasize medication. William Styron, the award-winning novelist, wrote bravely of a breakdown late in his life in *Darkness Visible*. Kathy Cronkite published a collection of interviews with notables who described their depression, including the late-night talk show host Dick Cavett and the intimidating *60 Minutes* reporter Mike Wallace. The emphasis in nearly every story is how medication saved the day, sometimes in combination with talk therapy.

Having well-known men speak about depression comforts me to a point, reinforcing this notion of brain chemistry that can be altered by drugs. But I know from my experience that moving through depression requires more than SSRIs and weekly conversations with a skilled listener. What about the power of positive thinking, a change of attitude? What about discovering the person that got stuck in childhood? What about creativity? I am more than a machine to be oiled with a pill.

Monday, January 3, 1994, two days after the conversation at the party, I have the day off from work. The kids are back in school, and I settle into my study, happy for time to reflect and rummage around my memory. I pull out little treasures from holiday visits and poke through my desk drawers, cluttered from too little use in recent years. I lay out papers and mementos on the large hearth that spreads the width of the room, fire crackling and warming the space.

I sit back and look at the photos and miscellaneous items that form a collage of sorts. In the center is a framed, black-and-white photo of Uncle

Bill, my namesake. He's about 22, just graduating from Georgia Tech in the late 1930s. He's a handsome, earnest man with a slight smile. In his lap he holds a book open, as if he's about to write the pages of his life. So sad, I think, that the notes that filled that book turned out to be records of hospital stays, without fond memories of family. My mind turns back on the previous year, starting with my dancing at Arts Together and the trip to Omega Institute. Fond memories of 1993 pile one upon the other.

The huge troll mask Dana made in a summer theater workshop pops into mind. It hangs in her room, along with an eerie and engrossing painting she made in her Art and Nature elective. She called it "Snake in the Night."

I pull out a church newsletter from the summer and see the little note from Lee, now 13. He described a retreat center in the mountains as "cold and foggy but still beautiful…a great self-esteem builder."

Flipping through random photos, I see the kids and Georgia with other friends, where we went for our fourth annual Thanksgiving holiday about an hour west of here at Recompense, the same retreat center where I've gone with the Men's Center Council. We had 16 at Thanksgiving dinner this year, ages 3 to 79. One of the photos shows Georgia with a camera around her neck, knee deep in the stream feeding into the Rocky River, recovering from a tilted canoe moment. She's laughing, happy that only her legs went in the water.

I stoke the fire before settling into the scrapbook from the initiation dance in the backyard. My next door neighbor captured moment after moment—my crane dance and other poses—and the other men as they took their turns on center stage. Another set of dance photos, not yet in a scrapbook, capture my role in a community dance performance in the fall performed at the Meredith College auditorium. The last time I performed on stage was 25 years ago, when I clogged before 2,000 Methodists at Lake Junaluska. This time at Meredith College, I jumped, skipped, and slid across the floor with three other adults as we pretended to chase a 10-year-old in a wheelchair.

My time alone winds down that day, with the children about to return home from school. I notice how good a year I have had, both within myself and with my family. But I also know I need to keep working at my healing regimens.

TO HELP ME UNDERSTAND MY DEPRESSION, I have tracked some
of the main times I've felt the worst. Often, my dark feelings have sur-
faced most frequently in the winter. Many Christmas seasons have been
challenging, when family rituals require more energy and attention. Also,
I have learned about the role that reduced sunlight can have on mental
health. Far northern countries with only a few hours of sunlight during
the winter have high depression and alcoholism rates. A literature is developing on this phenomenon, calling it seasonal affect disorder or SAD,
when too little light reaches a certain part of the brain and contributes to
low serotonin levels.

I discuss SAD and light therapy with Perilstein. We agree that using
my light box might do some good and certainly won't hurt. I have a home-
made box of 1 x 4's with two fluorescent bulbs attached at the top, put
together by Paul, a friend from the Men's Center. We have been discussing
for some months the role of depression in our lives, a matter-of-fact sharing of experiences and information—a big change from the once highly
charged topic I kept a secret. I've read some of the science that seems to
confirm the value of shining certain light frequencies just above the eyes.
Sitting and looking just below the light for 30 minutes a day seems to help
the brain counteract the effect of lower levels of sunlight.

"I don't feel like I need the box anymore," Paul says one day. "You
take it." And so, I bring it into my study for the winter, a three-foot-long
unpainted contraption that I pull out every morning before I go to work.
Sometimes, I put on the tape of Bantu I got at Omega, a guide through
a 30-minute meditation around the theme of "loving kindness." I sit in
my study on a big pillow, door closed, and look just below the light for 30
minutes, listening to Bantu guide me through my breathing with phrases
like, "May I be filled with loving kindness. May I be well."

IN *LISTENING TO PROZAC*, PETER KRAMER wrote that Prozac may
"only 'kick in' when [patients] are already psychologically and neurochemically on the mend." By the spring of 1994, I am clearly on the mend.
My life is so much better since Perilstein wrote my first prescription two
years ago. Therapy with him helped me understand my past, while Meade
and Daly gave me tools to move forward. The deep pleasure provided by

athleticism and clogging during my youth has resurfaced in the form of modern dance. I am learning about expressive arts with other men even while pulling off a dance ceremony honoring my midlife journey. I am talking about depression and Prozac with a few people, my embarrassment gone after singing with 35 other people, "I am on Prozac, there's no cause for shame."

Approaching my 47th birthday, I embrace my new hobby with both feet by discovering the Liz Lerman Dance Exchange. As a young, trained modern dancer, Lerman took her craft into nursing homes and elderly housing projects. She used exercises where the workshop participants told their life stories using shapes with their bodies. She then gathered movement and spoken phrases with members of her dance company, which she incorporated into performances, along with some of the workshop participants. "Any movement done with intention can be a thing of beauty," Lerman wrote in a slender book describing her process of using dance with non-dance communities.

Now, some 20 years after that beginning, Lerman basically does the same work, with performances at the American Dance Festival and other major venues under her belt. Besides working with non-trained dancers, the company includes dancers of all ages. During a week-long residency in Raleigh, the men from the Lerman Company come to my men's movement class at Arts Together. The two older men in the company in particular make a big impression on our class. One is a slim ex-military man who has learned dance in his later years, just like we are doing.

In the spring of 1994, Lerman returns to the area for another residency. One afternoon, she holds a workshop at a middle school for public school dance teachers. I know her company now and ask if I can attend. She agrees, and I join about 10 dance teachers. Her instructions at the workshop take me in an unexpected direction.

"First, we'll start with a little writing exercise, then add some movements," Liz says with her energetic and charismatic voice, penetrating but gentle at the same time. She is standing beside a desk in a small dance studio, her frizzy black hair a bit wild, like the emotions that can emerge in her work. "So, get settled in a place with your pencil and paper."

After we find our places, she says, "I want you to write down this beginning phrase: I come from a land of." She waits while we write it down. "Now, just continue with whatever story comes to mind right now. Don't worry about what comes out. Just free associate."

After just a moment, my story falls upon the page without interruption. "I come from a land that had a Civil Rights movement when I grew up." I write about the blood that was shed by the Freedom Riders on the buses that came through Alabama and into Jackson, and then scrawl out personal memories—getting my driver's license about the same time and taking my family's maid home not far from Millsaps College. I pour out phrases about the disconnection and hypocrisy I felt between race and the church, with its message of universal brotherhood. After about 10 minutes, she asks us to stop.

"Now look at what you've written and circle words that jump out at you. Whatever words grab your attention." She waits a few minutes to let us finish that part.

"Now, write the words you've circled down into a short phrase."

My phrase surprises me with its intensity. I was not planning to explore some difficult issue in the little workshop, which I squeezed into my work and family schedules. I came to learn her technique. But the words in front of me indicate my subconscious is ready for something more.

"I come from a land of blood," my phrase reads, "where any notion of God or Jesus is ludicrous when I take my maid home to her ramshackle house." Before I have time to ponder the power of the phrase, Liz is moving us into the movement phase.

"Now we'll put these words into a dance phrase. First, picture a place in the land you have written about, a very specific location, like a section of a yard or a room in a house."

She has us sketch the place quickly, very rough, just to get a few of the features of the space onto a page. I draw the patio at our house in Jackson, with the row of rose bushes, the basketball goal, and picnic table.

Now, she directs us through four movements. First, we are to move down a straight line, picking some line from the drawing. The next one, drawing on some other detail from the sketch, we are to change levels, taking our bodies down to the floor. Then, she says to play with the levels, perhaps rising back up or moving between levels, using another sketch detail. And, last, we are to use our head to accent some part of the drawing.

The dance teachers work quickly, building a simple movement phrase. Seeing that we are ready, she proceeds. "Now, I want you to put the written phrase into your dance."

She illustrates with a simple example, letting movements accent certain words, so that the body and story combine into a fluid visual and auditory expression. After about 10 to 15 minutes of practicing alone, we come back together. We talk about the experience a little, and then Liz says, "Let's see a few. Who wants to show their phrase?"

I hold back, since this workshop is really for dance teachers. Several of them show their phrases. Some are well trained dancers and extend into beautiful postures and extension, but the stories seem shallow, not taking advantage of how the body can accent the words. "Bill, do you want to go?" she says when it's clear there's time for me.

I move to the back right corner of the little staging area, take a deep breath, and perform my phrase. First, I walk down a diagonal to stage left, like the row of rose bushes on the edge of the driveway. While moving, I say, "I come from a land of blood," emphasizing "blood" with my last step near the little audience.

I pivot to the center and begin falling prone, body straight and extended, my hands at my chest. Just before landing, my arms break the fall and I say, "Where any notion of God …"

Then I lift my head and chest up and extend my arms and add, "and Jesus is ludicrous." Then I fall back down to the floor.

Now, I walk my hands towards my feet, arching my body up until I am standing again. I finish the phrase, "when I take my maid home to her ramshackle house." I accent the last words with a series of choppy nod-like notions with my head around a little circle. I hold the last shape a second and then go back to the group.

After a little silence, one of the others says, "Wow, that was really heavy."

"Yeah, I guess it was. I haven't thought about those things for a long time."

The afternoon is nearly over, and Lerman starts to wrap up. "I liked the power of the words and how the movement made them even stronger," she says to me. Then she turns to the group. "We all have profound stories to tell—teachers, middle schoolers, all of us. And, putting them to dance adds the artistic expression that can evoke some universal emotions for everyone."

Driving home, the words from my phrase rattle through my brain— God, ramshackle, ludicrous, and maid. I loved the exercise, how this set of words came up for me and then found their way into a movement phrase with such power, as I fell to the ground and rose back up. I don't understand the phrase but do know something is bouncing around now in my heart and thoughts.

I will need to come back to this, I tell myself as I turn the corner toward our house. *This is opening up some territory that I need to explore more deeply.*

In such workshops, time stands still for me. No worries cloud my vision or energy. The discovery process seems like I'm walking across vast continents, with so much to explore and to see and feel. Daily concerns about work and family fall away like layers of an onion. I feel like a little boy playing, and now with so many more ways to express myself than just clogging at Maggie Valley or playing tennis at Duke. That dwarf of a boy that I recognized as myself several years ago in Perilstein's office is growing up before my eyes.

Late in the spring, a brochure arrives in the mail announcing the program for the American Dance Festival or ADF, which begins early in the summer. This year, besides performances by modern dance companies and a school for aspiring dancers, it includes a week-long workshop on dance therapy. I am beginning to read about dance therapy, wondering if this is something I might pursue more rigorously. Still a small field compared to art therapy, it has evolved to include two main branches—working with hospitalized psychiatric patients and with a more mainstream population, using the wisdom of the body as a source of healing. I decide to go.

THAT SPRING OF 1994, MY WORK SEEMS less difficult and plodding. At my job at Family Health International, I take the lead on an issue of our quarterly magazine focusing on the theme of family planning and sexually transmitted diseases. This involves working with our Washington office, which coordinates the largest AIDS prevention project in the world, funded by the U.S. Agency for International Development. We are breaking new ground, synthesizing research from AIDS prevention efforts and conveying that information to a family planning audience. Also, that spring, maneuvering begins in our office to see who will get to attend the upcoming International Conference on Population and Development, to be held in Cairo, Egypt, the first time for such a meeting in a decade.

For two years, I have not thought of stopping the daily ritual of my Prozac pill. I have not told anyone at work that I take Prozac, including my boss, head of the information group. For an employee to travel internationally for the first time, I hear a rumor that the company requires a signed statement from a physician saying you are in good health, with a list of any medications you are taking. I am afraid to even check out this rumor, for fear that if I admit taking Prozac, I won't be allowed to go to Egypt. The trip to Cairo would be my first chance to leave North America since I returned from the Peace Corps in 1970. If I stop taking Prozac, I won't have to worry about it. I have not been seeing Perilstein on a regular basis. My energy level is high. All seems well. Maybe it's time to stop.

I also think about the upcoming dance therapy workshop as an opportunity not only to explore an avocation but to work on some difficult issue through the dance. The course is clearly designed as an introduction to the field, not as personal therapy. Even so, I feel that if I bring a specific issue to the workshop with me, I will get more out of the teaching techniques and perhaps experience some personal healing. I decide to explore my depression, especially the symbolic power that Uncle Bill has played in my life.

But how would Prozac affect this effort of focusing on depression and its connection with my Ratliff genes? I know from reading Kramer's book that the scientists don't know who the "real me" is—the one taking medication or the one who does not. It is as much a philosophical as a scientific question. Maybe through this dance therapy workshop, I can get some clarity. Maybe I can even alter my brain without the medication. Maybe

I can alter the kindling effect—where psychological stressors can trigger more frequent and more severe episodes of depression, due to progressive changes in the brain.

I decide that to explore the real sources of depression in me, I need to be functioning without the artificial changes that Prozac produces. I do not want the Teflon effect, the mind altered by modern medicine. I want the "real me."

Late that spring, I stop taking Prozac on my own, without consulting Perilstein. Like many men, I have not taken many medications in my life and do not know much about how medications in general work. I do understand that Prozac has a long life in the body and will take some time to clear out of the system. So I give it two months before the dance workshop in early July.

CHAPTER 18. Conversation with a Hawk

 IN JULY 1994, UNCLE BILL ARRIVES UNEXPECTEDLY in the week-long dance therapy workshop at ADF. "Go back 10 years," says Marcia Leventhal, the instructor. "You can pause at some event along the way if you wish," she says, "or go back exactly 10 years and be there with your body."

Nine workshop participants make shapes or move across the parquet squares that connect two large rooms. Now in the third day of the workshop, we have built cohesion, trust, and confidence. We start at 8 a.m., participating in a dance class at ADF, then work all day with Leventhal before attending an ADF performance at night.

"What did it feel like then, 10 years ago?" she asks rhetorically, as we move deeper into the exercise. "How did you move? Where are the stress points? What do you notice in your body?" She takes us back another 10 years, and then another.

"If you get to your infancy, decide whether you want to go back further into your family's psyche, before you were even born, or land at some year in your own life." The college students in the class nod, now with permission to play with their age. "Go back to the beginnings. See where your body movements come from if you like."

I gather shapes and movement phrases as I go, like I've learned from Liz Lerman and other teachers.

"Notice how you hold knowledge in your bodies," she says.

As I move back, memories dart through my body as if I am watching messages scroll down a computer screen. So far in the workshop, I have not focused consciously on depression, even though back in the spring I thought this might be a place to focus on its role in my body. Off of Prozac for several months, I have not gone into a tailspin. Quite the opposite. I feel energetic and bold in the workshop, trusting my body more and discovering more joy in expressing myself creatively through movement.

As I move back before my birth in 1947, I think of Carl Jung and his concept of the collective unconscious with its primal emotions and impulses that spring into each generation. Maybe a particular combination of magic, a spark of each self, arrives at a particular time and place, even choosing this life somehow. My linear thinking is dropping away as I spin back into time. What kind of spark came to me from this pool of life?

Leventhal moves through the room, encouraging us to linger wherever we land in time. "Just stay with where you are," she whispers to me, walking by in her bare feet.

Any sense of time floats further away. I find myself in a cave, or perhaps I am like a chick in the egg, trying to break out. Either way, I am exploring the edges, the rounded boundaries of a space that suddenly seems very real, with walls, like my primordial home. Images emerge in this time warp, and I begin to decorate the inside of the container, embracing it first rather than trying to break out of it. I want beauty here, no need to escape or find something else. I tilt my hands in small delicate movements, as if decorating a wall, recording my story in hieroglyphics. I tell a dark tale of an ancestor who appeared centuries ago, bringing his brain chemistry first to Uncle Bill and then to me. The person moving in this cave is not me but a primeval ancestor, a cave dweller. His drawings on the walls embody Uncle Bill, me, and all of our ancestors. Gradually, as I uncurl my long arms across this wall, a window appears in the cave. A rose vine climbs around the window, around the curve onto an outside wall and into the cave as well. I picture the rose bush at the edge of our real garden in Raleigh, not so far from the bamboo forest.

At last, Leventhal brings the exercise to a close, calling us gently back to the present, to our physical space on the floor, to our present personalities and bodies and age. She closes the afternoon session by warning us that we might not be ready to drive or deal with the real world outside. "Take it easy when you leave," she says. "Your psyche may still hold part of you in a distant place. Give yourself some time to move back into your present body."

I gather up my bag of clothes, still somewhat in a trance, nod to a few classmates without speaking, and walk outside. I am not ready yet even to put on my glasses, to bring the world back into focus. I sit for a few minutes outside the dormitory, noticing the large magnolias between the semi-circular driveway to the building and the pale sandstone brick wall near the street. Feeling connected somewhat to the present world now, I begin walking toward the small shopping area that borders the campus to get some supper.

Still without my glasses on, I look at the giant oaks in the field that stretches past the old stone building housing our studio. Suddenly, I stop and try to focus on a large creature on a low branch in the nearest tree. I cannot make out the details and dig about in the bag for my glasses. With clearer focus now, I see a large bird of some type with something hanging beneath it.

I walk closer, drawn by the bird as if it is some kind of guide. The creature opens its wings now, like a gesture. I stop and take a long look. Now, I can see the large hawk, holding some small animal in its talons, maybe a squirrel or rabbit. I walk several more steps, past the stone wall by the sidewalk and into the field. The bird takes off slowly but goes only a short distance to the next oak. It turns back and looks at me, perhaps signaling me to follow. Maybe the bird is simply keeping its distance from an intruder. But I move slowly his way and sense something more. The hawk stays for a moment as I approach and then glides to the next tree. We continue this dialogue, until at last, it flies away, conversation over, its prey dangling beneath.

Over the dinner break, I try to make sense of this encounter. Was it a messenger? How did this guide connect to the images I created with my dance? What about the cave and the drawings I imagined as I moved through the timelessness of the exercise? I reflect about my cave drawings and liken them to depositing the brain cells that came first to Uncle Bill and then to me. This biochemistry engages me. Uncle Bill brought this seductive power to me in the dream in my old office when his black cavernous eyes invited me in, but I resisted. Today, I sit alone with my light supper. Maybe I have stripped the rest of that dark world away from my true self and left it on those cave walls.

This hawk had a purpose in this conversation. "Uncle Bill's depression no longer lives in you but is on the walls of the cave," it seemed to be saying. "I will carry that depression away for you, from this cave, and will take it back to its source." I'm not a mystical person and have never had an experience of seeing an angel or hearing God speak to me. This conversation, though, feels like I was in that neighborhood.

After two years of taking Prozac, I believe now my brain is working in a new way, my serotonin re-uptake inhibitors unstuck, electrical energy jumping the synapses more easily. Today, perhaps my brain was altered in a complementary way. In the creation of my dance backwards in time, my genetic predisposition flowed backwards into this ancient symbolic cave. And then, a visitor from the spirit world took these deposits back to the great boiling pot of humankind. I get up from dinner, smiling, unsure what I really think or feel but happy with this proposition of rebirth and restoration of my brain cells.

AS THE SUMMER OF 1994 MOVES ON, day-to-day life involves more than symbolic hieroglyphics and messengers from beyond. I make preparations for going to Egypt, my attendance at the International Conference on Population and Development, or ICPD, approved by senior management at FHI. This will be my first trip to a developing country since India. While my life has changed a lot since that year after college, emotions from the Jabalpur journey are bubbling up.

When Rick and I used to sit on Mrs. Raza's verandah, we would think of the USAID workers as out of touch with the real India. Now, I am traveling for a USAID-funded project and will stay in a nice hotel. I feel nostalgia for that time in India but also relief that I have more focus to my work. I have confidence now in middle age that I can use my skills in whatever assignments will unfold over the 10-day event.

I feel proud of my growth and ready for this step in the public health field. But sorting out the parallels with my India year takes emotional energy that is challenging. For example, I begin to think of the trip as a new transition, functioning as an initiation process in the public health field, like the Peace Corps year served as my transition into independent adulthood. The event merits that kind of reflection. Between work and family, however, I don't have much time for pondering such issues.

The ICPD signals a paradigm shift in the family planning field, which only blossomed in the 1960s on the heels of the "Pill," the newly invented oral contraceptive. The conference is an official United Nations event, with a document to be debated by delegations from more than 160 countries. More than a year of preparatory meetings, organized primarily by women's advocacy groups, have triggered unprecedented international attention on the ICPD. In the draft document, the old vocabulary of "population control" has shifted to a new term, "reproductive health," emphasizing women's empowerment and choice. A parallel advocacy conference will be held where scores of international nongovernmental organizations like FHI and global advocates such as Jane Fonda will present information and calls for action.

At FHI, I am part of a small global fraternity of writers who think daily about the very large issues related to world population growth. But during the ICPD, reporters will expand our field to front page news. As a bonus, I get a call from the World Health Organization inviting me to participate in a pre-conference session among youth advocacy groups, which will develop a statement to the meeting on the needs of young people. I have recently worked with this WHO team. This opportunity sweetens the trip but means I leave a few days earlier. Plus, I've already arranged to stop off in England for two days of vacation on the way home.

I will be away from the family for nearly three weeks, longer than ever before. The children will be back in their same schools, starting the 8th and 5th grades, but the early weeks of a school year always bring surprises. Georgia will have to handle this alone; she also teaches art now at a local college. She will have to get the kids to the bus, walk the dog, cover my one-day a week after school, wash the dishes, and handle any unforeseen house problem—all areas I usually handle. The kids will chip in, and Georgia is resourceful. Many single parents handle such duties, but this will be new for us. We've worked hard at sharing family responsibilities as much as possible. I tell myself that many of my colleagues travel regularly and work out such family issues. Still, I feel conflicted and guilty about leaving her with these extra duties while I fly off to an exciting work assignment.

In August, a few weeks before I'm scheduled to leave, we have a vacation scheduled at the beach with Georgia's extended family. This is our last break before school starts, both for the children and for Georgia. At the beach, I need a full pail of energy for the children, cousins, family dinners, and my wife. Instead, I feel tired, not eager to join into games with our children and their cousins. I want to be by myself, to reflect on the summer and my upcoming trip.

Building sandcastles or checking crab nets at the sound requires more energy than I can easily muster. But taking my kids to our favorite beach restaurant, just the three of us, is fun. We're away from the larger collection of personalities and returning to a familiar spot. I find myself laughing, reminiscing about our previous trips here. We compete to see who can find the most unusual of the old license plates from around the world, which decorate the exposed rafters. But back with the extended family, I withdraw emotionally, even when I manage to smile and offer a piece of the conversation. I feel detached, with a familiar numbness starting to move in. And, I do not have Prozac to help.

THE EGYPT TRIP GOES WELL. A daily exercise routine of yoga stretches and swimming keeps me centered and present. Working at the FHI information booth and covering meetings for future articles in our magazine keep me busy, along with some sightseeing and networking with conference participants. I am stimulated to the brim, and any internal worries have no space to surface. Themes from India, my first international trip, surface often—adobe and mud houses, dusty streets, limitations of language, unfamiliar foods, protocols, manners, a very hot sun. But living in a nice hotel with a structured work day, so different from the long, lingering days in Jabalpur, keeps the similarities at a generic level. I do not have time to explore the more personal, unconscious patterns of how this trip may be affecting me in ways similar to being in India.

On my stop in England, I drive around for two days, braving the "wrong side of the road" to see cathedrals, Stonehenge, and village cafes.

Standing in the misty afternoon at Stonehenge, a double rainbow appears over the adjacent sheep fields. I breathe deeply and marvel at the beauty and history, and how this moment is flowing through me. I find a delightful bed and breakfast and join an elderly couple to walk about some off-the-beaten-track spots. So much fun, but I also miss Georgia. I feel enthralled but lonely at the same time.

I remember the carefree summer in college when I traveled through Europe with my three friends. We found a place to sleep on a moment's notice or slept in our rented Volkswagen van. But I also recall days on that trip when I walked behind my buddies across European cobblestones, an unexplained melancholy settling over me at a moment's notice. This stopover in England is mimicking at a psychological level that summer trip to Europe, just as the longer stay in Egypt reprised my year in India.

Returning now, almost a quarter-century after moving from Jabalpur to Boston, I think about the three stages of initiation, especially the third, the return to the community as a transformed person. After the initiation dance in my backyard, I have been reflecting on the concept of initiation as a way to view all transitions, from one life stage to another. When I returned from India at 23, I did not receive the blessings of the third stage of initiation, as we did in the backyard dance. In Boston, no community honored my transformation to manhood after the Peace Corp, and I fell into a deep depression. The challenge of the draft board is what revived me, not a transformation of my spirit.

This return in 1994 is different. Georgia, Lee, and Dana meet me at the airport and talk at once as we rush home and gather in the living room. I pull out gifts from my trip and they laugh, modeling long Egyptian t-shirts. Georgia has the same relaxed smile I remember from our fondest times over the years. She is relieved that I'm home.

Naturally, the excitement of the ICPD, the pyramids, the adobe huts, and the rainbows at Stonehenge mellow as I settle back into a routine at home and work. Without external excitement, I have to cope with a daily routine that begins to seem like drudgery. Chores, work, chores, sleep, and repeat the whole thing again. I look for opportunities to perk up my life, knowing now the power for me of dancing and of creative work.

I have the opportunity to coordinate a post-Cairo report by

nationally known journalists at the American Public Health Association annual meeting. Introducing reporters from National Public Radio and national newspapers is thrilling, hearing these top level reporters reflect on their experience covering the ICPD. But, with Cairo and post-Cairo over, I have to return to routine tasks, slogging through science articles for my research. I am grinding slower and slower to a halt at work. Because the magazine appears quarterly, I can get by with slow spells, if I work intensively to make the deadlines at the end.

To help me plug along, one day at a time, I find a helpful reading from James Hillman, the Jungian psychologist and writer, who worked with Bly at my first week-long men's conference. We want so much from work and make it a problem, Hillman explains. "I have a fantasy, for example, that I have a farm, and it doesn't matter whether I'm correcting proofs or writing footnotes or reading some tiresome paper," he writes. "I have to feed the chickens and hoe the potatoes and chop the wood and do the accounts and pull the weeds. And every one of those jobs is necessary, and none is more important than the other one."

With work going slowly, I draw four boxes, slanted so that they looked to me like fields to be planted. Each day, before I go home, I draw wiggly lines in one of the boxes representing the progress I made that day on my articles. Driving home, I'm grateful I'm not at a newspaper and don't have to churn out stories every day. I'm grateful to Hillman for his image and the idea that daily work does not always have to be exciting, like traveling to Egypt.

I have a chance to express myself in other ways too. I go with Dana's junior Girl Scout troop as one of the parents on a camping trip. The leaders want the girls to have some group morning activity, and I suggest simple stretches. They think it's a great idea. Standing in the misty fall morning, the girls and parents lean over toward their toes. The routine mixes simple yoga postures and athletic stretches. That night, at a small concert by local musicians at the park amphitheater, I lead the girls through a spontaneous square dance. The dance line fits clearly into the evening activities. All the girls and parents love it, and even Dana reluctantly dances along smiling with her dad. She cringes a little, but at least I'm not doing the crane dance. Walking back to the tents, I remember how much I like to dance and engage others in doing that as well—and see the impact on people's spirits.

WEEKEND CAMPING TRIPS and tricks to make it through my work day help. But they cannot disguise a deeper pattern that has returned to my thinking. I begin to reflect more on what Peter Kramer called the kindling effect, where smaller stresses trigger a familiar response from the brain and the serotonin re-uptake process gets interrupted. With no Prozac at work to counter the effect—and no hawks flying my way anymore—I'm in trouble. I wonder if what I felt at the beach before going to Egypt was part of this kindling thing. Now that the trip and aftermath are over, I notice long-familiar symptoms and signs virtually every day: a desire to be alone, a lack of patience at home, and a lack of energy at work.

I feel frustrated with these patterns. Why haven't all my efforts taken me beyond depression? I have used Prozac and worked with Perilstein, Meade, and others. I have discovered dance, connected with my past through movement, and held the initiation dance. Still the patterns appear. With the frustration, ironically, I also feel strangely energized. I now know what I'm dealing with—and do not fear it. I feel uncomfortable and restless going through the day, but I have more tools to understand and address this return of my depression. I've always written things down to at least record what's going on in my life. Sometimes, my journal notes help me understand things as well. As I begin to record this return of old patterns, I find myself more of an observer, a learner. I decide to give these reflections another form, just to see what happens. I pretend that I am talking with Dr. Perilstein, my psychiatrist, and start a series of journal entries addressed to him. I haven't seen him for nearly nine months, since he wrote my last Prozac prescription.

OCTOBER 12:

It seems time to get back in touch with you. Maybe I'll be in to see you soon, maybe start to take Prozac again. Even if I do neither, the impulses to do both are strong, so I need to sort these out in writing—going beyond the ruminations in my head and on my walks and jogs.... Part of the nosedive feels like symptoms of depression—low self esteem, lack of confidence, irritability, some sleep disorders, having to work very hard to see the joy in everyday life. I use lots of techniques to help me stay focused in the present: a daily reading from a 12-step book for men, jogging and chanting in the morning, stretching and dancing regularly, writing and ...

Georgia says I don't have energy for the family, although it's coming back somewhat.... From her point of view, she's been running
the family [alone] for a month and a half. In large part, I think she's
right. So, one side of me—the guilty, logical side—feels I should
start taking Prozac again. This will give me the energy I need to see
the daily routines in a more positive manner. I can cope with the
demands of my job, deal with my children in a kinder and more
even-handed way, and be more present and supportive of my wife.

I see from my journal that my nosedive has some positive benefits.
I can see some of the things in my life that I don't like. I realize that I
am resisting taking Prozac for fear it will smooth over this restlessness,
something fundamental that I need to change. Maybe the causes of my
unhappiness are appropriate—even my sadness, and yes, depression.
Maybe what I need to do is make some fundamental changes rather than
medicate my sadness. I know, above all, this sadness is not black and
white: medication is good, medication is bad. Sadness is neurotic, sadness
is appropriate.

OCTOBER 13:
Last night, I woke up at 2:30 and lay there until about four. Then got
warm milk and read the ADF history, which put me to sleep. Then
I had a dream.

I am driving with Georgia and an old man in the car. The road gets
more narrow until it's soft, very soft mud. Once, I manage to keep
on the slope of mud and back into the main path. Then, I find that
the road is closed altogether, the mud sinks down to railroad tracks.
We enter a railroad-type house, and then we find ourselves in a line
of people. It becomes a circular path; we're not first anymore, part
of a mass.

An official/policeman tells us to go down to the street and wait
near the housing project. It appears that it's near where we started.
Instead of waiting there, the old man takes us through a gate,
where there are intricate gargoyles—cupids intertwined, old men,
gods and goddesses. At one point, he opens a door and behind it
is another door carved magnificently with more heads. Then the
alarm goes off.

I see myself as the old man. Will I still be sitting in the car, getting stuck in mud, circling about, when I'm old? Or will I take these directions from the official guide and open new doors to gargoyles of gods and goddesses?

In the following weeks, journal entries are mostly about problems with my work, often juxtaposing my discontent there with the joy I feel when dancing. And, I focus on my efforts to be a more assertive and confident father. Each moment seems complicated, with so many layers to address.

OCTOBER 19:
If I go back on Prozac, it will smooth over my anxiety levels, give me more energy for everyday tasks with the children and at home. On the other hand, it seems that being in this better spirit also prevents the darker sides from surfacing, specifically whether to continue being a journalist indefinitely.

OCTOBER 25:
I realized once again how many good things there are about my job. Freedom and flexibility, not to mention the good it might do and the fact that some of the tasks themselves are satisfying, even fun, once I get into them.

I am cycling down to another level of depression, this time dealing more with work identity than relationships. I am more aware of my feelings and the symptoms of depression than in earlier episodes. I allow myself down time at work and home, without obsessing about a poor performance or less than a perfect day with my kids. I am less withdrawn, less numb, and less irritable. But I do lack energy for action. I plod along, putting one foot in front of the other. Throughout the fall, I stay engaged with the family, even getting them to participate in a community dance project with me. And, when I am in such a project, not only does the schedule get busier, but I get happier, especially with the family involved.

The theme of the project is families, and we join several other groups in an opening sequence of moves that shows aspects of play and chores and family life. I'm delighted that Georgia joins in, along with the kids, a true family ensemble. And, I negotiate with the kids to be in another scene with me.

"I'll do it if Rosebud can be in it too," Lee says.

"Yeah, so will I," says Dana.

So we choreograph a cameo appearance by our dog, working with my friend John. The first show in the two-night stand, Dana has a 102 degree temperature. But she still runs on stage, as John and I catch her and then Lee, circling about faster and faster until their feet leave the ground.

The rehearsals and performances and party at the end are so much fun, pure joy. I don't have to leave my family for a men's conference or dance class to have fun. I can do it with my family. As my concrete activities feel more integrated, so does my emotional health. The separate categories, where I put my emotions on hold in order to work, are at least in my awareness.

I also put together a dance based on the Leventhal workshop and call it "Conversation with a Hawk." It's a trio, with a bass player from the N.C. Symphony who's in the church and our wonderful pianist playing as I dance. This creative impulse, to put experiences into some kind of artistic expression, carries great power for me. Mostly, this joy comes when I am away from work. The letters in my journal to Perilstein help. Also, I visit a career counselor named Temple. But my energy remains low.

One day at Temple's office, we're discussing options for career aptitude tests I might take. I'm hoping he can help me think about new career paths or maybe a marketing plan for a freelance business. Then, Temple looks up and stops me.

"You're depressed," he says. "Bill, you're depressed. You need to deal with your depression before you continue with this." I have not discussed my depression with Temple. I am surprised it's so obvious. Another journal entry is also revealing.

NOVEMBER 8:
Each article at work does seem like a long trek, not like a whirling dance that brings me closer to God. I wonder what the whirling dervishes do all year to make a living, to cope with depression every day—does the Rumi poem help them?
Today, like every other day, I wake up empty and scared.
Don't go into your study and begin reading.
Stand beneath the tallest tree and sing and dance.

I adapted the last line in the poem to my morning runs! But there's a long day ahead, with each passing hour like a drip of Chinese water in many respects. I focus on the water as if it were the bubbling mountain stream in Madison County, surrounded by rhododendron, with Burnett walking beside me, standing beside me in his peacefulness and organic wholeness with the land.

The characters and images from past years fall onto the page like manna. I look up from my letter to Perilstein and picture Burnett in his 80s, walking with me across his mountain land in western North Carolina. I smile, remembering the regular visits we had for several years, and I think about the stories I've been reading by Wendell Berry, about characters like Burnett.

Maybe Wendell Berry does have it straight. The challenge is ultimately to find a way to connect with the land where you have chosen to stay—more than to accomplish a piece of writing or some other task that can be catalogued as your duty while on earth.

I now think about my condition as chronic, low-grade depression, with stress triggering symptoms that are less dramatic than suicide or chronic absence from jobs or lying in bed much of the day. I keep going, but carry along with me intense ruminations and obsessive analyzing of work issues. Making major decisions is difficult, as I lose confidence in my intuition. A dull preoccupation with myself hovers, even when ostensibly focusing on some other task. My attention always seems divided, and I rarely experience fully the details of life, except when rehearsing or performing a scene for a dance. Then, I am absorbed in the moment, just like a basketball game or clogging at Maggie Valley as a kid.

NOVEMBER 10:
It seems that I must start Prozac again. Last night at tutoring, waiting for the kids, I took a nosedive, mostly over work. It seems I'm becoming preoccupied with how hard my job is and how difficult it is to get motivated for it.

I appreciate the dependability of the job to support the family, the flexibility it allows, and the contribution it makes to an important public health issue. But despite all this, maybe I should make a gradual plan to change work.

Maybe I need to see you to get those juices flowing again. Figuring out this career thing is extremely challenging. So I can't be dealing with depression at the same time. That makes sense. All the best, my friend.

Two weeks later, I walk into the familiar office, where I haven't been for about 10 months, and start talking to Perilstein in person. By the dark days of December, not only am I meditating in front of the light box, I am on Prozac again.

I feel both relief and power. How much of this shift comes from the process of taking action versus the chemical-induced serotonin uptake? The answer does not concern me now, as I feel more present, more energetic, and more capable with my days.

CHAPTER 19. Mindful of Segregation, Work, and Joy

"ALLOW THIS TO BE A TIME IN WHICH we set aside the usual mode in which we operate, that of more or less constant doing, and switch to a mode of non-doing, a mode of simply being." The calm voice flows through my study at home, the cassette tape sitting beside the cold fireplace on this January morning of 1995. It's still dark outside, and the children are just starting to wake up for school. I have just enough time to sit through the 45-minute meditation tape.

"Becoming aware of our being, as we allow our body to become still," the gentle male voice continues. "Just bringing our attention to the fact that we're breathing."

The tape is familiar to me now after several months of daily practice. I have been alternating through the four-tape series that goes with the stress reduction program created by Jon Kabat-Zinn at the University of Massachusetts Medical School. The two yoga tapes are my favorites. I stretch slowly under his detailed instructions, always focused on breathing. The stretches are similar to what I do in dance classes, but with more focus on the breath and awareness of my body. I like the full body scan, too, where I lie flat on the floor. Today, I settle into the sitting meditation tape, the reminders from the smooth voice like rhythmic waves at the ocean.

"Now, of course, you will find that from time to time, your mind will wander off into thoughts, fantasies, anticipations of the future, worrying thoughts of the past, memories, whatever. But when you notice that your attention is no longer here, no longer on your breathing, and without giving yourself a hard time, just intentionally escort your focus, your attention back to your breathing, picking up wherever it happens to be, on an in-breath or out-breath."

Maybe 10 minutes into the tape, my left knee begins to hurt, the stretch on the tendons interfering with awareness of my diaphragm. I am sitting cross-legged on thick pillows on the floor. The cushions create an angle from my hips down to the hard floor under the rug. While stretching has improved my flexibility, I am far from being able to sit flat on the floor comfortably, much less able to cross one leg on top of the other in a lotus position.

"Now, as you observe your breathing, you may be finding that from time to time, sensations from your body come into the field of your awareness," he continues, after what seems like a long silence. "Some discomfort or agitation, which may be quite intense from time to time."

I smile hearing this familiar phrase from a voice that has become a daily friend. When the pain gets too intense, overwhelming my focus on the breath, I have two options, as he has taught me on the tape. I can shift to some new position to relieve the intensity, while being aware of the intention before I actually move. Or I can stay with the intensity further, "totally experiencing what your body is feeling, and responding by opening and softening rather than tensing. So that even within the intensity, you may find stillness and acceptance."

I breathe into the knee, identifying the exact spot an inch or so from the kneecap, on the inside of my left leg. I expand the focus of my breath to include this awareness of pain, imagining the breath going down to the cellular level. I picture the oxygen going into the actual cells causing the pain, bringing relief. The dull ache does subside for a time, how long I don't know. Time slows down in meditation.

Then the pain returns, more intensely. I decide to shift my knees and begin to move slowly, observing each part of my legs as I shift. My right leg moves away from my body, allowing my left leg to move out, stretching the knee and relieving the pain. I observe all the sensations of my right leg, as I move it back, now inside the left, the heel against my inner thigh.

I slowly move my left leg back now so that it goes across the right. And, I settle in for the next stage of the meditation.

The tape takes me through a focus on sounds next, not looking for sounds but simply being aware of what's there. I notice the deep drone of the trucks on the four-lane beltline around Raleigh, about a mile away. Birds are beginning to sing. The toilet flushes upstairs, water running down through the pipe hidden in the walls two rooms away. The coffee pot gurgles in the kitchen. I'm tempted to go fill my cup but instead notice my breath and stay. The tape turns now for its last segment to thoughts, simply noticing what goes through my mind.

The long silences allow plenty of space for my mind to wander. But after several months, I find the process easier, observing my thoughts just as I do my breathing, in and out, like an ocean wave, coming in and going out. Kabat-Zinn advises not to reject or embrace the thoughts, just to observe them. And, always, come back to the breathing, rather than riding the wave of thoughts that can carry me into wanting to make lists for work or the family.

The 45-minute tape ends just as I need to get breakfast ready for the kids. The closing words are my favorite. "And, as the tape finishes, recognizing that you have spent this time intentionally nourishing yourself by dwelling in this state of non-doing, in this state of being, intentionally making time for yourself to be who you are. And you might want to just congratulate yourself for taking the time and the energy to do this. And, to allow yourself the occasion to do it on a regular basis and to nourish yourself in a deep way. And to allow the benefits of this practice to expand into the active expression of your life in every domain."

I smile as I unfold my stiff legs and slowly walk to the kitchen. I feel grateful to Georgia for introducing me to this program. She gave me the set of cassette tapes and companion book, *Full Catastrophe Living* by Kabat-Zinn. She had used them for a time herself with a group but was ready to pass them on to me. The long subtitle intrigued me: "Using the wisdom of your body and mind to face stress, pain, and illness." That certainly sounded appealing. Stress contributes to my depression, but I am still trying to understand how to manage it.

The morning rush is on now, Lee getting off early enough to walk the three long blocks to middle school. We go together for about the first half, through an isolated stretch that doesn't seem safe enough for him alone, unfortunately. Then, back home quickly to get Dana to the bus stop, now in her last year of elementary school. Georgia will leave to teach before I get back from the bus stop today.

Kabat-Zinn calls the approach mindfulness. The term offers a way of standing in the repetition of tasks at work, in the unpredictability of my children, in the stress of a busy schedule, and the demands of being married. Mindfulness does not give me answers, but it suggests a way of living. I am learning to accept things as they are in the present moment, to enter each experience as if it's new, to cultivate patience, and to be non-judging toward myself. I am nourishing myself right here in my house, as much a part of my day as going to work or washing the dishes or tossing a ball with the kids. Each of those activities—all activity—can be a form of meditation, if done mindfully, without my thoughts wandering away from the present moment.

I savor these conceptual notions, studying the book with the title that suggests that dealing with depression is not so bad, only a certain life of catastrophe to be lived fully. The chapters flow into me like cool waters—attitudes towards mindfulness, descriptions of various types of meditation, glimpses of wholeness. Perhaps the nugget of the book that sticks with me intellectually is the basic notion of fight or flight, to re-act or respond. Whatever comes my way, I can observe my feelings, my thoughts, my temptation to withdraw or get overwhelmed or whatever. I can respond with mindfulness.

AS WINTER MOVES TOWARD SPRING, I see a notice for auditions for community members for "The Athlete's Project." The David Dorfman Dance Company, a modern dance group that has evolved from the Liz Lerman tradition of using community members, will incorporate local athletes into a dance with the six-person company. It will be the featured dance in two performances at North Carolina State University. With its promise of combining my new love of dance with my history in sports, the audition notice draws me in like a love letter. I can't wait to be a part of it. The audition goes well, and I join 19 other community members for three weeks of rehearsals.

I am standing backstage now at Stewart Theater, waiting for David Dorfman to call me into the group doing the core movement phrase for the dance. Several others have not yet been integrated into this group dance segment either. I feel capable of performing the athletic moves required, which involve quick rolls over the back and moving feet through the arms into a kind of hip-hop motion. Dorfman directs a new small group to run on stage, to perform a part of the phrase and then move in unison with those already on stage. The entries are tricky, demanding that each dancer roll into the unison phrase at the right moment, so that the group cohesion remains tight.

We are about halfway through our three weeks of rehearsals, six days a week, a major commitment for me and others with jobs and family. Two cross country runners are older than I am, but the rest are much younger, including an Olympic soccer player, dance teachers, a body builder, and a female martial artist who cleans houses for a living. Dorfman keeps working on the segment, with groups of threes or fours. Finally, only the two distance runners and I are left.

Watching the groups work through the phrase, I start withdrawing. I have learned to recognize this coping mechanism, which keeps me numb from any feeling. Noticing the pattern, I breathe in and concentrate on my breath. I watch my breath go deep into my belly. "Breathe in, my breath goes deep," I say, remembering the meditation tape. I notice my thoughts, which are about feelings. My bare feet feel the hard wooden floor. A slight sweat from the warm-up lingers under my arms.

"Okay. Let's go through it again," Dorfman says briskly, walking onstage. "Last group, come in one four-count earlier. Let's see how that works. So you come in on the roll. Got it?" I move back as the two groups who will enter stage left crowd into the wing.

I feel left out, not appreciated. Other feelings bubble up—resentment, self-pity, not good enough. I breathe into this unease, not judging it or wanting to do anything with it, but noticing the familiar feelings. My breath goes into my belly, where it seems to lodge into a memory. Breathing out, a feeling of sadness seems to sink through me. The memory comes into focus, and I keep breathing, alert to the thoughts as I watch the rehearsal.

The high school basketball game my senior year is vivid and clear. I was sitting on the end of the bench. (Breathing in, my breath goes deep.) After starting the first several games, the coach benched me, playing guys ahead of me from the football team that he coached through the fall. I have just moved to Nashville from Jackson for my senior year. My confidence was sagging and so was my playing time. I felt like a failure and considered quitting and playing in a city league, where I could get more playing time and have more fun.

Dorfman keeps rehearsing the group without seeming to notice me. Breathing in, I stay calm, alert even as the memory dashes through my awareness. My friend Jim encouraged me to continue on the high school team even though he said I was getting a raw deal from the coach and should to be playing. I stuck with the team the whole season. All of this flashes through my mind in a few seconds, and I notice now the pride I felt in sticking with the team, as well as the pain of a poor senior season. I breathe again, watching Dorfman put these athlete-dancers through this creative practice session.

Standing there on the sidelines, I breathe into the pain of the substitute's role, in the disappointments of a new team my senior year, missing out on the predictable starting role I would have had in my old school. Sports gave me an outlet then, from the transition of moving before my senior year and the race tensions that were escalating in Jackson and Nashville. Retreating into sports was harder on the bench, and the season reinforced my tendency to get numb, not know what I was feeling. Jim helped me get through the year. I smile, remembering his goofy smile, as we trudged through our senior year of high school together.

As I breathe, still in the wings of the stage, everyone rehearsing but me and the two older runners, images dash across my mind's eye. I see others who are left out—teenagers ostracized from groups for no apparent reason, often in a mean-spirited way. I feel their pain and mine. I see those who were not selected to be on a ball team. I feel their disappointment. I see those who are always chosen and feel pressure to perform, often forgetting the person beneath the performer. I feel blessed just standing here breathing, being alive, capable of running and jumping, being willing to try. Instead of being numb to resentments or self-pity or the pain of others, I simply breathe and notice these thoughts and feelings.

FOR ONE SCENE IN THE DANCE, we all introduce ourselves, much like an announcer does before a game begins. We give our name, hometown, and sport. I say, "William Finger, Jackson, Mississippi, basketball, tennis." And, then we say three words, each capturing something about our past, our present, and our future. I settle upon *segregation* for my past, *work* for the present, and *joy* for the future. During an early rehearsal, an exercise to help us pick our words leads to strong feelings surfacing. I feel obsessed with finding more clarity with work, meaning more than a job to make money. I want to embody my passions for life in the way I spend my time. *Joy* holds some hope, knowing that I am slowly but steadily moving in a direction where experiencing the joy of life is becoming more accessible.

Dorfman asks us to develop a phrase or routine as a way to make our introduction, either alone or with someone else. I work with Will, the body builder in the group. With a weight lifter's broad frame and rippling muscles, he competes in body sculpting contests. He is in his thirties with closely cropped hair and huge biceps that ripple across deep brown skin. I stand taller by several inches, lanky and pale-skinned, with longish, graying hair. Our physical differences are as dramatic as our racial divide, but we find a way to accent our common ground.

We run at each other from opposite sides of the stage, meeting in the middle with our arms against each other's shoulders. We take a huge leap up and yell as we land with a loud thud, locking our grasp at arms' length like two mighty warriors about to engage in a life-and-death struggle. We push at each other hard, as if trying to gain an advantage. Then we let our arms slip off the other's shoulders and slide our bodies past each other, as if barely missing a collision. We have to practice to get our balance to work with our disparate body strengths and sizes.

A gentle teddy-bear of a muscle man, Will hesitates to push hard, thinking he will break my skinny frame. With a wiry strength and in good shape, I urge him to push harder so I can push hard too in a counterpoint. But he can easily push me over if he exerts his full strength. We have to share our weight in a delicate but exuberant balancing pose, acting as if we're at full exertion. We finally find the spot where we can push to the edge of balance so that when we part and streak to the opposite side of the stage, we can barely keep our footing. We appear to the audience as if about to fall. When I dance in such a phrase, I am totally mindful, not because I am thinking of a particular yoga stretch or meditation technique, but because all of my body and mind is connected in the moment. Without being fully aware of mind and body, Will and I would collide or fall down.

After the first separation and run past each other to the other side of the stage, we run at each other again. We jump and lock arms, this time without the yell, and after struggling again in our push, we drop our arms and fall to the floor. We roll in opposite directions and then stand before the two mikes at the front of the stage. I speak first, my name, hometown, and three words. Then Will introduces himself.

During one rehearsal, I ask Dorfman if I can say something to the group. I feel an urge to share a bit of history. Many of the athletes are young and never experienced segregated schools or buses or restaurants. "I lived through segregation in Jackson," I say to the group, most catching their breath from practicing their own introductory phrases. "That's why I chose the word *segregation* for the past. I just wanted to let you all know that right here in Raleigh and of course in the deep South, we all went through it, all of us older ones." I gesture toward the runners in the corner of the stage. "I just want to thank David for letting us get these important personal and social themes into his dance. It's been a great help to me to get to dance with Will and include this theme." Many of the dancers nod an acknowledgment to me. Then Dorfman gets us back to work.

The performance goes great, exhilarating as we run through all of our steps, 11 women and 8 men from the community group, with the 6 members of the Dorfman company. Dorfman eventually works me into the full group doing the athletic anchor phrase for the dance. And, Will and I hit our timing perfectly.

"There were many wonderful touches throughout this aerobic work," reviewer Linda Belans wrote in the Raleigh *News and Observer.* "Will

Robinson, the muscles-to-die-for body builder squares off with long, stringy William Finger." I look up from the morning paper, basking in my moment of glory, beyond the dance with Rosebud and the family, or at church on a Sunday morning.

Then, I look at the clock and realize I've got to hustle or the children will be late to school. The Dorfman project was great fun and deepened my awareness of what being totally present in the moment felt like. Once again, however, I have to return to my daily work and family routine. The three weeks of practicing and performance are over. I have to find a way to incorporate these high moments into my regular life. Mindfulness helps. But transitions remain daunting, both in daily schedules and in major decisions.

CHAPTER 20. Breathing In, My Breath Goes Deep

7:20 A.M.

TRAFFIC ON INTERSTATE 40 OUT TO the Research Triangle Park varies this time of the day. Sometimes, I beat the rush. But other days, the pace slows to 15 or 20 mph. If there is an accident, the three lanes become a parking lot. In Los Angeles or Washington DC, drivers might be used to this, but not in North Carolina. Today, I'm stuck in traffic.

I say one of my favorite phrases from the Vietnamese monk, Thich Nhat Hanh, who writes a lot about meditation. "Breathing in, I know I am breathing in," I say out loud, as the traffic begins to clear and I move up to 50 mph. "Breathing out, I know I am breathing out." I am careful to stay alert and not get relaxed as if doing a meditation. Practicing meditation or listening to relaxation tapes in the car is not a good idea.

When an aggressive driver darts in front of me, I brake and do not get angry. Instead of absorbing another stress, I simply notice the reckless driver and keep my distance. When the traffic jams come, I sit more calmly, not as anxious. It is simply a traffic jam, and there is nothing I can do. "Breathing in, my breath grows deep," I say. "Breathing out, my breath goes slowly. Breathing in, I feel calm. Breathing out, I feel at ease."

Over the last six to eight months, I have carefully read Kabat-Zinn's book, *Full Catastrophe Living*, following the guidance on using the tapes and the theories behind them. If stress is highly charged emotionally, the body kicks into an automatic alarm reaction known as "fight or flight." The autonomic nervous system pumps blood into muscle tissue and adrenaline throughout the body. In ancient times, this impulse occurred sparingly to fight the occasional lion. Today's culture calls up the adrenaline from breakfast to bedtime.

On this typical day for me, my unconscious systems—the autonomic nervous system with its hormones—have been sending fight or flight signals steadily since the first jungle I've hacked my way through. I've learned that mindfulness can reduce stress, manage pain, or adjust an unhealthy coping mechanism—such as spiraling down into feelings of inadequacy or impatience or hopelessness, which is often my pattern. Today, I notice the horses grazing in the field, part of the North Carolina State University land that I drive past. I see the patterns of the cars, noticing the impatience of some drivers. Clouds move in animal shapes across the windshield.

8:05 A.M.

At the back section of the FHI parking lot, near the woods and swampy area, I shift to park and put on the emergency brake. Then I turn to another ritual to make the transition into the building and my computer. I pull from the glove compartment a book of daily meditations for men. The book is from a Hazelden Foundation series, which is based on the 12-step program that originated with Alcoholics Anonymous.

By now in my process of moving through depression, I consider myself a recovering "depression-aholic." I have begun to work with the 12 steps as part of my recovery. Depression seems to be my way of coping, my biologically and learned basis for response to stress and transition. Just as some have the disease of alcoholism, I have the dis-ease of "depressionism." I haven't shared this thinking with anyone, but it helps me.

The language of the meditation book is often tied to moment-to-moment awareness and acceptance of our powerlessness to control many things about the world we live in, including the behaviors of other people. Sitting in the parking lot, I read the quote at the top of the page, an Ethiopian proverb: "He who conceals his disease cannot expect to be cured." I think about depression as I read further, reflecting for a few seconds on my hesitancy to acknowledge this condition to myself for so many years and now learning how and when to tell others.

"Concealment and secrecy have been second nature to some of us," the reading begins. "We may have felt that our masculinity kept us loners....Maybe we could not bear to expose the truth because we feared the consequences." I sit in the car, wondering if I will tell co-workers about my depression, and then continue reading.

"Now we are learning to be open with our friends, and we are finding the healing effect of fresh air for our secrets." The final phrase rings true for me. "When we let others know us as we really are, we are casting our lot with good health and recovery."

As I shut the door and walk through the parking lot, I ponder the thought for the day at the bottom of the page: "Today, I will make progress in my recovery by letting myself be fully known."

10:43 A.M.

My mind is wandering at my desk, and I am feeling inadequate for the task at hand. I get up and walk to the men's room. As I walk, I am thinking that some yoga stretches might help me. At home this morning, I did not have time to do several of the balancing poses. I open the restroom door and notice no one is there. The hall seems quiet today. Many of the men must be traveling. I move before the long mirror over the three sinks and settle into my posture, feet about shoulder width apart, toes spread wide in my shoes. I'm pretty sure I will have the bathroom to myself for a few minutes.

Kabat-Zinn's instructions are well grooved into my body by now. Noticing each nuance in my body, I feel the weight fully in each foot, from the toes to the heel so that I feel anchored deep in the earth, as my mind travels down through three floors of steel girders. I extend my arms out to the side, feeling the shoulder muscles activated, as I slowly shift my weight onto my left foot. As I anchor my weight down the left side of my body, I slowly lift my right leg off the bathroom floor. I lift my leg straight up to the side as far as it goes and leave it there. I breathe slowly, noticing my belly rise and fall. And I hear Kabat-Zinn's voice in my mind, "A little bit higher." I lift another sixteenth of an inch.

My left arm and shoulder go further out as my right leg goes ever so slightly up. I keep my eye focused on a single point, which today is my nose in the mirror. Lifting my foot a little bit higher, my mind goes to a problem at home.

"You have such a big nose," Lee said recently, along with comments on my gray hair, my eating habits, and other details on how a teen sees his father. As his comments flash through my mind, I look at my nose and see my father's face. I decide that he's right. I do have a big nose, which I have never thought about before. My mind darts ahead to the next time he comments on my nose and decide that I will agree with him instead of feeling sensitive or criticized or responding in a preachy way about being polite.

Suddenly, I lose my balance and have to drop my right leg to the tiled bathroom floor to keep from falling. The large mirror, a third floor bathroom, the fluorescent lights, awareness of anyone coming in…. all present moment thinking has gone. My thoughts are flowing down like steep mountain streams, jumping from my son's manners to my father, over to acceptance of my ancestral nose, strategizing for talking to a teenager, feeling proud of my acceptance of myself and parenting savvy. But, alas, my self-congratulatory feeling has gotten me in trouble with my yoga pose, and my balance is gone. Thoughts cascade like a landslide that can begin with just a pebble. Even though my eyes are still looking at my nose in the mirror, my anchor to the present moment is gone.

All of this happens in less than 45 seconds, but it is long enough for my mind to move far from the feelings I had when I opened the bathroom door a few moments earlier—depleted, lonely, challenged, and inadequate. Staying in the present moment sounds so simple but is so complicated. Those were good, productive thoughts I was

THE CRANE DANCE 213

having, looking at the mirror. Another bond with my father through "our" nose, a tiny step toward being a better parent with a teenager. But in leaving the moment, in my thinking, I lost my balance. At this point it would be easy to judge myself for not being good at yoga, for not doing it right. I remind myself not to judge myself for "failing." In fact, I neither failed nor succeeded. What happened is what happened. I am fortunate to have been practicing with this tool long enough to be able to notice all of these thoughts, at that moment, in the third floor bathroom at Family Health International late in the morning of a typical workday.

So I settle in again, still feeling quiet and secure in this private-enough setting, and this time lift the left leg. In the full mirror, wearing a tie and nice pants, I form a striking pose. I hear Kabat-Zinn reminding me to go to my limit. "Wherever you land is exactly right for you. Just settle into it now, keeping the rest of your body relaxed." In the early days of using the tape, I noticed the tension in my jaw and face as I grimaced to go a little higher, like an athlete running one more wind-sprint. But now, I notice that the reflection of my long arms in both directions extending nearly the length of the mirror. I raise my left foot a little higher and smile. My tie hangs down like a carpenter's plumb line. My body pushes out in both directions at once, leg to the left, arm to the right. My right leg is anchored straight and true. "A little bit higher." I smile in the mirror. Slowly, after what seems like a very long time, I bring my left leg down slowly, along with both arms. I notice the gradual shift onto both feet.

10:48 A.M.

I return to my office, smiling, noticing the people I pass, the feeling of the floor from one foot to the next, like a walking meditation. My mind is on my walking, not the next task at my desk. Then, I reach my office and begin to sort through the information at hand, sorting through the nuances of a World Health Organization document describing how to introduce a new contraceptive device into a country.

My lunch routine varies. Sometimes I join colleagues in the canteen, which builds friendships and connections. Occasionally I leave the building campus for lunch or errands. At least two of the four days a week that I work in FHI, I either jog or eat alone, using them as another form of mindful meditation. Sometimes, I run with co-workers. The conversation is a release from work, usually entertaining, and certainly a diversion from the effort that the running takes. But I need diversion less than I need solitary time with my body and mind, to let thoughts, feelings, and unexpected connections bubble up. So usually, I jog alone.

Unlike other relaxation techniques, mindfulness does not try to take me away from pain with distractions. Instead, mindfulness actually takes me into whatever issue is bothering me, whether it's physical or emotional. But staying in a painful place is not easy. It's easier to turn to the addictive behaviors—to impatience, anger, rage, a cold distancing myself from loved ones. Without practicing mindfulness on a daily basis, finding alternative responses to pain is too hard. I need a lot of practice in this daily process. I learn to watch my mind, bring back the thoughts to my breath, breathe into a specific part of my body that is straining. On nearly every run, my mind gets carried away, endorphins driving thoughts too fast or far, and I have to bring it back to the cracks of the wooden bridge I hear jogging across a stream, chirping of mid-day birds, the heat or cold.

On this hot day in late May 1995, the saying, "breathing in, my breath goes deep," takes on a new meaning. After sweating heavily on my noon-time jog, I gradually turn the shower handle so that the water gets cooler and cooler. I breathe deeply, concentrating on "the breath goes deep" and the "breath goes slowly." If I think about it being too cold, like jumping into the mountain stream with the kids in the summer, I find myself gasping for air. But if I focus on breathing deeply, even saying to myself, "I know I am breathing in," I can stand in a completely cold-water shower and breathe normally.

I think of the television footage from the Vietnam War of a Buddhist monk sitting perfectly still after setting himself on fire—a dramatic peace protest. He never moved as the flames shot around him, burning him to death. That monk knew how to focus on his breath. When I saw this on television, I thought it was some kind of mystical ability. Now, I have some sense that a human being could sit that still under that kind of external stress. But it would take years of practice.

3:45 P.M.

Many times during the day, I need mindfulness techniques. I don't always remember to use them, of course. But this afternoon, in a meeting that begins to bore me, instead of questioning why I'm in this job, as I have over the years, I simply sit erect in a dignified posture and notice my breathing. I put both feet firmly on the floor. While the discussion does not interest me anymore, I feel better about myself. My mind does not begin wishing I were doing something else. I notice how fortunate I am to be sitting here, healthy, not in a war zone, not in a dangerous construction site. I am employed in a safe environment. I contribute. Some of the work is satisfying. I get a regular paycheck.

Back at my office, I make telephone calls. My energy wanes. When the phone rings, returning one of my inquiries, I try to remember to breathe once before answering it, so that when I say hello, I am truly connecting with the person on the other end. Often, I work without such conscious connections to people and to myself, especially as I get tired, discouraged, wanting to be dancing or working with others on an arts project. But I work at staying present in the time and place where I am.

5:45 P.M.

At home, pulling the Dodge Vista to a stop on the gravel driveway, I take a quick detour to the edge of the bamboo, breathe deeply and head in the back door. I greet the kids and Georgia and go directly into my room to change into "home" clothes. My mind is still at work in some ways, despite the commute home, but simply changing shirts and pants helps me get anchored in this present moment, in setting the table or sitting down with one of the kids.

I no longer head for the refrigerator and pull out a beer. I have quit buying beer at all, so that there is none there to get. I have not been an alcoholic in the traditional use of that word, of a person who drinks under pressure in an addictive way and loses the ability to think and act clearly. But I did turn to a habitual behavior, a single beer and occasionally two, to help me "wind down" and relax.

The more I work on noticing the thoughts and feelings in my body, the less I need to wind down. Tonight, supper will be a little late. Lee has finished his homework. "Come and walk with me and Rosie," I say. He comes out, and I ask about the party at school.

"Did we get enough soda?"

"Yeah, everything was fine."

Then, in one of those rare moments for a young teenager, he pushes me and races ahead. "Bet you can't catch me."

I race after him with Rosie, up the sidewalk in the lingering daylight of a late spring evening. I smile, content, happy, proud of my day, every breath.

CHAPTER 21. Gratitude Opens the Door

SEGREGATION. WORK. JOY. THESE words from the dance performance in early 1995 echo throughout the spring. My work as a kid was going to school—segregated schools. My father was my strongest role model, and work defined his life. Through the spring, I begin to think about Father's Day. When I led the Father's Day service at church several years earlier—when I told the African tale about Ogaloussa—I emphasized the mythological role of fathers. Now, I want to do something more personal, something that moves beyond ideas to gut-level experience, maybe even joy.

To help sort out some ideas, I turn to the large sketch book I'm using now, with its unlined pages. The spiral notebooks that I used for journals for many years rest in an old box under my desk, filled with notes from when I woke up in the middle of the night anxious and worried. Moving to the sketch books was yet another gift from Georgia. Over the years, I noticed how she developed ideas for her artwork in a large sketch book—drawing, pasting programs from art exhibits, writing notes, adding photographs, and more pencil drawings. I adapt her system to my own needs, even though I'm not sure of my own artistic vision. I fill my new sketch books with drawings, notes about dances, programs from art exhibits, and random ideas. The broad swaths of space on the pages hold more joy and freedom than linear thoughts on lined sheets

I am beginning to think about myself as being an artist of some sort. Teaching the dance class gave me confidence that I am more than a writer in a public health organization. Even though I often have to be creative in solving writing problems at work, a broader artistic side needs to emerge. Something about the dancing, the physicality and body memory, offers a gateway.

In the sketchbook, I start writing about Dad and making simple drawings of scenes I remember as a kid. On the top of the page, I sketch my dad at the card table in the corner of the living room. Sometimes as a boy, I would wake up early to a quiet house, the segregated world of Jackson, Mississippi, still asleep. The pre-Civil Rights caste system in jobs and housing and school assignments would crank into a morning rhythm soon. But at that moment, such issues were secondary to the privacy of being alone with my busy father.

"You're up early," he'd say to me as he worked at the card table, sipping his coffee. "Are you ready to get dressed now?" he might ask, looking up from a stack of index cards. I might linger briefly, absorbing the familiar smell of his coffee and the image of how men begin their day with quiet and thoughtful work. Sometimes, I would go to my little desk, back-to-back with my brother's, and make lists of tasks ahead—school assignments or stations for the safety patrol boys.

I learned later as an adult that he was outlining his sermons on those cards. He would incorporate those notes into Sunday morning sermons, spoken without notes across Mississippi, where he linked the work of the Methodist-supported Millsaps College to the message of the gospel hour. Or sometimes, he would be working with a different set of cards, one for each incoming freshman at the college. By the time the 300 or so entering students came to our house for a welcoming "Coke party," as we called it at home, he knew all of their names and hometowns.

Underneath the drawing in my sketchbook, I write, "Thank you, Dad, for teaching me about discipline." Over the next weeks, I write other thank you's, things I have not even realized I appreciated about him. On May 19, now birthday number 48, I put these notes from my sketchbook into a kind of a poem, or maybe it's a liturgy:

Thank you for sitting so still, for being up early in the morning,
For the smell of pre-dawn coffee

Thank you for the discipline I see in you

Thank you for the work you did, the way you stuck with the task

Thank you for being handsome, for having a good smile

Thank you for playing ball with me, for going to my basketball games

Thank you for supporting me at the draft board

For paying tuition at Duke

For crying when I was mean to my sister.

Meanwhile, I approach our student minister, who is scheduled to lead the Father's Day service. "I am thinking about ways to thank our fathers," I tell her. "I think it would be effective to tell stories about our fathers with movement—like a liturgical dance."

"I've been thinking about gratitude as a theme too," she says. "Tell me some more about your dance idea."

Over the course of several meetings, I explain the work I've done with Liz Lerman on developing dance phrases using personal stories. We discuss some ideas and agree to a tentative plan.

Three others are participating. John danced with my children and me in the community dance last fall (when our dog also participated). Laurie and Andrea, two women in the church, are exploring various career shifts. Andrea is working with yoga, and Laurie is considering various artistic avenues. I explain the approach for creating a small dance, incorporating storytelling into movements. They decide to give it a try.

In our first rehearsal, we draw a picture. "Make it simple," I say. "Don't worry about the art. Make it something that you want to thank your father for." The three of them move into a separate part of the little fellowship hall of the church, which has carpet on half the floor and tiles on the other. After a few minutes, I see that Laurie is still looking at a blank sheet of paper.

"Is there anything you did with your dad?"

"Well, he did like to throw balls with me. I think he wanted me to be a boy."

The dance gradually emerges. Her memory of her father works itself into a phrase where the four of us, two in each backstage corner run on a diagonal to the front of the stage in rapid succession and finish with a dive. Laurie has been playing in an ultimate Frisbee league that involves lots of diving. After her dive, she stands and says, "Thank you Dad, for your playful love of sport." But Laurie's "thank you" barely sounds across the little rehearsal space.

"Speak up," I say emphatically, standing in the back row of the small sanctuary a few days before the service. "I can barely hear you."

She tries again, her voice only a little louder. I say her line, projecting my voice. "See what I mean." Again, her thin voice barely reaches the back row, unconvincing in its gratitude. After several more tries, I suggest, "Just yell it. Pretend you're yelling."

This time, we slide across the floor, energy pouring across the room. Our student minister, Julie, is in the corner, watching. Laurie gets up and says in a loud speaking voice, "Thank you Dad, for your playful love of sport." Her words match her energetic body now. We all laugh and congratulate her. She smiles, feeling the breakthrough. Julie comes up and gives her a hug. Laurie starts to cry.

"You found your voice," I say.

"I guess I did."

On Sunday morning, we feel well prepared. John tells a story about finding his dad's fishing pole in the garage. His dad left the family when John was very small. John had no memory of his father at all in the early rehearsals. Then one night, he remembered the fishing pole.

"I feel like I can thank my father now," he said that night. "This will help me be a better father, with a little of my resentment gone."

In the performance, after John finishes his story, I end the dance with a memory of Christmas morning. "My father opened a present from my little sister. It was an ugly pottery paperweight—she was in the first grade. My brother and I laughed. She went running over to Dad and climbed in his lap." As I tell this, I'm crouching on the stage, the other three dancers behind me. Then, I form into a ball and they gently lift me up, cradling me. I look up from the curled baby-like pose and finish the story.

"Instead of getting mad at me and my brother, my father just held my sister and began to cry with her. Thank you, Dad, for crying when I was mean to my sister." They carry me off stage.

After the dance, which comes early in the service, Julie asks the congregation to think of ways to thank their fathers and to write them on the paper they received with their bulletin. They can put them in the offering plate if they wish. During her sermon, Julie has the stack of papers on the pulpit and pulls out several at random, integrating them into the sermon in a litany of thanks. Then, at the end of the sermon, we come back onstage and do the improvisational yoga poses from our dance. As planned, we add to our poses phrases we have just heard her read in her sermon, made individually and sometimes joined together into a single shape.

"Thank you, Dad, for going camping with me," I say, repeating a phrase Julie read. Later, Julie tells me that the little girl who wrote that phrase was thrilled to hear it repeated during our dancing. I smile.

"You know, I probably heard that one because my dad didn't really take me camping when I was little. But he did many other things. I don't feel regret or anger at him for that anymore."

Over the next few days, a sense of pride and deep accomplishment sinks into me. This creative approach helps me move past resentments and disappointments—the process of the rehearsals and the performance. I feel privileged and touched to have seen Laurie find her voice and John remember his father—and proud of the role I played in their growth. I feel excited to explore this artistic approach in a more focused way.

The story about my own father also takes me to a new point of strength. I feel more completely adult, going beyond functioning as a father to actually feeling like a father, even in my vulnerable moments. I can't blame my father forever for perceived losses or lack of attention during his most stressful years in Jackson. Thanking him in a public way, in an artistic way, opens up the present for more joy—and for sorrows, as they come now, not memories of the past.

OVER THE NEXT YEAR, our little dance group performs several times at church. And, I get more training through a week-long workshop with Lerman and her dance company in Washington. In one of our dances at church, we use a phrase from the poet May Sarton as our text: "Whatever the wounds that have to heal, the moment of creation assures that all is well, that one is still in tune with the universe, that the inner chaos can be probed and distilled into order and beauty."

I love the thought of the moment of creation itself healing wounds, and that chaos becomes order and beauty. The dances we're creating at church out of our own experiences—as rough as they are if measured by standards of modern dance companies—are in fact transforming bits of chaos into beauty. I think of the process as community art, like the creations of visual folk artists without formal training.

Creating order out of chaos is what I need for another issue that shaped my childhood. In my late 20s, the same year I married Georgia, I worked with an interracial organization where church and civil rights leaders supported textile workers seeking a union contract. By the mid-1970s, the all-white textile workforce in rural North Carolina was increasingly transitioning to a younger, bi-racial group of millworkers. This shift led to more focus on economic justice for blacks and whites alike. The campaign gained national attention, which led to the award-winning movie *Norma Rae* starring Sally Field. For the first time, I worked and socialized with black Southerners on a regular basis, living in an integrated culture. The work was exciting and heady, but I quit after about 18 months, without another job waiting.

At the time, I didn't realize I was depressed, much less understand why I felt the way I did. I just knew I had to change something. Turning 30, I had not yet decided on a career, was newly married, and lived in an old rambling house. I felt pressure to make money, decide on a career, be a good husband, and take care of our first house. Then, during that time, Georgia and I got the news about infertility. All of these transitions tumbled together into a pile of pressures. My patterns of withdrawal and anxiety took over. My capable, outgoing side went into a hibernation mode. Gradually, without Prozac or dancing, I rebounded. I found the editing job at the N.C. Center for Public Policy Research and began to feel better about myself. I did creative work, provided for my family, and was involved as a Dad. But I also no longer focused on race.

Now, nearly 20 years after working on that union campaign, I find myself scratching out ideas in my new sketchbooks about race. Gradually, my next major project takes shape.

In the fall of 1996, I lead a community dance project called "Growing up Black/White—Finding Common Ground." Our church, the Unitarian Universalist Fellowship of Raleigh, sponsors the project, including a Sunday morning service in November that concludes the workshop. Meeting for an hour and a half, one night a week for eight weeks, we draw on the storytelling/movement techniques developed by Liz Lerman. We will find order and beauty, I say in the flyer, working with the chaos and pain of what James Baldwin called America's "racial nightmare."

My personal appeals along with the announcement in the church newsletter yield six people committed to the workshop, two of them men. Four participants are white, one is African American, and one is Chinese American, a teenager who works in the church nursery. Through the fall, we tell our stories and construct simple dance phrases that gradually develop into a seamless story of race in America, as we experienced it in our unique ways.

The November 10th service is the first dance performance for everyone except the young Asian American and me. The group plans the service, including choosing the cover of the bulletin for that Sunday. I bring a *New Yorker* cartoon to a rehearsal that all endorse. In the cartoon, a businessman stands before his boss, skyscrapers visible out the window. Balancing on his left toes with his left arm extended to the ceiling, he grasps his right knee as high as it will go, his head leaning down to almost touch it. The boss, balding and looking to be near retirement, sits stone-faced behind a heavy desk and has the only line: "Say what's on your mind, Harris—the language of dance has always eluded me."

In the service, we read from Studs Terkel's book on race, and from James Baldwin and May Sarton. In the children's corner, the little ones make a shape based on what they think of when they hear the word *race*. How refreshing to see young children imitate running, hearing *race* as a physical activity on a playground instead of a social issue with a complex history. I'm smiling as they leave the small sanctuary, heading to their Sunday school classes. The dance we prepared during the fall workshop and a discussion fill the sermon slot.

The performance opens with each member of the ensemble, the six participants and me, walking across the stage, announcing where we grew up and in what time period. We arrive in two rows of three facing each other with me at the back, facing the congregation.

The full group then performs the phrase I created in the Liz Lerman workshop with middle school dance teachers several years earlier. As I drove home that day, I knew the phrase needed more of a performance. I did not know exactly why the words seemed so important to me, but I knew they said something deeply personal as well as more broadly about how segregation and church intersected in those of us growing up in the deep South. The race workshop and this dance give me the opportunity for full expression and the healing power of a community.

"I come from a land of blood," the full ensemble says. The two rows of dancers fall toward each other to the floor—bodies straight, hands at their chest to break the fall. I fall in unison with them from the back, my head landing at the top of the two rows, so that our heads form a kind of arch on the floor.

Just before our hands meet the floor all of us say in unison: "Where any notion of God"—emphasizing "God" as we hit the floor. And now, we lift our heads and turn toward the congregation, arms still on the floor and continue, "And Jesus are ludicrous when I take my maid home to her ramshackle house." We walk our hands back to our feet, body arching up until we are standing again.

Edd, the only African American, tells a story about his mother, a maid for a white family in a small central North Carolina town. "One day, I must have been about eight or nine, I was with my mother walking downtown, and we met the family she worked for. The little white child let go of her mother's hand and came running to my mother and hugged her. I felt like I had to share my mother with a white kid. I felt funny, maybe I was angry or sad but also proud that a white child would hug my mother. It was complicated." Others tell their stories: the first years of integration in their schools, an international elementary school where being Chinese American was a natural part of a diverse ethnic mix.

The ensemble then tells another of my stories, the one I recalled when I returned to Jackson a few years ago. During that visit, I remembered the shame I felt in high school. This performance provides an opportunity for further healing of the racial nightmare, perhaps even redemption, one might say. The ensemble stands bunched together—I run up to them and suddenly stop.

"It was my junior year in high school," I say to the congregation. "Our high school chorus was performing across town at lunchtime. I was riding in a car with six guys, in the backseat behind Larry, the driver. The light turns red and he stops. Throngs of Negroes—that was the word our family used in the early 1960s—crossed directly in front of us, inches away from Larry's front bumper." The ensemble ambles across the stage towards the congregation.

I continue with the story. "As we waited at the stoplight, Larry said, 'I wish I could drive through and kill 'em all.' The light turned green, a few stragglers scampered out of the way, and Larry accelerated into the barely open space. Not one of us five young men in the car spoke. I felt shame, confusion, guilt. All of those feelings sunk into my soul, and I let them stay there, silent, for more than 30 years. I never told anyone about that before today."

The dance closes with Karen's story. She grew up in Chicago and went to a girls' Catholic school near Marquette Park. "There was a large monument near the school where neo-Nazis held rallies," Karen says to the congregation. "I would come out of school and hear them saying slogans to keep the blacks out of the area. They were filled with hate." As she tells the story, she places the cast members into positions so that they resemble the monument.

"No one in school ever talked about the neo-Nazis and their hate talk about the blacks, but we all heard it. The nuns never mentioned it either. But today at least, I'm saying something."

As she finishes, we freeze, holding our final pose in the dance. Then we disassemble the monument and line up for a bow. The congregation applauds. I move to the small pulpit as the others return to their seats on the front row. I stand silently for maybe 30 seconds as the impact of the dance settles and then ask for any comments, feelings, experiences from people's own past. People share about racial patterns when they grew up and more recently. Then, I hear the clear sounds of a man sobbing near the back. I ask if he would like to speak.

A white man, he stands and collects himself. "I was in Chicago, not so many years ago," he manages. He loses his voice as he sobs again. The 100 or so people in the congregation seem to be breathing with him as he regains his voice. "I was there when a man did in fact drive into the crowd." He gasps his breathe in. "He was white. The crowd was mostly black. And, he did kill somebody."

HELPING PEOPLE TAP THEIR MEMORIES, crafted into shared presentations with others, brings great satisfaction to me. At the same time, I am opening doors that have been jammed in my psyche for many years, allowing fresh air to blow through stale rooms that need to be reclaimed as part of my true self. The next year, I lead another project, "Race Matters—Continuing the Conversation," working through a small dance studio, with a performance this time at a downtown art gallery that has a large performance area. I work with a homeless shelter where six residents participate in a six-week project, drawing pictures of their last home and putting gestures to their memories of home. All of the participants are African American.

At work, after many years of being limited in my job to writing scientific articles for Family Health International's quarterly magazine, new opportunities seem to be coming my way. The more energy I feel outside work, the more new assignments seem to land on my desk. Working on curricula for family planning providers leads to a trip to Jamaica, to participate as the editor with local providers during a field test. I attend a meeting at the Rockefeller Foundation's Bellagio Center in Italy, where scientists finalize modern-day standards for framing breastfeeding as a contraceptive method; my job is to publicize these findings.

While the new projects are exciting, at times I still feel limited by the job—needing the salary for family security while my passion for the community dance projects remains a time-consuming hobby. I remind myself of how fortunate I am to have a job that allows me to work with good people, to make a decent living, and to contribute to important international public health issues. I know that many writers would love to have my job.

I look for people who are trying to juggle jobs with artistic and other interests. Several of us begin meeting every other week to discuss these issues. During one Sunday afternoon gathering, six of us are pondering our jobs and future directions.

"Even though things are better, I still feel trapped sometimes," I say. "Sometimes I feel like I'm in jail."

One person responds that since I'm not in jail, how can I know how that feels. Instead of calmly saying something about this just being a metaphor, I snap back: "I DO feel that way. Why don't you believe me? I'm telling you how I feel. I feel trapped." The response offers little sympathy.

"Why don't you believe me?" I'm nearly yelling now, crossing a line of decorum for an informal Sunday afternoon with friends.

Several days later, I run into the friend who questioned the image of jail. "I had a big insight about the other day," I say, a little sheepish about my behavior. "I hope you didn't feel offended."

"Well, a little. But I figured something was going on that I didn't understand."

"What I realized later was that you reminded me at some primal level of my mother, and a child-like emotion burst out." I pause. "My mother tried to help me achieve things—in school, in sports— but I don't remember her trying to help me understand how I felt. So I learned a lot more about how to think than how to feel." I let this thought settle in. "I'm surprised I still had that kind of anger at my mother. Actually, we're good friends now."

"Maybe something about your mother is holding you back from sorting out any changes you might make in your career."

"Yeah, maybe so. But you know, I don't feel as restless, even since our exchange the other day. I think things will work out in due time."

Part of understanding segregation, work, and joy, for me, is going back to Perilstein and sorting out the role of medication. We decide together this time to phase down the dose, instead of me trying it on my own. Over many months of transition, I alter my brain with fewer and fewer man-made chemicals and finally stop taking even a portion of the little green and white pill. But I know I can go back to Prozac if I need it.

I don't feel graduated from Prozac, only ready for taking the next steps without it. I can feel the air blowing through the many unused rooms of my inner mansion. I am only beginning to know what riches lie latent, ready to blossom into this elusive feeling called joy.

CHAPTER 22. From Dis-Ease to Manhood

 IDEAS ARE BUZZING—NOTES in my journal for communi-
ty arts projects, options for career changes, dance possibilities.
Gradually, I address the issue that has been driving all these
activities: the role of depression in my life.

On a morning run, my friend Mark asks me what I've been doing lately. When we manage to jog together, we usually talk about
something meaty. "I've been doing a lot of work on dealing with
chronic, low-grade depression," I say. He is a physician, and we've
discussed medical and mental health issues before, but not so personally. We run a few more steps, breathing in the crisp October
morning air.

"I've been working at it for a number of years now. I've been developing a lot of tools to complement therapy and Prozac—I've used both
of them. But I needed a lot more."

"What do you mean, a lot of tools?" Mark asks, slowing a bit as the
conversation deepens.

A few strides go by in silence. "Well, first I found some ways to talk
about it with other people, in small groups and then in a ritual at a weekend retreat. So I didn't feel so ashamed and isolated. Getting past the
shame was a big step." I catch my breath as I turn and see his interest in
these details. "Two other important tools for me have been meditating
and expressing my creativity." I breathe again, running a little slower.
He looks toward me, waiting for more.

"Creativity has been really important," I continue. "I found a person who uses storytelling and dance movements. This has opened a lot of doors and been really helpful. And I've used my creative interests to help others who participate in my projects. Service seems really important too—realizing how much we have to be grateful for. There's a lot of stuff."

We run a few more steps. Mark has a serious look, his eyes focused on the ground. "So many people leave our clinics with medication," he says, talking about the hospital where he works. "They think the pills will cure them. But even with therapy, many have recurrent depressions and come back later. They don't want to look at themselves in a holistic way."

"Depression is more than just something to cure with drugs." I'm even more animated with my story now. "Prozac has helped a lot but I don't think of it as healing me as much as giving me the energy I needed to understand the role depression has played in my life and to move into new roles where I don't need it anymore—if that makes any sense."

"Yes, that makes sense," Mark says. "A little booklet on other tools and techniques to help in the healing process would be a great thing to give to my patients."

I begin to think about a workshop on depression, maybe at church, like the one on race. But I'm not sure if I can take on that topic. The news media is so focused on medication and brain chemistry; my ideas go against that conventional wisdom. Moreover, I'm not a professional and can't offer therapy. But if the content is about depression, how can I avoid mental health issues?

I call my minister to see if we can have lunch to discuss the project. Michael has been in Raleigh for about half of his year-long stay as an interim minister. This energetic and engaging leader offers original ideas and sermons.

He picks a Japanese restaurant. "I don't eat sushi as much out here in North Carolina," he says as we drive the few blocks to the inexpensive restaurant. It looks more like a fast-food stop on the outside, and the tables inside seem as much like a southern café as an ethnic option. Settling by the window, we chat about some of the dances I've done at the church, which he had not heard about. I begin to tell him about my experience with depression, much like my conversation with Mark on the run.

"Nearly 10 years ago, I lost my job and went into a bad place. Gradually, I realized it was low-grade, chronic depression. Over the last decade, I've been on a kind of journey through depression, figuring out the role it has played throughout my life, even since childhood." He nods, scooping up the raw fish expertly with chopsticks. "First, I had to accept depression as part of who I was, not just get on meds to get rid of it. Make sense?"

He's nodding enthusiastically, chopsticks down now. His arms move through the air with the gusto of his sermons. "Yes, too many people think of depression as something to run from, to cure."

"Exactly." Hearing his enthusiasm feels like finding a long-lost brother in the woods, so different from news stories on new medications and adjustments to brain chemistry. "Depression for me has been a place of retreat, to go when I'm under stress or in a big transition. It's a familiar place. Even though I'm hurting, it sounds funny to say, but it's also kind of comforting. Or it *was* until I kept waking up in the middle of the night worrying, being exhausted after a day of work, snapping at my kids. I had to change, but I had to transform myself somehow, move through the part of myself that relied on and needed depression."

"That makes total sense," he says. "Moving through depression, not curing it." His eyes are sparkling, but also darting about with a kind of restless energy.

"In fact, I think of depression as kind of like alcoholism, for me at least. After all my work the last ten years, I have come to think of myself as a recovering depression-aholic."

Michael throws his chopsticks down now with a clatter against the plate. He claps his hands together. "Yes, that's it exactly. It's an addiction."

I smile, my ideas confirmed by at least one person. "I think of depression like a dis-ease." I say the two parts of the word distinctly, emphasizing the separation with my right hand, drawing a dash in the air. He's nodding so hard I think he might bob his head into his empty plate. "Like alcoholism, it has a biological, psychological, social, and spiritual dimension. Does that make sense?"

He smiles. "Yes, great sense. Keep thinking about all of this."

I call Michael later and tell him that I am planning a workshop at the church to explore some of these ideas. He says it's fine so long as it focuses on information, not counseling. I find a small group who is willing to attend a four-week workshop. I'm careful to explain that I'll be sharing my own experiences, that the workshop is not meant to function as therapy. The sessions will include some of the approaches that have helped me. Most of the group have seen some of the dances at the church and know what to expect.

I decide to frame the workshop around what I see as the three phases of my decade-long journey. The first night, the small group sits in a circle of chairs at the end of a trailer that the youth group uses, the only space available in the church. The top page of the flip-chart beside me is numbered: 1) Going In, 2) Tools for Transformation, and 3) Maintaining Health. I introduce these three stages as the way I had approached depression. "Tonight, we'll focus on the first one," I explain.

The Persian poet, Rumi, provided a perfect example of what I mean by going into depression. I turn the first flip-chart page over to show the poem, folded and taped so that they can see only the first short verses. I read the lines and ask them to write down what comes to mind for them.

This being human is a guest-house, every morning a new arrival

A joy, a depression, a meanness.

Some momentary awareness comes, as an unexpected visitor.

Welcome and entertain them all!

Even if they're a crowd of sorrows

Who violently sweep your house empty of its furniture.

For me, the poem captures this stage perfectly—accepting depression not as a burden or an unfortunate circumstance, but as a gift to embrace. As the participants share what they have written, I struggle to remember how much sorrow I felt in my depression before I embraced this poem. No one wants to welcome depression, especially if it sweeps "your house empty of its furniture." They do not want to be immobilized, to worry excessively, to be anxious and impatient with their family members. I push on with the poem, hoping the message that has meant so much to me will sink in a bit.

Still, treat each guest honorably,

He may be clearing you out for some new delight.

The dark thought, the shame, the malice,

Meet them at the door laughing, and invite them in.

Be grateful for whoever comes

Because each has been sent as a guide from beyond.

By the end of the first night, the group has generally agreed that some value does exist in understanding the lessons of depression. But, no one wants to stay in depression to get those lessons. People want to function better, be happier, have a brighter view of the future. I come home that night wondering about the three phases, especially the first. When is a person in depression ready to engage the "going in" phase?

Another evening, we brainstorm about things that have helped them with depression at different points in their lives. And, I add my own list of tools. This second phase, developing tools for transformation, seems more logical to everyone, but most participants identify primarily with therapy and medication. Some add to the list diet, exercise, and cognitive therapy. Creativity and meditation, after some discussion, resonate with a few. An accountant feels best, he says, when he finds time to play around on the piano, losing himself in the jazz improvisation that unfolds. Another echoes such positive feelings when she creates art. No one mentions initiation into full adulthood, a theme that was important for me, leading up to the dance in my backyard.

The workshop ends on a good note, the participants glad to share experiences and get some new ideas. I successfully focus on information sharing, without sliding into intimate personal memories that might have taken us into more of a therapeutic setting. A lesson I take with me is realizing that my experiences with depression may be different from what others have gone through.

SEVERAL MONTHS AFTER THE WORKSHOP, I catch a cold and have a slight fever. I stay home from work, rare for me. Resting in bed, I find myself thinking about how difficult it will be to do more expressive arts work. "I can never be a dancer at my age," I think. "I'll never make enough money for the family if I leave my job. How can I afford to go back to school?"

Unlike in the past, though, the negative thinking does not burrow its way into old habits. I see the thoughts for what they are, the worst case scenario. At first, I draw on my analytical skills, recognizing the need to avoid thinking in terms of "never" or "all or nothing"—like quitting my job and trying out for the Liz Lerman dance company as the only way to find more joy. Tossing about on the bed, I notice my restlessness and decide to use my meditation skills.

I lie flat on my back, arms to my side, and notice my inhalation. I notice the thoughts—the negative, my corrective analysis, the humor I see now in my mind, noticing these shifts. All are just thoughts, nothing more. I observe them and stay in the present, with each breath. I look around at the big quilt spread over me on the bed, gazing out at the trees and the sunlight slashing down into the yard. A mini-journey has gone through my head, but I am still lying there.

Even with a slight fever, I find myself with energy. I begin to think about depression and timelines—like the one Tom Daly had us make at a men's workshop when we reflected on the feminine energy in our lives. And, I have recently read *Drumming at the Edge of Magic*, where Mickey Hart, the Grateful Dead drummer, traces the history of the drum and its influence on him. To help him see the details, Hart used a long timeline, putting bits of random information across the walls of an old barn.

I get out of bed, feeling a little gimpy, but manage to find some colored markers, paper, and a large book to write on. Then, I climb back under the covers, prop the pillows behind me, sit up, and start free associating. Perhaps the fever is driving the process as much as conscious thought. The details fall like rain on the page, up and back through time—family life, my job at FHI, dance classes, therapists, the Peace Corps, the draft board, marriage, a new high school my senior year, my job at the legislature, and the annual treks from Jackson to Lake Junaluska as a kid. I draw a line across the center of the pages. I mark the times I remember feeling depressed below the line. The stronger the depression, the lower

I plot the time on the page, as if graphing data. Above the line, I mark feelings of joy; the happier the occasion, the higher it goes.

After maybe 90 minutes of pouring out my life story in a depression timeline, I feel exhausted and fall into a deep sleep. When I wake up later in the day, the fever is gone and I feel ready to return to the routines of life. I tuck the timeline away into my files and head back into the fast pace of job, family, and community arts projects. But the timeline stays on my mind. In quiet moments at the end of the day, I pull it out and look at the data, looking for patterns.

The tools are easy for me to see, as I study the timeline:

MEDICATION—gaining energy to explore new ways of living

THERAPY—understanding old patterns

RITUAL—finding the safety to go beyond shame to acceptance

CREATIVITY—discovering how dancing with stories gives me joy

MINDFULNESS—learning how to stay in the present moment

INITIATION—moving into full manhood

THE LAST ITEM, INITIATION, never resonated with the group in the workshop.Even so, I remember the dance in the backyard, its power and impact. I sort through ways the idea of initiation helped catapult me into a new phase of life, past my old habits of depression.

Across the stream in our backyard hang huge, wild wisteria and grape vines tangled through the six-inch wide bamboo. After my first men's conference, I took a bench and an old table to these woods. I would go there and sit sometimes and say aloud, "This pole is for you." I thought of the bamboo as poles, like those in the corral containing the horses in the pig herder story Michael Meade told over several days at my first week-long men's conference.

When the boy struck the bargain with the witch, she agreed to give him his choice of horses to leave the forest, if he could return them to the corral at nightfall for three straight days. The corral holding the horses had a human skull on every pole but one.

"If you fail," the witch said, "this pole is for you." That's how I thought of my life as I moved into my forties. If I failed to break through from the patterns of a lifetime, my imagination with life would die, even if I lived another 40 years.

I decided to pursue the theme of initiation with another group, working with the Sunday school class for high schoolers. I've led this group a number of times, usually on a theme using one of the Unitarian Universalist curricula. This time, I propose to the religious education director leading a four-part session on transitions into young adulthood, how they see this as an initiation process. The first week, I have them brainstorm about the major steps in their initiation into being young adults. Most mention getting a driver's license, among other things, and leaving home for college. The next several weeks, I tell them the pig herder story that I learned from Michael Meade, and we discuss which parts of the story they see as relating to their lives.

The final Sunday of class, we go outside to the stream beside the church property, and they make little sketches in the ground, using twigs and stones and other objects to represent a scene from the story. Many depict a scene with the magical horse that takes the pig herder out of the forest. The next Sunday, we have a youth service in the regular morning worship service, where the senior high class share their thoughts on transitions in life. The engagement by these teenagers with this theme resonates with my instinct that the concept of initiation links with issues connected to major life transitions.

Other memories help me to validate the role that initiation played for me in addressing depression. I find notes from a session with Perilstein. "I was riding down a street in my red VW," I said to him, describing a dream about my first car. "The open, country road becomes more like streets in downtown Raleigh, then more like alleys behind buildings, really narrow."

"Then what happened?"

"Well, finally, I just stopped. The street got so narrow I couldn't go any further."

"So what did you do?"

"I got out of the car and started walking. I just left it there and never went back for it."

As we talked about the dream that day in his office, the image got clearer. I was ready to walk away from thinking about the past, from living in my red Volkswagen's memory. In 1972, more than 20 years before this dream, the car was totaled where I parked it on a Boston street. It was time to move on. But how could I move past unresolved issues in my psyche?

At the second and final week-long men's conference I attended, Meade gave me the answer. It was one of those "aha" moments. Standing before more than 100 men at the California lodge where I first started to dance, he turned sideways, facing the end of the hall. "You can look backwards, separating from your parents," he said, "or"—and he turned to face the other end of the long room—"you can look this direction, ahead." In either case, he said, you have a choice of which direction you face, and you need to take control of that choice.

The physicality of his turn hit the mark with me as much as what he said. When Meade turned his body 180 degrees, my view of my own story took a turn too. Since that day, when my symptoms arrive, I realize I am choosing to be in the grief behind the symptoms. Rumi's poem helps me stay in "the dark thought, the shame, the malice," and to "meet them at the door laughing, and invite them in." Lines of a poem provide a new tool, but the daily workings of the mind remain challenging. Many days, this poem helps me to remember that I can see whatever may come not as a problem but as a "guide from beyond."

THE TOOLS FROM MY TIMELINE and the ideas from the workshop need more expression. My journals are filled with notes and dreams, impressions, and sketches. Mark, my doctor friend, encouraged me to write down lessons from using various tools to move through depression. My own experiences seem valuable, but I don't have the credentials of a mental health professional.

On a series of morning runs through the woods, I think about my options. I am working in Washington, covering a conference for my job and staying with my sister-in-law in Arlington, Virginia. As I run along the Potomac, geese, wood cranes, and other river birds skim across the water, occasionally diving for fish. I slow down to navigate the rocks as the path veers close to the edge of the river. I pause to breathe deeply, as I watch the birds. A crew team shoots their sleek craft against the current, each set of arms dipping the oars in silent unison. Then, as the path turns into the woods, I pick up my stride, hopping over branches and tiny streams. The mist off the river carries the smell of a fresh rain. The beauty of the moment seeps into me like a guide from within.

As I move deeper into the woods, I realize that I want to share what I have learned through my recovery from depression in a more structured way. I know it will be valuable to others, if I can find a way to do it. Maybe I can do this as a writer. Maybe as a mental health professional. Maybe through community dance and the expressive arts.

I return to my friend Temple, the career counselor, for guidance. On my last visit to him, several years earlier, he told me I needed to get help with my depression before he would work with me again. Now I'm ready. I take the Myers-Briggs assessment, which is supposed to identify personality preferences—such as being either inner-directed or stimulated by external forces. I had never taken the test.

"I felt odd taking the test," I say to Temple, returning in several weeks. "I kept thinking, 'Should I answer this question as how I feel today or as how I've felt at other times, say, when I was depressed?' I didn't know which side of me should answer."

Temple listens and then moves onto his role as a career counselor, pulling out lists of various professions he has matched with my scores. The assortment of professions ranges from minister to the guy who headed the Esalen Institute, a humanistic, adult education and retreat center in California. We talk about options I have been thinking about. A health education degree in the public health school would be the most logical connection to my job but wouldn't provide an easy link to the expressive arts or to addressing depression. We talk about a Masters in Fine Arts, and I wonder if I'm really that much of an artist. Also, what kind of job could I get with that degree?

Gradually, pursuing a Masters in Social Work emerges as the best route, where I can explore expressive arts, therapeutic issues, and broader themes that connect with public health. The degree would allow a new career as I approach retirement years, if I wish. I can learn more about depression, to help put my own journey into a more grounded and professional context.

I research my options and talk to friends who have this degree, one a long-time therapist and one who has gotten it more recently. The University of North Carolina has a part-time program that requires classes only on Fridays for the first two years. The second year, I would also work part-time in a field placement. The third year would be full time, between courses and a half-time field placement.

Can I manage this with my job? Fortunately, FHI will let me drop back to half-time and keep benefits. But I'll have to borrow money to cover tuition and family living expenses. Plus, our older child is nearing college age, but we have saved for this. My wife and I discuss the decision at length. I feel an urgency to keep up the momentum that I have from moving through my depression. I want more than leading random services and workshops at church and reading mental health books on my own.

At age 51, I decide to pursue this dream with the seriousness and the imagination of what I consider to be a fully initiated man. Georgia and I reach compromises on money, household responsibilities, and support for each other. I agree to delay the pace of school if necessary. But I don't let go of my dream.

One of the first steps is to take the Graduate Record Exams, the famous GREs that I thought about but never took 29 years ago when I decided to go to the Peace Corps. The day of the test, I go into a room of little cubicles, each with a computer. I feel a little nervous but have a work deadline on my mind as well. Life is different in 1998 than in 1964 Mississippi, when I took the SATs as a high school junior.

As a boy, not so many months after Larry drove his car past the mid-day throng of Negroes in downtown Jackson, I sat at a desk in a large gymnasium-like room and quickly realized that a Negro boy about my age was only two seats away. No one else sat near him. We exchange a quick, uneasy meeting of the eyes. His dark face carried emotions I could not read, perhaps some mixture of gratitude that I chose to sit that near and pain because I left a seat between us. Some ambiguity and confusion swept through me as well, recalled now after decades of being lodged in my belly.

Today, at age 51, as I become aware of unprocessed emotions I take a first step toward graduate school. "We will begin shortly," the GRE test monitor says. I focus on the computer screen, no No. 2 pencils needed today. I take a deep breath and punch the keyboard. My timed test begins.

The year races by. I assemble letters of recommendation and craft the required essay articulating my purpose and hopes in pursuing this degree. My work at Family Health International, ironically, has become more interesting than ever, with a range of activities that include regular trips to Washington. Family pressures have evolved from sorting out depression and gender roles in child-rearing to working with the complex gamut of teenage issues, demanding in new ways that bring Georgia and me together as a parental team.

Following my instinct to pursue this degree makes me feel stronger. I'm not sure how this decision relates to the journey I've been through with depression, but I feel a connection. I understand that depression functioned as an addiction for me for many years, a pattern of reacting to life's stresses in habitual, predictable ways. As I moved through this awareness, I gradually began to accept the role of depression—not thinking of it only as a problem but as a gift. I gained a willingness to stand in the darkness, in conflict, in uncertainty, in stress—and sometimes, to even welcome whatever feelings come.

Over the final months before school begins, I retrace my journey through depression. I remember the grace, grief, and grandeur of the backyard dance, and the ritual where the large circle sang "I'm on Prozac and I'm not ashamed." I remember my interviews with Mahan Siler, his emphasis on the word "grace" and how he spoke of the role of darkness in the worship service I attended. Through these years, my family held a safe and sacred space, even in the darkest night. I learned from my kids the joys of constellations and sunsets, the "double delight seen in the glow of trust and affection," as J.B. Priestley said. Georgia's loyalty and love were daily reminders of my blessings. She listened, endured, and accepted me as I found my way to a new flight pattern in midlife. I survived, and as I became stronger, our family became stronger too.

Entering the social work graduate program feels exciting to me. I can't wait to learn more about mental health issues, developmental stages, counseling approaches, and how mindfulness and the arts can be used in therapeutic ways. This step feels like a culmination of all the actions I have taken along my journey through depression. Paradoxically, as I move forward to this new plateau, I also feel like I am returning to a familiar place—returning to the self, to the spark that preceded my disease, to the unique spirit that arrived on earth in me.

CHAPTER 23. Standing in the River

IN MY CLASS PRESENTATION near the end of the first semester of graduate school, I ask for a volunteer to participate in a role play. Our teacher, who is about my age, offers to help. I explain that she will act the part of a family member who is being blamed. "The blamer points at the other person, and if taken to an extreme, the person actually goes to her knees, into a submissive position," I say to the 22 other students and our teacher, Iris Carlton-LaNey.

"Okay, are we ready?" I ask Iris. She gamely gets on her knees. I begin the role play.

"You never do anything right around here," I say, using language from the writings of Virginia Satir, one of the founders of family therapy and the subject of my presentation. Standing at my full six feet, with my long arm extended directly at our teacher, I am menacing. Iris plays the role perfectly, bowing her head as I speak, as if wounded emotionally. I repeat the phrase, pointing now in an even more threatening way. She cowers more.

Then, I drop my pointing arm and mean expression, and go back to the lectern to continue with presentation. "When the blamer takes this aggressive stance with his body," I say to the class, "the blamer feels something like 'I am lonely and unsuccessful.' The blamer has a tension in his body and a sharp voice."

Some residual anxiety seems to remain in me and the room. Then I notice Iris is still on the floor on her knees. I obviously have left my role and didn't think to tell Iris to get up and de-role too. "Thanks, Iris, for playing the role. I really appreciate it. You can get up now." I turn back to the lectern, to go on with my presentation.

"Help me up," Iris says laughing, looking up now in a playful way. "You can't leave me down here!" The whole class breaks into laughter. Any tension slips away as we hear the funny, familiar voice of the teacher whom we all love. I reach down and help her up. All roles are over now and I can continue to explain why Virginia Satir has been so important to me.

Iris designed the course on foundations of social welfare and social work with an emphasis on what she calls intellectual biographies. Beyond the textbook and discussions on policies, the course is anchored in a semester-long individual project. "I want you to find a person who will stay with you as you work in the field, as a guide or a model for your work," she explains. "Find a person who will inspire you and teach us all." Our choice has to appear in the *Encyclopedia of Social Work* (all entries have died and have played some significant role in the field), and each student has to pick a different person.

The name of Virginia Satir popped into my head immediately. In the last 10 years, I have bumped into her work in various settings. At a workshop, a therapist used what he called "sculpting," where participants played various family members, connecting to each other spatially, close or apart, maybe touching or pointing. Virginia Satir helped develop the technique, he said. I saw a poster at a clinic called "My Declaration of Self Esteem" written by Satir in response to a 15-year-old's question, "How can I prepare myself for a fulfilling life." I discovered that one of the leaders in the Satir approach lived in Chapel Hill, and coincidentally, the School of Social Work was sponsoring a weekend workshop on Satir that fall. Iris agreed with my choice, and I immersed myself in Satir's life and work, with its emphasis on family therapy.

I discovered, for example, that among the handful of pioneers credited with adding "family therapy" into the psychotherapy field, Satir was the only woman and non-psychiatrist. As a school teacher, she visited students' families, where she first saw the impact of family systems. After social work training, she again visited families of clients she counseled and then began counseling families. Gradually, she formulated her approaches into books and monographs. Later, she led human development workshops, exploring unresolved childhood issues in large groups.

I pored through the writings, worked with the local expert, and attended the school's workshop. There, I saw the leaders demonstrate the four patterns of communication in families that Satir identified, with names and distinctive gestures. The blamer is one of them.

As I reflect on the blamer, I reluctantly acknowledge in my journal that I acted that role. After losing my job at the legislature, now more than 10 years ago, I felt vulnerable, sometimes unsuccessful. Although I was a good father and husband in many ways, when I was tired and depressed, at times I would use the blamer. I also used a pattern that Satir called the "super-reasonable," where I reverted to analysis, either ignoring my emotions or not making any effort to know what I was feeling.

Another of Satir's theories brought into focus the notion that crisis can also offer opportunity. From years of seeing individuals and families come to therapy in a chaotic moment, Satir identified her "theory of change" as one of her guiding principles. Usually, what triggered the crisis was what she called a foreign element, which interrupted the status quo—like losing my job. With help and the proper tools, a transforming idea entered the system, leading not just to a resolution of the chaos but an integration of new ideas into the family system. Then some kind of transforming idea or actions occurred, and the system transformed itself to a higher order: a new status quo. This led to more self-esteem among all of the individual members, better family performance, and more peace.

I feel a huge relief as I learn and reflect on the Satir change model. The idea of transformation in times of major transition grounds my work with the concept of initiation into full manhood. Drawing on the Satir system, I now see the patterns of depression—my depression timeline—as a series of transitions. With change comes chaos, sometimes a crisis. What I know now, after a decade of work, is to draw on other tools, rather than falling unconsciously into old patterns.

MEDITATION HAS BEEN ONE OF MY MAJOR ACTION TOOLS. The graduate program gives me a chance to find out how meditation functions beyond my individual experience and the Kabat-Zinn stress reduction approach that I followed. Can stress reduction techniques, especially meditation, fit into formal therapeutic settings? What research evidence supports this approach?

During the first semester, while learning about Virginia Satir and a lot more—and working four days a week at FHI—I find time to develop an independent study course on mind-body therapeutic approaches. An energetic young professor, who worked with biofeedback at a hospital before coming to UNC, agrees to sponsor the course and my research.

As part of the course, I take the Kabat-Zinn eight-week, mindfulness-based stress reduction program, which has been incorporated into the Duke University Center for Holistic Medicine. A psychiatrist administers the program, working with social workers, psychologists, and a yoga instructor, all well trained in the Kabat-Zinn approach. When I first went through the process, I worked alone in my living room with only his tapes as a guide.

Sitting with 20 other participants in the front of a teaching auditorium, part of the modern building in the massive Duke Medical Center, I feel on both familiar and new territory. The tapes on stretching, sitting meditation, and body scan are similar to what I used several years earlier alone in my living room, as are the 45 minutes of practice every day at home. Now, I am also practicing once a week in a community with discussion afterwards led by trained professionals. I gain more confidence about this as a healing and therapeutic approach. But where does this work fit into such constructs as cognitive therapy?

"You need to dig harder," Liz Arnold says early in the semester in her small office at the Social Work building. "Meditation is a good focus. And I want you to look at the literature on biofeedback. I know there's some there. I think the other areas will get clearer. I think we can get something published if you keep working at it."

"I don't know, I've been looking hard," I protest feebly. Thoughts of more work and too few hours in the day flash through my mind. "But it is exciting, actually. You think we can actually get something published?"

"Maybe. Let's see what you find."

On Fridays, after the lunch with my colleagues in the part-time program, I practically run over to the health and social sciences library, excited by the new articles I'm finding. Searching for research on my topic, I pull down copies of *Oncology Nursing Forum* and *Headache*, along with pivotal articles in mainline resources like *JAMA* (*Journal of the American Medical Association*). Framing the entire study through stress reduction broadens the topic from depression to include anxiety, physical reactions, even cancer. To decide how to focus the investigation, I first have to understand the context of the research.

I learn that ancient cultures did not divide the mind and body as modern Western medicine has done. The Greeks at the time of Hippocrates incorporated imagination into their healing model, recognizing that images from the psyche could affect how the body felt and responded. In Eastern cultures, meditation and other daily practices were part of a person's health and healing. Racing ahead toward the present, I find the first description of the "fight or flight" reaction by Harvard physiologist Walter Cannon in the early 1900s, the first connection between environmental stresses and the body's reaction to that stress by Hans Selye in 1956, and into the present a growing cascade of pivotal studies on diet, exercise, group support, positive thinking, and meditation. Seeing my own journey framed in this march through Western history is exciting, seeing it as part of broader cultural themes.

On one hand, scientists are pushing on the frontiers of brain chemistry with new medicines being formulated to shape the mind. Meanwhile, a wide range of alternative practitioners are trying to re-establish the connection between mind and body. During the 1990s, the portion of Americans using one of 16 approaches to alternative medicine jumped from about 33 percent to 40 percent, according to nationally representative random surveys published in *JAMA*. More people visited alternative practitioners than primary care physicians. What an exciting time to be thinking about and practicing such approaches as meditation!

In our meetings through the spring, Liz keeps pushing for rigor and clarity. Finally, we decide on four areas of focus: meditation, guided imagery, biofeedback, and progressive muscle relaxation.

"A lot of the studies don't necessarily fall neatly into those four," I explain.

"That's OK. Add a fifth category that covers combined approaches."

So, I go back to the piles of studies on my desk at home, copied from the journals in the UNC health and social sciences library. The pieces of the puzzle fall into place, just in time for me to finish my paper during the semester. I find enough evidence in all four areas, as well as the combined approaches, to conclude that these specific stress reduction interventions affect behaviors. For example, progressive muscle relaxation that followed a specific protocol was most successful in reducing tension headaches. The mindfulness-based stress reduction approach to meditation was successful in reducing anxiety, depression, and skin conditions.

In our closing meeting at the end of the semester, Liz says, "I think you could get this published if it had more about social work practice."

"But I don't know enough about such applications. I'm just a student here."

"I could do a little research and summarize that material from my experience."

I hesitate, wondering if she wanted to take over my hard-earned research. As if reading my mind, she continues, "You would be the first author. You've done all this work. I'll add some credibility for a journal and focus on the new social work practice material."

During the summer and fall, now no longer connected to the course, we go back and forth on a new draft, incorporating her material. She suggests possible journals, and we send it out. A positive response comes back, but with some rigorous questions about both my research and hers. We work more, finding more studies and clarifying assertions. Finally, more than a year after I started the independent study, *Social Work in Health Care* accepts the paper. All my efforts in connecting my mind and body—from meditation to guided imagery—seem more authentic and supported. I feel stronger, more confident, even vindicated that my ideas have solid grounding in the social sciences.

THE SUMMER AFTER MY FIRST YEAR, I squeeze in a summer-school course on the mental health diagnostic system, driving to Chapel Hill after work three nights a week. The course focuses on the *Diagnostic and Statistical Manual of Mental Disorders, Fourth Edition*, or DSM-IV, the manual used by mental health systems to classify symptoms into disorders.

Our professor frames the context for using the DSM-IV before we start through the sections on different disorders. We learn that words like illness, disease, habit, addiction, or personal weakness are commonly used and often misunderstood by clients or professionals. Symptoms and conditions, for example, are understood as deviations from normality, with a combination of symptoms classified as a mental disorder. A summer school class races through material at a dizzying pace, but I want to get the details. The discussions on many topics fascinate me, both intellectually and as part of my personal reflections. The concepts can seem abstract: risk and protective factors, interventions proven to have positive behavioral outcomes, and relationship of psychological makeup and adaptation to stress. And, how all of these issues relate to diagnoses in the DSM-IV.

Major depression and alcohol dependence are the most common disorders in the country. "Men are more likely to have addictive disorders while women are more likely to have mood disorders," reads one of my professor's slides. I know Perilstein diagnosed me with some sort of depression, because of the prescriptions for Prozac. But I think of my behaviors as more addictive, leading to mood disorders. The DSM-IV system doesn't incorporate that subtlety.

After the overview and framing sessions, we charge through the DSM categories, from anxiety disorder and depression to schizophrenia and alcohol dependence. Naturally, I'm most interested in the categories of depression: major depression, dysthymic disorder, depression not otherwise specified, and a group of others related but not specific to depression, including bipolar disorder, adjustment disorder, mood disorder, and seasonal affective disorder.

Studying the diagnostic categories, I see my symptoms fitting closest to dysthymic disorder, a chronic low-grade depression. But I wonder if I really met what appeared to be the essential criterion: having a depressed mood "for most of the day, for more days than not, for at least two years." I was always able to escape into work or one of my kid's activities some of the time. The criteria for depression raise another basic issue: Why are women twice as likely as men to be diagnosed as depressed? About one fourth of women but only one of eight men will have a depressive episode at some time in their lives.

As I research papers for this and other classes, I find that a growing number of practitioners and researchers are addressing questions specifically related to men and depression. The reported lower incidence among men may reflect the fact that women are more aware of their feelings, seek help more often, and consequently get diagnosed more often with mood disorders. Rather than internalizing problems, men tend to externalize distress through anger, irritability and self-medication, and they seek psychotherapy less often than women.

New books use terms like "unmasking male depression" and the "covert depression" of men. *I Don't Want to Talk about It* by Terrence Real focuses on the connections of covert depression in men with domestic violence, alcoholism, and other addictive behaviors. "Alcohol both provides relief from depression and simultaneously creates more of it," he writes. "What is true for alcoholism is true for all of the defenses used in covert depression…. While the capacity to externalize pain protects men from *feeling* depressed, it does not stop them from *being* depressed."

Richard O'Conner, in *Undoing Depression,* focuses much of his analysis on men. Men are "good at depression," meaning that depression functions as a coping mechanism that serves them well in many ways, he says. Depression helps men cope with "the gradual numbing of feelings and experiences that the child learns are unacceptable." Men are taught to tough things out, to go to work no matter what, to get back in the battle—regardless of what they are feeling, even if they know what they are feeling.

But depression can be "unlearned" as a way to recover the missing pieces not developed fully during life, to return to the spark of our unique personalities and gifts we bring to the world. Recovering the missing pieces means a lot of work beyond a quick fix with brain chemistry. Or as O'Connor puts it, "the symptomatic relief of depression provided by medication or brief therapy may only help the patient regain a previous level of functioning that was depressed to begin with."

I incorporate this new wave of thinking into my papers in various courses, along with more traditional research. For example, a major study reported in 1999 in the *New England Journal of Medicine* identified the key factors precipitating battering of women to be alcohol or drug use, employment stress, and below high school education. This finding meshes with my experiences at field placements—first at an alcohol and substance abuse treatment program connected with the UNC medical center, and the final school year at a domestic violence treatment program in Raleigh.

At the UNC substance abuse treatment program, a client said, "I didn't realize I was trying to control my wife until I started to recognize my substance abuse problem." During group sessions, he talked sometimes about attending a separate domestic violence treatment project. Themes of control and taking responsibility underlie my other field placement, a program called Domestic Offenders Sentenced to Education (DOSE). One man at his second session was furious at the program itself for causing him to have a problem with his car.

One of the available parking areas near the DOSE program has some large pot-holes. "If I didn't have to go into that parking lot, I wouldn't have gone over that drop off," he said angrily at the group.

"You mean the program caused you to drive that way?" a veteran of the group asked, pushing the man to go beyond his complaint.

"Well, yeah. If I didn't have to come here, I wouldn't have been there and hurt my car."

Other men in the group pushed the newcomer to examine his logic. He was driving, not the program staff. How could the program be responsible? That night, the young man finally acknowledged the obvious—that he was driving the car and made choices of how fast he drove or how careful he was in the poorly paved parking lot. Many more weeks passed before he began to focus more on his own behaviors, rather than blaming others for his actions.

I pull together my experiences and readings in a presentation for a course my final year on therapeutic approaches. Called "Substance Abuse and Depression among Men," the presentation identifies patterns unique to men. One slide on dual treatment for both substance abuse and depression encourages social workers to see the client in a holistic manner. A key part of that is to be aware of tools to complement medication, therapy, and substance abuse treatment.

The list draws on my research in school, my experiences in field placements, and my experience in moving through depression. Social workers need to consider incorporating support groups to address isolation, after-care mentoring to nurture a sense of service, positive initiation rituals to move beyond boyhood behaviors, creativity to find a route to life desires. I love pulling these threads together into academic presentations, complete with literature citations on the required handout.

THE DANCES AT CHURCH AND other community events provided a way to express difficult parts of my past. I felt creative in a new way, in an artistic way. Although these projects required focused effort, just as writing articles at work did, the expressive process felt freer than my normal job. I felt like I was tapping all of my gifts, not just my intellectual and journalistic competence. Workshops and books gave me techniques and confidence that I could function as an artist.

Entering the Masters in Social Work program, I wanted to learn more about expressive arts and to integrate the techniques from the dance performances into mainstream psycho-educational and therapeutic settings. Dr. Paul Smokowski, who taught the DSM-IV course I took, had once worked in theater. When he turned to social work, he became certified in the field of psychodrama, one of the earliest expressive arts areas with a formal therapeutic training process. I discuss with Paul my interest in expressive arts, and he agrees to sponsor an independent study course. It is my last semester.

I research psychodrama and other expressive arts approaches and examine therapeutic concepts. My practical experience is to design and lead a four-week expressive arts workshop. To reflect on all of the work, I write two papers—one describing the workshop and one linking the literature and therapeutic framework with the outcomes of the workshop.

"I'm not sure what to call what I do in these workshops I've led," I tell Paul in one of our early meetings. "I have used primarily movement, writing, and storytelling, usually with a simple performance of some sort. I've taken a dance therapy workshop and created some dances with groups in churches and workshops. I've also read a lot about using writing and dance in therapeutic ways. But I want to learn more about using these expressive arts approaches in a therapeutic setting rather than a performance."

"Let's start with the psychodrama literature," he says. "That will help ground you in the drama part of it. And, you will need to start thinking about the therapeutic context as well."

Seven students, all women, respond to my announcement and participate in the workshop, called "transitions." Most of them are graduating, and I assume that will be the focus of the transition. Paul reviews my plan for the first session. He sees me focusing more on the first of the three-part psychodrama structure, warm-up, with less on the action/enactment and sharing stages. He also requires that if any participant shows particular vulnerability, I make sure she has another person in the group to talk with during the week.

In the first session, after a brief explanation of the process we will follow, the seven participants and Paul move through the room in an opening exercise, exploring different movement patterns, rhythms, and speed while thinking about a transition they want to share. I ask them to stop moving and arrange themselves in pairs. Each person then tells a short transition story. The partner responds with two movements reflecting the feeling that the story inspires, an approach called authentic witnessing or listening. The witness can add a word or two to the movement as well. I demonstrate some sample types of movements and explain that they should be discrete, simple, and easily repeatable.

I move about the room, watching the pairs work. In one, "Sally" is crying as she listens to her partner's story. "I feel confused by the exercise," she says to me. "I don't feel I'm doing justice to my partner's story with my responses."

"Just keep on going with the exercise," I say, encouraging her. "We'll have a chance to discuss that later. Can you do that?" She nods.

After both have told their stories, they have a total of four movements and perhaps a few words between them. The next step is to develop a simple duet using this material. I show how to tie the movements together, adding a four-count rhythm and connecting body movements to make a fluid phrase. The four groups continue their work and create duets. When I see that they are finished, I re-assemble the group.

"Does anyone want to say anything at this point, before we go on to the next step?"

Sally shares her confusion with the group. "Was I supposed to just focus on my own feelings as I listened or how my feelings related to my partner's story?" She catches her breath and goes on. "I felt like I was letting my partner down if I didn't say something about her story."

"The assignment was to focus on your own feelings as you listened, and to express those," I say. "In this exercise, what begins as a single story becomes a shared story." I encourage everyone to trust the process and move on to the next step. I look around to gauge their feelings. Sally seems okay. She's not crying and nods again. Others seem eager to proceed. No one wants to discuss Sally's question at this point.

I now group the pairs into two quartets, based on the movement patterns and words I saw as the duets took shape. They agree to do a simple performance for each other. I instruct them briefly on how to use our classroom space as a stage. I demonstrate a beginning pose and how to alter their movements a bit spatially, and I encourage them to be aware of the other duet as they function as a foursome. "Use the same authentic witnessing approach, focusing on your own feelings that may arise."

After both performances, participants describe feeling "nervous but exhilarated," as one says. Witnesses were touched and moved by what they saw.

"It was like the creation of the world. They were like puppets being set in motion." Another says, "It reminded me of my divorce. They broke off and they created something new." Still another adds, "I saw it as nurturing and giving order, like gardening does for me."

We are nearly out of time in the first session and do not get to the "sharing" portion of the psychodrama structure. I do make sure that Sally has a partner during the week to discuss the feelings that arose for her. She appreciates that but says she's fine.

The next week, we share a good bit at the beginning, including learning what was going on with Sally the week before. "Last week, I had come directly from meeting with a lawyer regarding selling my house. This is part of the process of ending a relationship of several years," she says. "All that stress and emotion came up as I listened to the story."

"I can understand that there was a lot of stress," I say.

"I felt guilty letting my own emotions flood into the exchange with my partner. I didn't feel I was being responsible to her." She pauses. "Sometimes, I worry more about another person than I do about myself. I think that's what was happening."

As I move through the four-week workshop and the writing of my papers, the intuitive process I've followed over the last years in building dances gets more organized and structured. I can plan and anticipate where a dance or story needs to go in terms of the group, in the process and the therapeutic issues. I have a lot to learn, but this course has given me confidence and insights into how my experience with the expressive arts stands in a stream of learning and practice over many decades.

AS I BEGIN MY FINAL YEAR IN SCHOOL, FHI wins a large grant from USAID. This global leadership project will work with youth in developing countries on reproductive health and HIV prevention. I have been bid on the project to help with information and publications. I am now working half-time at FHI during my third year of graduate school, scrambling to juggle classes with my field placement at DOSE. With this new project, I begin to shift my tasks at work. The assignment holds a lot of excitement, moving from a focus on contraception to more diverse issues such as youth development, sex education, parents, and community norms. And, I may have a chance to assume more responsibility and leadership, which could be exciting.

In my final spring semester at school, the stress of the new youth project is building—launching a website, completing research briefs to be ready for the bi-annual international AIDS conference in June, developing a project brochure, revitalizing the color scheme for materials, and more. Working half-time is not enough to complete these tasks and keep up with school. So, I cut back on my hours at DOSE and develop a plan with the field placement office to spread the required field hours through the summer and fall. I make an arrangement with Paul to take an incomplete so that I can finish my research paper on expressive arts in the fall. Everyone is happy, including me. I get to walk with my class at the graduation ceremony, just not shift my tassel.

In May 2002, standing in the back of the huge basketball arena at UNC, with my classmates around me, I am more excited than when I graduated from college 32 years earlier. I borrow a cap and gown, my wife is beaming and takes loads of pictures, and my sister, herself a social worker, comes from across the state for the ceremony. We have a great party that evening at a classmate's farm, with food spread out in a section of their barn. It is cozy and fun, with music blaring, and family and friends swapping stories along with our pride and hopes for the future.

Several weeks later, I am off to the AIDS conference in Barcelona, and the excitement of my new job builds. I work with youth producing an on-site newsletter at the conference, helping build attention to the growing HIV infection rates among young people globally … all heady stuff.

In the fall of 2002, with only the final paper and field placement hours left to complete for my degree, I move to 80 percent time at FHI. I graduate from UNC officially in December 2002 with my Masters in Social Work. Also, my boss at the youth project resigns to take another job. As senior management reshuffles staff to cover her responsibilities, I have the opportunity to direct all information programs for the project. Now comes the real decision. I can remain part-time at FHI and begin a social work career part-time. Or, I can take the promotion and help build this new project.

I feel more creative in planning, managing, and writing in the youth project than I have in many years. The reason is not because the job is that different from my other FHI assignments but because I have changed. I have brought long-buried emotions to the surface, expressed them in dances, used Prozac and therapy, accepted who I am, and learned to meditate when stresses prompt old patterns.

Practical considerations play a role as well. Struggles with money have always added pressure to my decisions. I can get a raise in this new role and feel much more secure. When I had chances early in my career to advance, I held back because the path did not feel right. Now, I feel my social work training merging with my public health on-the-job experience into a more coherent career path. I can still return to the expressive arts or other social work opportunities in future years, certainly in retirement. As the baby boomers mature into old age, I have a feeling there will be plenty of work to do. I talk the choice over with my wife. I feel drawn to what appears to be an obvious decision: take the new full-time position.

Through graduate school, the burden of working through depression gradually fell off my shoulders. Unresolved emotions settled into themes from research-based constructs, like unorganized scraps of paper landing in well-organized file folders. The research, learning, papers, and field work invigorated and challenged me, reaching beyond intellect and even feelings into a spiritual place, like a series of reflections on a very long hike in the woods. Instead of feeling that my path through depression has been too eccentric or eclectic, outside of grounded theories and other's experience, I now feel I am standing in a broad river of human learning and growth. In stepping firmly into this mighty flow of water, I am adding my own knowledge, experience, and perspectives for those who will taste and feel refreshed in their own ways and in their own time.

I feel an abundance of gratitude for having this chance to synthesize my thinking and feelings about depression and the steps I've taken since losing my job in 1988. I'm proud of what I have learned and know I have the credentials to move into a new career in social work. But for now, I have a new and exciting job at FHI.

BOOK 5. RETURN
(2003)

CHAPTER 24. Slow Down, You Move Too Fast

 IN 2003, THIRTY-FOUR YEARS AFTER MY FIRST arrival in Jabalpur, India, I step off the Gondwana train at dawn. My FHI duties in Delhi ended the day before, and I rode the train all night.

I am planning to take a taxi to Roshan's house. (I began calling Mrs. Raza by her first name in our correspondence leading up to this trip.) Instead a young colleague of Taqi's picks me up and drives me to the compound. Taqi can't come himself because he is very busy with a conference.

Roshan explained in her first letter that Taqi—the bright, older of the two boys I played with on the verandah so many years ago—had become a prominent doctor, a professor at the Jabalpur Medical College of Orthopedics and secretary of the All India Orthopedics Association. This weekend, he is hosting the 22nd annual meeting of the Madhya Pradesh Chapter of the Indian Orthopedic Association, a conflict with my visit that he cannot avoid.

The ride through the city at dawn stirs forgotten memories but also alerts me to the sweeping changes that have gone far beyond Delhi. Internet cafés and ads for telephones and televisions dot our way toward the Razas' house. As we pull into the old compound, I mentally scroll through images from so many years ago of rickshaws taking me back home down the same drive: Rail-thin men of indeterminate ages, stooped by years of physical labor, pedaling me through the garden, around the circular drive to the back of the compound, and up to the house under the roofed porch of the bungalow.

But this time, I will not see the verandah. Three years earlier, "our lovely bungalow collapsed due to the heavy rains and water logging," Roshan told me in a recent letter. An earlier earthquake had damaged the walls. "I had repaired it but little did I know the foundation had suffered too." The walls of mud bricks, more than 100 years old, could not hold up. "Thanks to God we were able to get out before it fell."

The Razas had a place to go, the modest building that now stands before me at the front of the compound. Several years before, the family had constructed this 16-bed hospital to serve mostly poor families. Since the bungalow collapsed, the family has lived in what had been the simple administrative areas of the hospital, keeping rooms open to patients in the back.

Taqi's young associate honks our arrival. I get out and stretch my legs, watching the early morning haze burning off. The acrid smell of cooking fires welcomes me back. The strong, high-spirited woman I remembered appears and walks forward with the same energy and no-nonsense directness but now in a 72-year-old body that is starting to stoop. We hug warmly.

Drawing back, Roshan looks at me closely, hands reaching up to rest on my shoulders. "You look just the same, Bill," she says in the non-sentimental way that I remember, as if the time that has passed is four years instead of 34. Her steady strength shored her up as a Muslim widow in the middle of Hindu India, as she raised her boys and maintained what was once her father's elegant compound.

"You look the same as well," I say. "Just a little smaller, I think."

She smiles and takes me to the door that opens into their makeshift home. Soon, a large man with a touch of gray in his beard appears.

"Do you know who this is?" she asks. For a few seconds, I don't have an answer. Then I recognize the quizzical smile that the younger brother, Moin, carried about with him as he played with us on the verandah instead of doing his homework. Moin helps direct the small family-run hospital. His wife, Afreen, a schoolteacher, has left for the day with their three children.

Taqi is finishing his morning prayers and about to rush out to make last minute preparations for the conference. We greet with a quick hug in the small living room and dining area, the family gathering spot. A long hall goes down to several family bedrooms and past a divider to the hospital rooms still in use.

"I am so glad you are here and regret so the conflict with my conference," Taqi says quickly but earnestly, his warm eyes calm and slow for a moment. He is as intense and charming as I remember the 12-year-old, seeming to be the man of the house even then. Taqi moves nimbly past the dining table, gathering his papers and materials for the conference. Then he agrees to join us briefly outside for a photo before he leaves.

Five of us pose in the early September morning, the heat that will come later in the day not yet a concern. I have the same kind of knit shirt and khaki pants that I wore daily in 1969. Only the high-tech, all-purpose running shoes reflect the new consumer age. My Indian family, as I have thought of them all these years, gathers around me.

Next to me, only a few inches shorter, Moin has a piece of fabric wrapped around his head in the informal Muslim style, a large shirt loose over simple trousers and flip flops. Taqi, on the right end, is more professional with his white shirt tucked neatly into trousers. Slightly in front are Roshan and Kehkashan, Taqi's wife, who is a gynecologist and works with the family hospital. The women wear kurtas, colorful shirts that reach below the knee, and a dupatta thrown across their necks (a long piece of fabric with the ends hanging over both shoulders down the back). The garden behind us has bright red flowers, with a miniature palm tree reaching above the low roof-line.

After the click of the shutter, Taqi hastily waves goodbye and heads to one of the two small cars he and Kehkashan keep behind the house. Their son is away in medical school in Pune, a large city near Bombay, and their daughter left for secondary school earlier. Taqi pulls out into the crowded traffic of cars, school children on bicycles, bullock carts, and rickshaws, all much denser and with more cars than I remember it.

Roshan turns, her face somber. "Do you want to see what's left of the house?"

We walk around to the back of the compound, maybe an acre of land behind the surrounding wall. She points to what had been the side of the house, with the remains of several walls still leaning under a portion of the crumbling tile roof. "The mud walls simply couldn't withstand any more rain," she says. "We were in the house that night, and we noticed a crack in the wall that kept widening."

As we walk along what had been the verandah, she continues, "The cracks grew wider. Taqi and Moin tried to shore them up with old posts, even old bedsprings from the hospital, with whatever they could find, but things were not stabilizing. They called an architect friend on a cell phone, and he said to get out of the house, that it sounded like it could collapse. Moin scooped up little Ridha, then just two, and we all left with nothing."

Within an hour, most of the interior walls collapsed, bringing down much of the roof, including where the little two-year-old had been sleeping. Roshan speaks with determination but clearly is holding back the emotion that is close to the surface. I feel her anguish as if she is a close relative whose story is partly my own.

That disastrous night, Roshan left the house where she had raised her two boys and welcomed their wives and grandchildren in the traditional Indian style: three generations living under one roof. The five adults and five children rushed into the hospital for safety. The family heirlooms were destroyed. I remember the large hand-carved room divider with inlaid ivory of Indian scenes, near where Rick and I sat and played our ragas. These lost family art pieces came from her grandfather, a barrister in Bengal who practiced in the British court and married an Irish woman.

Stepping through the rubble, I take photos of what's left of the walls around the room where Rick and I slept under our mosquito nets, Motilal's kitchen, and the dark bathing room. Cold water ran through the single pipe, where Motilal would fill his metal pot to prepare the water before announcing, "Shaving *kar liya.*" Memories wash through me from another era, when I felt more boy than man. I feel sad that with the passage of time, this house where I started on my road to adulthood now sits broken. But this space served its function of helping me to begin to discover the spark within me that lies deeper than achievement. A spark defined more by grace.

I rejoin Roshan in the yard between the ruined bungalow and their temporary home. As we walk back to the tight family quarters at the front of the little hospital, I think about fate and human response, acceptance and pushing forward, how I happened to land in Roshan's life so many years ago and what happened when I went home. Returning from India the first time and living in Boston was something like the monsoon that occurred here. While physical structures around me did not crumble and collapse, the foundations of my inner self began to crack, eventually requiring a total rebuilding.

THE VISIT WITH ROSHAN AND HER FAMILY is operating in slow motion, more like two months than two days. Each nuance of the discussions conjures up connections—with my own story, with changes in global culture and Indian society, with the aging of the family constellations.

The movie title *Back to the Future* comes to mind as I sit in their modest living room, on the single hard couch, watching the hustle of the extended family unfold. As Roshan stands before me, my own parents dash across my mind. The grandchildren are running in from school now, and I see my own children at that age. Lee and Dana are facing new challenges as young adults now, and I can see myself moving toward Roshan's time of life. But at the same time, this stately Indian woman takes me back to when I first came to India, and I see at a glance how our stories have played themselves out.

Despite the time warp spinning me backward and forward, I find myself aware of each moment—perhaps the single most important skill that I have been practicing for a decade as I have moved through depression. The kids tell their mothers and their granny lively tales from their day in the Indian sing-song English that I adapted for my time here. I slow down still more, listening to each detail. Then I smile as I hear the tune sound through my mind, *slow down you move too fast...* Many times in my last months at the Raza compound so many years ago, the Simon and Garfunkel phrase kept me anchored in the day.

I absorb the sights and sounds about me: laughing children, crinkling of wrapped presents being brought to the table, and aromas that I could once name wafting across the top of the wall between the dining area and the kitchen.

Moin remains at the mosque, and Taqi is working on his convention. The females of the household assemble with me and the children. Roshan insists I begin the opening of gifts. She has picked handicrafts from local artisans. A large red and yellow batik depicts seven horses pulling an archer in a royal exotic carriage, preparing to launch his arrow. My gifts from America and from the market in Delhi make their mark. Falaq, the 17-year-old home from school, beams with joy as she holds the American t-shirt up, before racing to her room to change from her school uniform to model it with modern jeans. I cannot remember seeing a girl in blue jeans on my first stay in this city.

That afternoon, Moin and his family take me to one of the notable sites in the few guidebooks that cover Madhya Pradesh, the "marble rocks." At this geological wonder, the rocks on both sides of a river are made of a soft material like soapstone that can be carved. We make the hour-long drive through crowded city streets past the hospital where Taqi teaches and the convention center where his meeting is underway, and into a rural area. Little 5-year-old Ridha falls asleep in my lap, after sleepily saying things like, "Look, Uncle," pointing at a shrine being decorated for a Hindu holiday coming in a few days. Her sister and 10-year-old brother, Fatir, are in the back seat.

At the rocks, merchants sell all types of carvings from the stone. We leave the path and make our way across a small field of rolling rock formations, like walking across a rocky section of the Maine or California coastline, except that instead of reaching the ocean, we reach the edge of a small canyon with a river about 40 feet wide gushing between us and another plateau of marble rock on the other side of the river. Moin and I carry the little children until we finally reach a flat area near the river. We pose for photos at the edge of this rock, which juts out onto a cliff. The high water from the last of the rainy season keeps the river high on both sides of the canyon, obscuring much of the molded patterns shaped by the current over the centuries.

When we return, I rest in the room where Moin's children sleep. The girls agreed to their mother's request to perform the songs they recently sang at the school open house, the same Catholic school where Roshan taught chemistry and sent her boys for their education. Little Ridha, who slept in my lap on the drive to the rocks, sings a sweet little song about God creating the world. Her seven-year-old sister follows.

"Thank you God for the nose we have that can smell the flowers," Rifat sings, her beautiful dark eyes dancing like an angel as she tilts her head in a choreographed pattern with the music. She goes through all the verses, thanking God for eyes that can see and hearts that can feel.

Rifat's song speaks to me of paying attention to the blessings of the day and expressing gratitude for what we have now. Her beauty, innocence, and performance echo with a song I try to bring into each of my days. The mantra of gratitude for a positive approach and living one day at a time, even one breath at a time, is alive in a schoolroom in Jabalpur, just as it is in spiritual meetings in North Carolina.

Listening to Rifat and Ridha sing in their cute outfits, I remember more about my Simon and Garfunkel ritual. Thoughts of my youth and my own children zip through my mind at 21st century speed, and I laugh out loud, grateful for my ability to observe my mind and not be consumed by it. I come back to my breathing and stay focused on these two beautiful little girls. I think of my own children, Lee now 22, the age I was when I first went to Jabalpur.

After the rest and performance, we have a late dinner, including miniature hamburgers, like those advertised on the television shows that beam into the Raza dining room. But Roshan also serves the spicy vegetable curries that I remember, and the sweeter-than-syrup dough balls called *gulab jamun* for dessert, as we watch the soap operas from Bombay. In one favorite, a mother-in-law can make things disappear, a cross between *Casper the Friendly Ghost* and the *Our Miss Brooks* characters from my childhood television years. Roshan watches the soaps regularly with the kids before they do their homework and then go to bed. It is a ritual in the joint family where any of the three women might be in charge of any of the kids.

Moin joins us for this meal, but Taqi is still dealing with some emergency at his conference. When Taqi does finally arrive around 10 p.m., the phone is ringing as he walks in the door. Another detail settled, he hangs up and eats his supper with his wife, his mother, and me. I remember how my boyhood household revolved around my father's busy schedule.

The second day of my visit, Taqi's wife Kehkashan, Roshan, and little Ridha, the only child who did not have Saturday school, take me to Taqi's meeting at the modern convention center on the edge of town. We stroll through the outside exhibits, and I peak into the main hall with a presentation in progress. The precocious little boy I remember has grown up to master the management of all of these details. Taqi walks with us for a few moments, always speaking to people who pass by us. I feel like I could be the little child, my father so busy with details at the college. Taqi returns to the details of lunch, presentations, and other logistics. And, my time in Jabalpur is starting to run out.

As we get back into the car, we have a choice. Roshan and I have discussed my work in family planning and AIDS prevention, which had brought me to the meeting in Delhi. She is happy to take me to meet the man who pioneered family planning programs in the area, one of several community activities with which she worked as a volunteer. Or we can visit Ala, Roshan's best friend her entire adult life, and the woman I remember as the Parsi who visited and heard Rick and me play.

THE CHOICE FOR MY LAST OUTING IN JABALPUR is easy. I feel something important awaits at Ala's house. Kehkashan negotiates the small van through the crowded paved road back toward Jabalpur, dodging potholes, bicycles, and animals. Roshan's role as the matriarch in this family is slipping as the two daughters-in-law, Kehkashan and Afreen, increasingly direct the household. But this visit back to Ala's is Roshan's time. Turning off the main roads into what Americans would call a subdivision, Kehkashan and Roshan begin a vigorous exchange about the best route. Kehkashan, the gynecologist, stands her ground on her choice. Finally, Roshan announces with authority, "I am from Jabalpur," and Kehkashan turns obediently in the direction Roshan prefers. Kehkashan drops off Roshan and me, and takes little Ridha home for a nap.

Ala greets us warmly at the second floor walk-up apartment in a compound with flowers, gates, and quiet streets. She looks the same as I remember her, striking high cheekbones, an exotic Middle Eastern look.

Nearly 35 years later, her straight black hair is not yet totally gray. Ratan, her husband, older and not well, greets us with a welcoming spirit, as he remains seated in a comfortable chair in a spacious living room. He has not dressed for the visit, remaining in his short pajamas to accommodate the heat.

Away from her own home and the competing new matriarchs, Roshan takes on the schoolgirl flare I remember in her. Laughing and telling stories, she and Ala recount their friendship, dating from when Roshan was just married and Ala moved to Jabalpur. They chuckle as they recall some of my bumbling efforts to accommodate myself to India, how they nursed me back to health during several bouts with dysentery. I push the conversation to other matters that I have been pondering, how Indians cope with illness, hardship, and depression.

From my book-bag, I pull out clippings I have gathered from my week in the country, mostly from *The Times of India*, a sophisticated international newspaper. The editorial page carries a column called "The Speaking Tree." One column discussed the seven sacred chakras in the body, linking them with sacred cities and rivers. Another addressed awareness, how a careful attention to the details of daily life leads to freedom. "It's amazing to me that this major paper has this spirituality column on the editorial page," I say.

"It's a very spiritual country," Ala says. "Indians are spiritual, even if we have different beliefs."

"How is it that you two were such good friends and from different religions?"

They laugh, as if the question is irrelevant. "We're friends. The differences in our faith do not matter," Roshan says. There is a pause. The tone has taken a serious turn.

I break the silence. "My year here, I felt lost a lot, even depressed."

"It was a real challenge to be so far away from home at that age. India is a lot to get used to," Ala says.

"India made a big impression on me. Even though I've never been back, that year changed my view of my whole life, of religion, of Americans not being better than anyone else. At times in my life when I've been depressed, I often think of India, how I handled the year here and how hard life is for so many people here."

"I get depressed from time to time too," says Ala. "I always feel better when I get together with Roshan and visit."

"It helps us both," Roshan says smiling. "When the house collapsed, I kept saying, 'Oh, My God. What will we do now?' Taqi was there, of course, and made plans for us to live in the hospital. But when I visited with Ala I felt so much better."

"I think about my daughter often," Ala says, her smile disappearing into a solemn, sad face that looked her age for the first time.

"Ala's daughter died in the Air India crash off of Bombay," says Roshan. "She was a stewardess."

"I get quite depressed sometimes," says Ala. "Reading about prayer in the newspapers is comforting. And, of course, I get a lot of comfort from my faith." After a moment, she continues. "When I think of my daughter, I feel a darkness. It's the grief of her death, but it's some other kind of sadness—beyond her death. A deeper sadness."

I'm not sure whether to comment about her daughter. "I've dealt with depression often in my own life," I say. "Coming back to India, it's interesting to me to think about the role depression has played in my life and how I've changed since I was here before."

"You were so quiet when you were here. Rick was the talkative one," Ala says, ready to change the subject. "He could play so well." She talks more, recalling our mini-concerts for them in Roshan's living room, remembering us as "those two American boys living with Roshan."

Animated again, she invites us to have a snack in the kitchen. The simple apartment has not moved to the modern style that has begun to sweep through the growing middle class in India, with gleaming white refrigerators, washing machines, kitchen counters with new gadgets that Americans take for granted. This is an Indian kitchen, with a large table in the middle, cupboards with biscuits, a sink, and small fridge, as Ala calls it. As we are finishing our tea, Kehkashan and Ridha arrive to take us home. They join the tea party.

I'm eager to explore the large verandah, the roof of the apartment below, and Ratan guides me outside. The street and the rooftops beyond are so much quieter than I remember India, where loud film music played throughout the day.

"They passed a law against the loud music," Roshan explains. "And, this is a much quieter neighborhood."

The verandah stretches around the apartment back toward the front door, where we pause at an air conditioning system that uses homebuilt trays, water, and a fan to generate cooler air. The simple but effective set-up prompts a memory of a night I spent in Katmandu, the capital of Nepal, near the end of my India year, when I took a vacation. That night in a tiny hotel room—we were in the middle of the intense hot season—another volunteer and I tried everything we could think of to cool off. Finally, we soaked our sheets and pulled them over us. The ceiling fan directly overhead, which had only blown hot air, making things worse before, now cooled us, as the sheet gradually dried. Several times I soaked the sheet before I could sleep. The scene races through my brain as I follow Ridha around the corner and back to the living room. I see my own daughter back at age 5, like Ridha, in a bright dress, barefooted, smiling, happy in the moment.

Now in my late 50s, I feel my memory dash about sometimes, at an increasingly warped speed, as if my brain needs to add more memory chips to absorb all of life experiences. Paradoxically, this avalanche of detail forms patterns that seem to slow down at moments to offer insight and clarity. Like tracking animals in the bush, I see clues in my life story, which lead me to finding what I need to know, especially as I have more material with which to work.

DEPARTURE TIME IS APPROACHING. I take a last walk up to the clock tower, down the busy market street and back to Roshan's home. The sights and sounds seem both familiar and foreign. The loud music is gone, but the crunch of traffic has increased. Two boys draw water from the same spigots where I stumbled along early in my first arrival in Jabalpur, and the veteran volunteer asked if I was depressed. The shops and street vendors offer all the basics of life. A paint store named "Colour World" is next to the mobile phone shop, which is next to the bicycle shop. Bullocks and motor scooters pass by, and a man pushes a vegetable cart piled high in a beautiful arrangement of tomatoes, beans, eggplant, and several long varieties of squash. The Chinese restaurant is still at the roundabout, where the streets meet at the clock tower. I buy some bottled water and chat with a young man who is the grandson of the man who ran the restaurant when Rick and I ate there once a week on Motilal's night off.

The clock tower appears freshly painted, with four ornate cupolas at the second-story level, sparkling whitewash and brown trim. It stretches tall above the little shops, another four to five stories in a single cylindrical shape, interspersed with carved collars encircling the clocks. The four timepieces face in each direction, and I notice they have the correct time. I feel as if the clock speaks to me in multiple dimensions, with correct time whether I'm looking backwards or forwards. I feel overcome with memories, contentment, joy, and sadness at leaving—all joined together like so many religions.

My visit back to Jabalpur has been a homecoming on multiple levels, a time of renewed healing and deepening faith. The depth of my connection to Roshan, not nurtured over the years, surprises me, as if our earlier bond has been simmering in some universal energy source that reaches beyond oceans, time, and circumstances. Roshan and her world lodged deep within me, and have emerged, just as *kahan hai* did when I needed to find my seat on the Gondwana express. I returned to the home that held me in its aging mud walls as I passed through that initiatory year after college.

The women of the house gather for lunch with me. Taqi is at his meeting. Moin must be at the mosque. We review the two days, marveling at how much like family we all felt and so quickly. Roshan packs me sandwiches for the return train ride.

As I am about to leave, 17-year-old Falaq gets her brother at medical school on one of the cell phones, and I talk with a young man in Bombay who is sorry to miss this family occasion. I hear a quivering voice, as if he may cry from missing such a family event, but he holds his poise. I feel the same quiver of nerve that shot through me that Christmas of 1969, when I waited for hours at the government poultry office for a phone call with my parents, scheduled by letter. The call was delayed again and again, trying to move through wires connecting my parents' home in Tennessee through cables under the ocean to Australia and up to Jabalpur. Amazingly, I did hear my parents' voice crackle into the receiver briefly but the operator could never patch me in.

CHAPTER 25. Coming Home

MY TWO TRIPS TO INDIA IN 1969 and 2003 stand like bookends for the primary story of my adulthood: finding the spark within me as I moved through the depression in my life, returning to my unique self. Coming home in 2003, I have a plan. This time, I will not isolate as I did in Boston in 1970.

I put a notice in the bi-weekly church bulletin announcing I will lead a discussion on issues related to returning from major trips, including my recent visit back to India. I decide not to work hard at rounding up an audience, as I did with some of my dances. Wednesday nights, after the dinner at church, many meetings are planned as a means to combine fellowship and getting the church business done. Whoever comes will come. That will be who needs to be there, I decide.

That Wednesday, as the last stragglers drift off to the various meetings, only three people are left with me at a table in the corner of the small fellowship room. Jane and Jim Hunt sit side by side, my friends for many years. One of the high points was the dance celebration in my backyard when they served as the elders in the initiation ceremony. We have often talked about India, where they have traveled several times while Jim worked on books about Gandhi's life. Dorothy, another long-time friend, joins us.

After we settle in at the table, the clean-up of the dinner over, I begin talking about visiting Roshan, the grown up boys, the new generation, the songs and gifts. "Still, there was the issue of coming home," I said. "I want to tell others about how differently I feel coming home now, and why I wanted to talk to Roshan about being depressed 35 years ago. I wanted to share my feelings and stories this time, not just move to the next task now that I'm home. What better place to do this than in a spiritual community, where I've done my dances and sorted through a lot of stories in my life."

Jane, in her normal style, gets right to the point. "So, how do you feel?" We both laugh.

"I feel great. At first, when I saw we would be such a tiny crowd, I had a quick pang of not feeling important enough, that hardly anyone wanted to hear my story. But, then I saw you over here and realized that was just perfect. Our little group would be just fine."

We talk about the discussion I had with Roshan and Ala about depression. "But the serious challenge, I've come to realize, for me, is not depression per se, but how I manage big transitions—how I move through change, especially if the change is about a life issue that has been difficult, such as something related to work." We sit silently for a minute or so. "What do you make of this issue of transition?" I ask.

After a little silence, Dorothy says her elderly mother is considering moving to Raleigh to be near her. "This prompts some ambivalent feelings," she says. I look over at Jane and Jim. Jane is uncharacteristically quiet. Jim starts to move his bushy eyebrows.

Over the years, Jim grew to take on more and more of the quizzical look of Gandhi, in his work on his books about the great Indian's life. Like Gandhi, Jim is a lean, wiry man with a wry smile, and always full of the kind of joy and irony that Gandhi projects in his photos. "Actually, I'm in a big transition," Jim says. He pauses, his dark eyes darting about and then settling on mine. "I'm not able to remember as much anymore."

His eyes zip away and I look toward Jane. The tears are starting to roll just onto her nose. Jane has told me about Jim's diagnosis, but I have not heard Jim discuss it. "It'll be hard," Jane manages, the tears flowing now in front of Jim. "But that's life." She looks up, her face vulnerable but strong. She took care of her mother, who lived well into her 90s. Now, her husband is starting to lose his capacities.

Then Jim looks back at me. I can't tell if he heard Jane and if so, if he can process her thought. Then he says, "And, it's going to get worse."

I feel a shared sadness at the table, but some collective strength as well—from the telling, these words said aloud. Jane is so strong, even when her emotions are exposed. Jim sounds courageous, but already his tone has a slight childlike quality, what I understand to be the early stages of Alzheimer's. I feel blessed to be hearing this intimate sharing in this small community of four friends. It's a tender moment.

Jim has been my hero. This strong, quiet man played the role of elder at my midlife initiation ceremony. He quietly marched through his life, true to his values in his choice of jobs, writing, and family priorities, finding ways on a modest professor's salary in a small predominantly black university to travel and see the world. Now, he is telling us of the final passage ahead for him.

I needed Jim as my elder once, and he was there. Now, in my second return from India, this community event turns out to be of service to him—and to Jane, as hard as it is for her to hear him say these words. Perhaps this is the purpose of my re-entry this time, returning from India, not to establish my new role but to be there for others as they share important details about their own transitions.

I AM ENTERING A NEW THRESHOLD. My hard wiring and the circumstances of my upbringing led to low-grade depression as my primary coping mechanism with life's difficulties. I no longer need this response to transition, stress, and change. The transformation of my midlife years resulted from good fortune, hard work, and above all, the love and support of family and friends. Georgia, my best friend and life companion, stood at the center of this pack of soul mates, present with me on each slippery slope and every solid step.

As I move forward, ancestral wisdom guides me. My father gradually has settled into my psyche as an emotional lodestone. An adjacent space now holds the power of my mother, reconciled with herself. And Georgia remains beside me. Gratitude and grace encircle me within communities of love and faith.

I've forgiven myself, let go of shame and embarrassment. Today I celebrate the yellow and purple of spring and the golden crimson of autumn. I stand smiling in a sweaty August heat wave and breathe deeply in a January freeze. Sometimes, I turn to my crane dance, remembering to smile and notice the miracles around me. My long skinny arms now extend gracefully, the old awkwardness transformed into beauty.

I frame my life now with acceptance. My best is good enough. I am worthy of love. Every day remains full of imagination and adventure.

EPILOGUE. OBLATION MEANS FORGIVENESS

A FEW YEARS AFTER MY LAST TRIP TO INDIA, we celebrated my father's last birthday, his 91st, at his favorite restaurant. Mother had died 18 months earlier; if she had been with us, the evening would've been their 65th wedding anniversary. The tales that night revolved around childhood memories.

I began talking about Jackson and Galloway Church, including my time as an acolyte. "Do you remember that, Dad?"

"Vaguely." His eyes looked up slightly above his thick glasses, his head remaining stooped. No more response, so I continued.

"Every Sunday morning, I felt a strange peace in that little chapel, hearing the communion ritual, the words rolling off the minister's tongue." No one jumped into the conversation, so I went on. "The phrases became so familiar, part of the routine in that quiet, sacred place." I drifted deeper into the memory.

"One word sticks out from the readings that I heard every Sunday… *oblation*." Quiet again. "I never knew what it meant. Still don't. I never looked it up."

To my left, Dad suddenly lifted his head as erect as I had seen it in a year. He looked as if ready to make a point in a sermon and spoke with the same authority that rang loud in both lofty and humble sanctuaries. "Forgiveness. *Oblation* means forgiveness."

After dinner, I drove Dad back to his little cottage, thinking about forgiveness. A series of phrases I had learned in a meditation class came to mind. I noticed my in-breath and said to myself, *May I be filled with loving kindness.* Out-breath: *May I be well.*

As I pulled the car into the little garage, I inhaled again: *May I be filled with gratitude.* Exhale. *May I be calm.*

I helped Dad out at his slow-motion pace. He took his cane and gripped my left arm. At the back door, he pulled up on the extra railing built into the door casing. As he moved inside, I breathed in and smiled with the third line: *May I be filled with patience.* Exhale. *May I be at ease.*

The house still seemed quiet without Mother. Dad headed to his chair in the living room. My siblings were about to arrive. A moment of silence remained. I breathed in and said the last line. *May I be filled with forgiveness.* Exhale. *May I be at peace.*

When I returned to Raleigh, I opened our large Webster's to *oblation*, this word from my childhood. It refers to the Eucharist or some other form of penance, in order to feel some serenity—or, one might say, some forgiveness. I looked up from the heavy dictionary and smiled. Dad cut to the chase—*oblation* means forgiveness.

NOW AS I WRITE THIS IN 2016, I am 69 years old. Thirteen years have passed since that last trip to India. In this time I've had many opportunities to return to old self-defeating patterns. Immediate family members have died. My wife and I have retired. I've celebrated lives well-lived, mourned lives cut short. I've held my new granddaughter.

At times, familiar forces raised their seductive banners: worry, numbness, sleeplessness, and more. Behind these unhealthy behaviors lay feelings that I now accept, even embrace as being human: sadness, loss, disappointment, and loneliness. I also learned to feel and celebrate feelings of joy, hope, gratitude, friendship, and love.

My hard-earned insights and transformation from the crane-dance years remain my default setting today. Walking within old as well as new tribes, I stand tall on emerging paths, taking one step at a time through the next threshold. The poet Stanley Kunitz in "The Layers" helps me name where I am today:

I turn, I turn
exulting somewhat,
with my will intact to go
wherever I need to go,
and every stone on the road
precious to me.

ACKNOWLEDGMENTS

About a decade ago, Claire Guyton co-founded a new writers' group that grew out of a class she had taken through the North Carolina Writers' Network. This group provided a supportive and vigorous structure to help me shape my musings, manuscripts, journals, essays, and research into a cohesive shape. After Claire moved away, her colleague Andrea Wenger took over the leadership role and continued Claire's tradition of kind but hard-nosed comments. Our group settled into a three-year run, three men and three women. I owe immense gratitude to Claire, Andrea, and the others: Drew Bridges, John Brothers, Noor Shehzad, and Jeanne Ketterer.

In addition, many friends have supported the development of this book. I am especially indebted for the comments from three people who carefully read the entire book: my wife, Georgia Springer; Gloria Hunt, a high-school English teacher for 31 years; and Jane Hunt. I also appreciate the wisdom and support of these readers: Donald Davis, MariJo Moore, Jim Neill, Peggy Payne, Jim Prevatt, R.C. Smith, Larry Sorkin, Steve Taravella, Alice Weldon, and James Wilson. Still others offered a kind ear and reflections as I read aloud or discussed sections related to their interests: David Kiel, Cy King Sr., Doug Lester, Doug Jennette, Bennett Myers, Bob and Marion Sigmon, Fred Stephens, Paul Tierney, and Bill and Prentice Weldon. My brother and sister, Ellis and Betsy, supported me as I shared segments of the book with them. My mother and father supported this project and gave me their blessing, although they died before its completion.

Joyce Hopkins, Kim Marley, and Amanda Shurgin at the Hopkins Design Group in Durham, NC, provided artistic and production skills to transform a manuscript into a book. Mark Theriot allowed me to use his photo of a crane taking flight; see his work at *soaringart.com*.

With permission of the publisher, I have adapted two of my previously published essays into this book: "Finding the Door into the Forest," in *Wingspan: Inside the Men's Movement*, editor, Christopher Harding (St.

Martin's Press, 1992); and "The Healing Power of Community" in the *World* (journal of the Unitarian Universalist Association, November/ December 1999).

I appreciate permissions to quote material from these publications: "The Guest House" by Jelaluddin Rumi, translated by Coleman Barks, 1997 (*The Illuminated Rumi*, Random House), permission by Coleman Barks; *Landing Zones* by James R. Wilson (Duke University Press, 1993), permission of the publisher; and recordings of Jon Kabat-Zinn's guided mindfulness meditation practices, Series 1 © ℗ 2002, permission of Dr. Kabat-Zinn.

All of the stories in *The Crane Dance* are true. I changed a few names for privacy but did not invent or compress any characters or scenes.

Above all, I thank Georgia Springer, my wife of nearly 40 years ago. Her support went far beyond reviewing a manuscript to revisiting many aspects of her life as well as mine. I feel gratitude beyond words for the grace Georgia has shown in embracing *The Crane Dance* for what it can and cannot do. So many joys, sorrows, and uplifting adventures in our marriage and family have not made their way into this story, and thus it lacks the breadth of a full history of my life and our family. For Georgia, I offer the words of the Celtic poet John O'Donohue:

And so may a slow
Wind work these words
Of love around you,
An invisible cloak
To mind your life.

RESOURCES THAT HELPED GUIDE THE DANCE

Resources that helped me during the midlife period in *The Crane Dance* (1988-2003) appear below. The categories link with the tools that became clear as I worked through my "depression timeline" near the end of the book (Chapter 22). Novels and poets who helped guide me are also listed. For an update of these resources, see *www.journeycakespirit.com*.

EXPRESSIVE ARTS, CREATIVITY

Cameron, Julia with Bryan, M. 1992. *The Artist's Way: A Spiritual Path to Higher Creativity*. New York: Tarcher/Putnam.

Hart, Mickey with Stevens, J. 1990. *Drumming at the Edge of Magic: A Journey into the Spirit of Percussion.* San Francisco: Harper/SanFrancisco.

Humphrey, Doris. 1959, 1987. *The Art of Making Dances*. Princeton, NJ: A Dance Horizons Book/Princeton Book Company.

MIND-BODY HEALING, MEDITATION, MINDFULNESS

Goleman, Daniel and Gurin, J., Eds. 1993. *Mind Body Medicine: How to Use Your Mind for Better Health.* Yonkers, NY: Consumer Report Books/Consumers Union.

Hanh, Thich Nhat. 1993. *The Blooming of a Lotus: Guided Meditation Exercises for Healing and Transformation.* Boston: Beacon Press.

Kabat-Zinn, Jon. 1990. *Full Catastrophe Living: Using the Wisdom of Your Body and Mind to Face Stress, Pain, and Illness.* New York: Dell Publishing.

Moyers, Bill. 1993. *Healing and the Mind*. New York: Doubleday.

MENTAL HEALTH, DEPRESSION, MEDICATION

Bradshaw, John. 1988. *The Family: A Revolutionary Way of Self-Discovery.* Deerfield Beach, FL: Health Communications Inc.

Cronkite, Kathy. 1994. *On the Edge of Darkness: Conversations about Conquering Depression.* New York: Doubleday.

Kramer, Peter D. 1993. *Listening to Prozac.* New York: Penguin Books.

Miller, Alice. 1981. *The Drama of the Gifted Child.* New York: Basic Books (1997 edition).

O'Connor, Richard. 1997. *Undoing Depression: What Therapy Doesn't Teach You and Medication Can't Give You.* Boston: Little, Brown and Company.

Real, Terrence. 1997. *I Don't Want to Talk About It: Overcoming the Secret Legacy of Male Depression.* New York: Fireside.

Seligman, Martin. 1991. *Learned Optimism.* New York: Alfred Knopf.

Solomon, Andrew. 2002. *The Noonday Demon: An Atlas of Depression.* New York: Simon & Schuster, Inc.

Smith, Jeffrey. 1999. *Where the Roots Reach for Water: A Personal and Narrative History of Melancholia.* New York: North Point Press/Farrar, Straus and Giroux.

Storr, Anthony. 1988. *Solitude: A Return to the Self.* New York: The Free Press/Macmillan, Inc.

Thompson Tracy. 1995. *The Beast: A Journey through Depression.* New York: Penguin Books.

Men's Movement, Initiation, Ritual

Bly, Robert. 1990. *Iron John: A Book about Men.*
Reading, MA: Addison-Wesley Publishing Company, Inc.

Gilmore, David G. 1990. *Manhood in the Making: Cultural Concepts of Masculinity.* New Haven: Yale University Press.

Meade, Michael. 1993. *Men and the Water of Life: Initiation and the Tempering of Men.* San Francisco: Harper/SanFrancisco.

Moore, Robert and Gillette, Douglas. 1990. *King, Warrior, Magician, Lover: Rediscovering the Archetypes of the Mature Masculine.* San Francisco: Harper/SanFrancisco.

Raphael, Ray. 1988. *The Men from the Boys: Rites of Passage in Male America.* Lincoln: University of Nebraska Press.

Novels, Poetry

Forster, E.M. 1924. *A Passage to India.*
New York: Harcourt, Brace, & World, Inc.

Godwin, Gail. 1991. *Father Melancholy's Daughter.*
New York: William Morrow and Company, Inc.

Matthiessen Peter. 1978. *The Snow Leopard: The Astonishing Spiritual Odyssey of a Man in Search of Himself.*
New York: Viking Penguin.

Oliver, Mary. 1992. *New and Selected Poems.*
Boston: Beacon Press.

Proulx, E. Annie. *The Shipping News.* 1993.
New York: Touchtone/Simon & Schuster.

Warren, Robert Penn. 1946. *All the King's Men.*
Harcourt, Brace, & Jovanovich, Inc.

Bill Finger has been editor of a public policy quarterly, a consultant for the N.C. Legislature, and from 1989 to 2013, a writer and communications manager at an international public health organization. He grew up in Jackson, Mississippi, went to Duke University, was a Peace Corps Volunteer in India, and completed a Masters in Social Work in 2002 from the University of North Carolina at Chapel Hill. Since 1977, he has lived with his wife in Raleigh, NC, where they raised their two children.